100 YEARS OF SPANISH CINEMA

Tatjana Pavlović
Inmaculada Alvarez, Rosana Blanco-Cano,
Anitra Grisales, Alejandra Osorio, and Alejandra Sánchez

WILEY-BLACKWELL

A John Wiley & Sons, Ltd., Publication

This edition first published 2009
© 2009 by Tatjana Pavlović, Inmaculada Alvarez, Rosana Blanco-Cano, Anitra Grisales, Alejandra Osorio, and Alejandra Sánchez

Blackwell Publishing was acquired by John Wiley & Sons in February 2007. Blackwell's publishing program has been merged with Wiley's global Scientific, Technical, and Medical business to form Wiley-Blackwell.

Registered Office
John Wiley & Sons Ltd, The Atrium, Southern Gate, Chichester, West Sussex, PO19 8SQ, United Kingdom

Editorial Offices
350 Main Street, Malden, MA 02148-5020, USA
9600 Garsington Road, Oxford, OX4 2DQ, UK
The Atrium, Southern Gate, Chichester, West Sussex, PO19 8SQ, UK

For details of our global editorial offices, for customer services, and for information about how to apply for permission to reuse the copyright material in this book please see our website at www.wiley.com/wiley-blackwell.

The right of Tatjana Pavlović, Inmaculada Alvarez, Rosana Blanco-Cano, Anitra Grisales, Alejandra Osorio, and Alejandra Sánchez to be identified as the authors of this work has been asserted in accordance with the Copyright, Designs and Patents Act 1988.

Wiley also publishes its books in a variety of electronic formats. Some content that appears in print may not be available in electronic books.

Designations used by companies to distinguish their products are often claimed as trademarks. All brand names and product names used in this book are trade names, service marks, trademarks or registered trademarks of their respective owners. The publisher is not associated with any product or vendor mentioned in this book. This publication is designed to provide accurate and authoritative information in regard to the subject matter covered. It is sold on the understanding that the publisher is not engaged in rendering professional services. If professional advice or other expert assistance is required, the services of a competent professional should be sought.

Library of Congress Cataloging-in-Publication Data

100 years of Spanish cinema / Tatjana Pavlović . . . [et al.].
    p. cm.
    Includes bibliographical references and index.
    ISBN 978–1–4051–8420–5 (hbk. : alk. paper) — ISBN 978–1–4051–8419–9 (pbk. : alk. paper) 1. Motion pictures—Spain—History. I. Pavlović, Tatjana. II. Title: One hundred years of Spanish cinema.
    PN1993. 5. S72A15 2009
    791. 430946—dc22

                                                                    2008028051

A catalogue record for this book is available from the British Library.

Set in 10.5/13pt Minion by Graphicraft Limited, Hong Kong
Printed and bound in Singapore by Utopia Press Pte Ltd

001   2008

Contents

Figures

About the Authors

Tatjana Pavlović is associate professor of Spanish at Tulane University in New Orleans. Her first book is *Despotic Bodies and Transgressive Bodies: Spanish Culture from Francisco Franco to Jesús Franco* (2003). Her research and teaching interests are twentieth-century Spanish literature and cinema, cultural studies, and film studies. Her next major book project, entitled *España cambia de piel: The Mobile Nation (1954–1964)*, focuses on this key moment of transition in the history of Spanish mass culture.

Inmaculada Alvarez received her PhD in Spanish from Tulane University in 2006. She was a visiting assistant professor at the University of California, Riverside, and is currently a visiting assistant professor at Clark University. Her research and teaching interests include transatlantic studies, contemporary Spanish cinema and literature, film theory, and Caribbean studies.

Rosana Blanco-Cano received her PhD in Spanish from Tulane University in 2006. Currently she is an assistant professor at Trinity University in San Antonio, Texas. Her research and teaching interests are twentieth-century Mexican literature and film, performance, and feminism.

Anitra Grisales received her MA in Spanish from Tulane University in 2004. She worked in editorial acquisitions at Duke University Press prior to moving to Oakland, CA, where she is now a freelance editor and translator specializing in film and media studies. She is also a reporter and independent radio producer who focuses on Latino/a issues and on political relations between Latin America and the United States.

Alejandra Osorio is a professor in the Communications Department of the Universidad Autónoma Metropolitana-Cuajimalpa, Mexico. Her areas of interest are Mexican cinema and photography.

Alejandra Sánchez is a PhD candidate at Tulane University in the Department of Spanish and Portuguese. Her research interests include the body in Latin American performance in the twentieth century and contemporary Latin American literature and cinema.

Acknowledgments

We have many people to thank for their support, guidance, and encouragement at various stages of this project. John Charles, Laura Bass, and Henry Sullivan each gave the manuscript detailed and insightful readings. We are deeply indebted to them for their friendship, ideas, and critical suggestions. Tulane University provided research support and a stimulating intellectual milieu in which to test our project. Thanks also to Anthony Geist and Marvin D'Lugo for years of personal and intellectual support that goes well beyond the pages of this book.

We would also like to thank the Program for Cultural Cooperation between the Spanish Ministry of Culture and United States Universities, whose grant for the dissemination of Spanish cinema in the United States provided funding for the film festival "Politics of Memory, Memory of Politics: Film and History in Contemporary Spain" (Tulane University, spring 2007).

We thank our editor Jayne Fargnoli and her assistant Margot Morse at Wiley-Blackwell for their efficiency, patience, and commitment to the project.

Preface

Trains thundering toward the camera, workers leaving factories, worshippers coming out of churches, and theatrical screen gags were some of the images that thrilled the first moviegoers in Spain in the early 1900s. The birth of cinema at the dawn of the twentieth century was marked by a fascination with moving images and optical illusions. However, this interest was also accompanied by questions regarding the limits of artistic expression, film financing and distribution, the porous boundaries separating art from entertainment, and technological innovations that rendered previous forms obsolete. The allure of film – its ability to captivate, entertain, and delight – persists to this day. At the same time, the challenges that faced the pioneers of Spain's silent film industry also persist, and many of the same questions continue to confront its cinema. These include ongoing debates surrounding foreign markets and co-productions, political and economic censorship, questions of national identity, and artistic vision and aesthetic autonomy in the face of market demands.

Prompted by these queries, *100 Years of Spanish Cinema* provides an in-depth look at the most important movements, films, and directors in twentieth-century Spain. Examining film in terms of its cultural and technological dimensions, this book combines aesthetic analysis with considerable attention to industrial and historical contexts. Cinema, a medium of modernity and witness par excellence to the past century, is a privileged site for grasping tensions and conflicts that have shaped the modern Spanish nation and its identity. *100 Years of Spanish Cinema* is a comprehensive study of Spanish film, from the silent era to its contemporary phase. The book is divided into nine periods: *Silent Cinema and its Pioneers*; *Surrealism and the Advent of Sound*; *Spanish Civil War*; and *The Autarky: Papier-Mâché Cinema*,[1] all covering the first half of the century. Beginning with the 1950s we examine *Neorealism: Status Quo and Dissent*; *The "Liberal" Dictatorship and its Agony*; *Cinema of the Transition: The Period of Disenchantment*; *Post-Franco Spain: The Pedro Almodóvar Phenomenon*; and finally *Contemporary Trends* from the early 1990s into the new century.

The nine periods that make up the framework of the book were structured around historical and political junctures (e.g. the Spanish Civil War, the transition, the socialist period) as well as national and international artistic movements (e.g. surrealism, neorealism). Some of the proposed categories, like Spanish Civil War film, are more neatly aligned with their historical markers than others. However, all of the nine periods we study are firmly grounded in their political and historical context. By the same token, while certain periods of Spanish cinema are more tightly connected to the international movements that mark them, others are not as clearly referenced, or they coexist with other, sometimes contradictory tendencies. While our conceptual schemes fit the accepted canon and chronology, the gray areas and overlaps between the proposed categories are as important as the borders that separate them. Pre-Civil-War cinematic practices, for example, persist into the Civil-War era, and the politics of production during the autarky are still vital during the neorealist period. Furthermore, our project concurs with the recent theoretical revisions of "monolithic" entities that until recently prevailed in textbooks on Spanish history and culture, such as Francoism vs. Resistance, or elite vs. popular culture. This textbook therefore features Spain's most renowned and accomplished filmmakers alongside marginalized directors and movements, several of which have not been studied systematically before. More canonical films and their directors are tempered or de-centered by more obscure figures and texts. We also include directors who have ambiguous political postures, such as Benito Perojo and José Luis Sáenz de Heredia, both of whom served and challenged the interests of the dictatorial regime. Their work resists unambiguous classifications, adding to the complexity inherent in the study of Spanish cinema.[2] While *100 Years of Spanish Cinema* is organized chronologically, it also invites the defiance of borders and the re-inscription of both the mainstream and margins through an active mode of teaching and studying.

100 Years of Spanish Cinema studies several directors and films of the various national cinemas in Spain – Catalan, Basque, and Galician – but their treatment is nevertheless limited due to the reduced availability of these films on the market. National cinematic traditions in Spanish film history are recounted in the "Historical and Political Overview of the Period" that opens each of the nine chapters. Furthermore, several of these films address Catalan, Basque, Galician, and Andalusian subjects or themes, but are filmed in Castilian and marketed to a more general Spanish public, mostly because filming in a language other than Castilian radically limits audience, commercial appeal, and national visibility. We faced a similar dilemma with the inclusion of women directors. Until the end of the twentieth century, female-produced films in Spain were, as Susan Martin-Márquez claims, a "sight unseen," for reasons ranging from a lack of women in the profession and poor distribution of their works to patronizing dismissals and analytical oversight.[3] Recently, however, there has been a boom in women's filmmaking in Spain, with some twenty new female directors making their feature debut during the 1990s. For these reasons most of the women directors we study appear in either the *Cinema of the Transition* or *Contemporary Trends* chapters.

100 Years of Spanish Cinema is systematically structured around the nine chapters or periods, from *Silent Cinema and its Pioneers* to *Contemporary Trends*. Each chapter is prefaced by a "Historical and Political Overview of the Period" that outlines the social context in Spain, sketches cinema's industrial framework, charts major film movements and schools, and concludes with the directors and films that have impacted each period in question. We then provide a more detailed exploration of nine movements, illustrating each period with two to four films (22 in total). We divide the analysis of each film into three parts: the first, "Context and Critical Commentary," examines the film's historical, technical, and thematic properties, engaging with the opinions and interpretations of leading critics in the field, and includes a concise summary of the plot and technical data (director, year, actors, score, etc.); "Film Scenes: Close Readings" presents a detailed study of three representative scenes from each film, exposing the student to the specific visual and technical aspects and aesthetics of the movie (camera work, frame, mise-en-scène, color, performance, sound effects, and music), as well as analyzing historical, political, socio-cultural, and aesthetic context; and finally, "Director (Life and Works)" provides an overview of the filmmaker's career and its importance to the film studied. The book also includes an extensive bibliography, a glossary of film terms, and a concise historical chronology. The glossary provides definitions of essential technical, aesthetic, and historical terms.

Spanish cinema is increasingly considered an essential part of under-graduate and graduate college curricula in the United States, but this trend is at odds with the materials currently available. While a growing number of introductory texts appeared on the market in the last few years, from

Spanish Cinema for Conversation to *Hablando de cine* to *Más allá de la pantalla*, they are mainly written for intermediate-level conversation and culture courses.[4] *100 Years of Spanish Cinema* is a textbook for upper-division Spanish film courses. The book's main objective is to create an educational resource of material for the study of Spanish cinema that integrates historical data, political context, industrial infrastructure, aesthetic tendencies, and visual elements of film. *100 Years of Spanish Cinema* promotes student-centered learning, enabling users to actively draw connections and contrasts between films, directors, and genres. The stress on the acquisition of conceptual skills in film analysis is an invaluable tool in students' academic formation. This book offers a step-by-step guide for students as they explore the visual elements, critical perspective, and cultural contexts of 22 featured works, helping students to be more analytical, sophisticated, and engaged spectators, while also enabling them to interpret and examine the films in their socio-cultural contexts. Our textbook references the most recent theoretical texts in the field of Spanish film studies and reflects current developments in cinema studies. Thus, it enriches students' experiences with, and comprehension of, film art within twentieth-century Spanish culture.

100 Years of Spanish Cinema's structure lends itself to a web of possibilities and creative explorations, making it an ideal primary text for Spanish film courses. The 22 films, 20 directors, and nine movements or periods enable various paths of exploration. Reading or teaching the sections "out of order" or combining them in a different manner could yield equally productive results. The nine chapters connect through various axes; their interpenetrating layers encourage the reader to move through the various interrelated realms. The variety of possible pedagogical approaches that we offer with this project should suit traditional methodologies as well as support innovative ways to teach film.

Displacement, a strong thread that begins with Buñuel and runs through many of the directors we feature, proved to be prophetic for us as well, its meaning resonating in our own experience. We, the authors, hope that our labor, collective spirit, and enthusiasm come across to the readers and users of this textbook. We were sustained by filmophilia, collaborative ideals, team spirit, and friendship, in spite of the different directions Hurricane Katrina scattered us in. Years after its inception in New Orleans, we finished the project in Mexico City, Boston, San Antonio, Oakland, and New Orleans.

Upon the completion of the textbook we were reunited once again for a Spanish film festival, "Politics of Memory, Memory of Politics: Film and

History in Contemporary Spain," organized in conjunction with this project in the spring of 2007 at Tulane University. We wish to acknowledge our plenary speakers Anthony Geist and Marvin D'Lugo, who moreover thoughtfully provided us with feedback on this project. The new entering graduate students at Tulane University were also involved with the festival organization and paper presentations. Their presence signified a symbolic passage to the next generation, just as we were remembering our own indebtedness to the previous, pioneer scholars in the field of Spanish cinema studies. The project and the event were a celebration of collectivity and continuity, of our department (Spanish and Portuguese), our university (Tulane University), and our city (New Orleans), as well as a gesture of gratitude to a larger context (an academic community) that stimulated us intellectually throughout this process.

1

Silent Cinema and its Pioneers (1906–1930)

1 *El ciego de aldea* (Ángel García Cardona, 1906)
2 *Amor que mata* (Fructuós Gelabert, 1909)
3 *Don Pedro el Cruel* (Ricardo Baños, Albert Marro, 1911)
4 *La aldea maldita* (Florián Rey, 1930)

Historical and Political Overview of the Period

Spanish silent film history is a tale of lost patrimony and its ghostly remnants. The number of lost and destroyed films is astonishing; only 10 percent of pre-Civil War (1936) films remain in existence. The advent of sound films in the early 1930s rendered silent film technologically obsolete. Additionally, due to the chemical value of the celluloid, countless silent film negatives simply became "raw material in the manufacture of combs, buttons, and sequins" (Gubern, "Precariedad y originalidad del modelo cinematográfico español," p. 12). The scarcity of records and reliable data on early Spanish cinema considerably hinders the reconstruction of a consistent historic outline. Histories of Spanish silent film are written in a speculative manner, based not on the films themselves, but on secondary sources such as popular film journals of the period, anecdotal testimonies of film professionals and critics, or early critical works on the subject.[5] Given this context it is not surprising to find contradictory and multiple periodizations for this early era. While some film historians and histories focus predominantly on silent pioneers and the genres they worked in, others cite the Barcelona/Madrid dichotomy or the industrial weakness of the incipient Spanish film industry. This introduction briefly outlines the most significant features of silent Spanish cinema, including pertinent historical and political background, while bearing in mind the complexities of the period.

The era in which cinema was introduced and consolidated corresponds to a turbulent period in Spanish history, marked by intricate political and economic upheavals. The first moving pictures were seen in Spain in 1896, just two years before the country's defeat in the colonial wars that would result in the loss of the final remnants of its empire (Cuba, Puerto Rico, the Philippines, and Guam). It is significant that the arrival of cinema, a medium of modernity, coincided with a traumatic colonial loss symbolic of Spain's crisis of modernity – a crisis that would only continue to intensify.[6]

In 1896 Spain was a constitutional monarchy. After King Alfonso XII died at the age of 28 in 1885, the throne was occupied by his widow María Cristina of Habsburg (the archduchess of Austria), whose reign lasted until her son Alfonso XIII, known as *el hijo póstumo* or "the posthumous son," ascended to the throne in November of 1902. The regime of this period, known as the Restoration regime, was comprised of two political parties: the liberals (Sagasta) and the conservatives (Cánovas de Castillo). Under King Alfonso XIII, Spain remained officially neutral during World War I (1914–18). However, the political and economic crisis that had already been felt during Alfonso XII's reign progressively intensified. In an attempt to ensure social and political order, Alfonso XIII supported the military dictatorship of Miguel Primo de Rivera, which lasted from 1923 until 1930. Nevertheless, the monarchy did not survive. A civil uprising culminated in Primo de Rivera's fall. In 1931 general elections resulted in the abdication of Alfonso XIII and the proclamation of the Second Republic (1931–6).

As this brief history illustrates, the first moving pictures in Spain were projected against a volatile social and economic backdrop. In addition to governmental instability and the widespread fear of military takeovers, some of the most problematic issues were uneven industrialization and urbanization, poverty, the exploitation of peasants by the landed oligarchy, the offsetting of war debts with tax increases, fear of working-class movements and unrest, and the need for educational reforms. When the first Cinématographe arrived, Spain was an agrarian state. Peasants comprised the majority of the population, while 35 percent of the active population worked in agriculture. Only a small minority of Spaniards lived in cities with more than 100,000 inhabitants (Madrid 540,000; Barcelona 533,000; Valencia 203,000). The illiteracy rate was remarkably high; 60 percent of the population could not read or write at the turn of the century.[7]

The development of cinema in general, and of Spain's in particular, was drastically influenced by economic and technological factors. Cinema as a popular art and a form of entertainment was tied to technological advances that were crucial to film recording and projection. Captivating optical illusions were inseparable from the complex mechanics of movement that enabled them. Cinema, a kingdom of illusion and shadows, was bound to its contiguous material reality. It was an artistic product as much as a commercial one. The inseparability of economics, institutional aspects, technology, and aesthetics is noteworthy in Spain, a country fraught with poverty and underdevelopment. Nevertheless, despite the country's lack of political and economic progress, Spain's cinematic history reflects larger patterns in the expansion of the seventh art – those of more advanced industrial societies.

Optical and mechanical apparatuses that were circulating, competing, and participating in the evolution of the moving image – the Thaumatrope, Phenakistocope, Stroboscope, Zoetrope, Praxinoscope, Chromatrope, Eidotrope, and Cycloidotrope among others – made their way to Spain as well. Spanish film beginnings can be traced back as early as 1896, the year Spain held a competition between the Animatograph (Robert William Paul) and the Lumière Cinématographe. The royal family professed their preference for the Lumière Cinématographe, represented in Spain by Alexandre Promio. He expanded his activities in Spain and in June of 1896 filmed *Plaza del puerto en Barcelona*, acknowledged as the first film actually made in Spain. The Lumière brothers, Louis and Auguste, were thus as triumphant in Spain as in their native France, where they are credited with the "birth" of cinema on December 29, 1895.

The Lumière brothers had a direct impact on the beginnings of film in Spain, where French cinema's pioneering patterns of filming and production were being replicated. Similar themes and genres, such as *actualités* (short documentaries), screen gags, and short comic films, abounded. Because of the Lumières' expansionist politics, their cameramen were scattered around the world filming *le catalogue de vues Lumière*: a catalogue of general, military, comic, and scenic views. This collection of picturesque panoramas was precisely what Alexandre Promio was filming in Spain. In addition to the aforementioned *Plaza del puerto en Barcelona*, Promio's *vistas españolas – Llegada de los toreros, Maniobras de la artillería en Vicálvaro*, and *Salida de las alumnas del colegio de San Luis de los Franceses* – were the first moving images taken in Spain.

Spanish nationals were as involved as foreigners were in this turn-of-the-century filming frenzy. In October of 1896 Eduardo Jimeno Correas shot the "first" Spanish film, *Salida de la misa de doce del Pilar de Zaragoza*. There were also numerous other *salidas de/llegadas a* (leaving from/arriving at) in the Lumières' hyperrealist style, such as *Llegada de un tren de Teruel a Segorbe*, an anonymous film shown in Valencia in September of 1896. Therefore, as in other countries, workers leaving factories and trains thundering toward the camera were some of the images that thrilled Spain's first moviegoers. Several chronicles of Spanish film history emphasize that the train, an icon of the Industrial Revolution, has been outnumbered as a cinematic subject by the church. This gesture highlights Spain's adherence to traditional, pre-modern imagery over symbols of industrial progress.

A look at the figures and technology integral to Spain's early film history highlights the technical, national, and aesthetic crossovers characteristic of film culture and exposes the fragile boundaries between foreign influences and national "origins," between colonization and co-productions. The silent period pioneers – the innovators, experimenters, visionaries, nationalists, internationalists, and foreigners – were as diverse as the medium itself. While several figures had radical proposals and projects, many others were conservative, formulaic, and conventional; some were successful, while others were ruined in the enterprise; some were seeking a lucrative commercial enterprise, while others were carried away by technology, science, and the invention of machines; and while some people received belated recognition, many others encountered oblivion. Fructuós Gelabert, Ricardo Baños, Albert Marro, Joan María Codina, Ángel García Cardona, and Adrià Gual are just a handful of the pioneers that should be recognized as important figures in the development of early Spanish cinema. With more then 500 films, one of the most brilliant, innovative, and prolific of the early pioneers was Barcelona-based Segundo de Chomón. He was a master of illusion and the creator of technically adventurous masterpieces whose innovations in cinematic special effects brought him international fame.

This chapter includes three films from this period: Ángel García Cardona's *El ciego de aldea* (1906), Fructuós Gelabert's *Amor que mata* (1909), and Ricardo Baños and Albert Marro's *Don Pedro el Cruel* (1911). These films are part of the creation of "the preliminary industrial and expressive framework for Spain's budding cinema" (Pérez Perucha, "Narración de un aciago destino (1896–1930)," p. 35). These filmmakers' trajectories reflect a collective cinematic drive, illustrating most of the traits that marked filming, production, and distribution in early "silent" Spain. *El ciego de aldea*, directed by Ángel García Cardona, is representative of Films Cuesta and its thriving production activities in Valencia; *Amor que mata* was filmed by Fructuós Gelabert, the director of the first fiction film in Spain; and *Don Pedro el Cruel* is representative of the successful and profitable Hispano Films run by Ricardo Baños and Albert Marro.

These films were also characteristic of the larger aesthetic, formal, economic, and political trends of early cinema. In addition to displaying noteworthy technical traits and tendencies of "primitive" cinematic expression, these three films also point to the exploration and rethinking of national themes and Spanish cultural identity. *El ciego de aldea*, with its central blind character, originates from a long Spanish literary tradition by incorporating a popular theme of orally transmitted ballads such as *Romance del cordel*. Popular melodramas and successful theatrical works were frequently adapted for the silent screen, *Amor que mata* being one of the most representative. This film also reflects cinema's search for a more "sophisticated" audience who may have been tired of the usual vaudeville acts and comic chases. Filmmakers therefore embraced the theatrical model in an attempt to attract the theater-going middle class to the cinema by increasing its aesthetic and intellectual appeal. As can be seen from *Amor que mata* with its papier-mâché and plaster sets, the film frame functioned as a proscenium arch,[8] contributing a highly theatrical feel to the productions. The film also illustrates the discrepancies and tensions between the two dramatic forms; the actors perform with archaic facial grimaces inherited from the theater as they also develop new acting styles and conventions particular to the movie screen. Finally, *Don Pedro el Cruel* is a historical drama of monarchic betrayal and succession, a mise-en-scène of the nation's history and its moments of tension and conflict. The film is contemporary with lavishly produced Italian historical costume films such as Giovanni Pastrone's *Giulio Cesare* (1909) and *La caduta di Troya* (1910), or Enrico Guazzoni's *Bruto* (1910). While *Don Pedro el Cruel* does not share the extravagance and grandeur of its Italian counterparts, it still fits the trend of historical cinematic superproductions.

El ciego de aldea, *Amor que mata*, and *Don Pedro el Cruel* enable us to better understand the early politics of film production in Spain. We see a burgeoning industry whose financial mechanisms required caution, and the subordination of creativity to profits. In the Spanish milieu this meant supporting more creative, risky, and original projects with cheap formulaic ones such as inexpensive newsreels, cheap comic flicks, and familiar literary adaptations. Furthermore, as we can perceive from these films and as Marvin D'Lugo points out: "On the one hand, Spanish film innovators struggled to harness the artistic and commercial potential of the rapidly evolving technology of film as an international mass medium; on the other, artists and commercial promoters of Spanish cinema, as well as early audiences, tended to see in the motion picture the reflection of local and national culture" (*A Guide to the Cinema of Spain*, p. 1).

Don Pedro el Cruel coincides with the end of the first silent period, also known as *un prolongado pionerismo* or "a prolonged pioneer period," encompassing the years between 1897 and 1910–13 (Pérez Perucha, "Narración de un aciago destino (1896–1930)," p. 25). According to several film historians, this prolonged early period would account for the relatively slow development of Spain's film industry and infrastructure. Its inadequacies also set the framework for Spanish film production's future economic, political, and aesthetic dependency on other more powerful film industries.

Most of the filmmakers discussed so far – Marro, Chomón, Gelabert, and Baños – worked and filmed in Barcelona. Neighboring Valencia also boasted significant film production, especially Antonio Cuesta's company Films Cuesta. Barcelona's dominance as the most important and powerful film center was indebted to Catalonia's industrial superiority to the rest of the country. Nevertheless, even industrialized Barcelona could not keep up with growing foreign competition. The situation deteriorated further, mostly due to the increasing weaknesses in the film industry's infrastructure. Spain's early cinematic trajectory, the years between 1911 and 1922, can be seen, as Pérez Perucha says, as the "apogee and decline of Barcelona's production" ("Narración de un aciago destino (1896–1930)," p. 47). The slow but steady decline brought on an irreversible crisis that finally resulted in the end of Catalan silent film production.

This "pre-history" of Spanish silent cinema is marked by Madrid's absence, which can be tied to the capital city's idiosyncratic entertainment history. Across the globe, early cinema competed with other entertainment spectacles that it progressively displaced, such as vaudeville acts or shadow melodramas. Madrid, however, had a solid tradition of following the "native" genres: *el sainete* (short comic play), *la zarzuela* (musical theater), and the bullfighting spectacle. Enjoying great popularity among Madrid audiences, these popular forms of entertainment were only gradually displaced, mostly once an unanticipated theater crisis coincided with the increasing infiltration of American and European films into Spain.

Once Madrid embraced filmgoing and filmmaking, among some of the most important personalities of its budding film industry was Benito Perojo, a producer, cameraman, director, screenwriter, and actor. In 1915, Perojo, together with his brother José, established the prominent Patria Films. Antonio Martínez (more widely known as Florián Rey, the pseudonym he later adopted), another actor and later an important director, also contributed to Madrid's emergence and consolidation on the peninsular cinematographic scene.

Political factors intensified the peculiar economic, technological, and cinematic differences between Barcelona and Madrid. The capital's belated but powerful rise to primacy as a film center corresponded to the military dictatorship of Miguel Primo de Rivera and his centralizing tendencies. By the same token, Primo de Rivera's ascent to power in 1923 signaled Barcelona's descent as an important film hub. However, these inner dynamics, industrial power shifts, and domestic rivalries obscured the actual competition that threatened national Spanish cinema from the outside. The principal foreign competitors were French monopolies, dominating until World War I, followed by the United States, especially during its international expansion (1907–18). Around the world, cinema was transformed from a risky commercial venture to a full-scale industry and a lucrative commercial enterprise. However, unlike elsewhere, in Spain early "cinematic craftsmanship" did not evolve into a powerful industry. Spanish production lacked modern studios, a sophisticated star system, and significant investment in competing technologies. The problem was further exacerbated by a lack of originality, evidenced by the overuse of tired themes and formulas that were, as Pérez Perucha argues, fundamentally influenced by, when not literal copies of, foreign styles ("Narración de un aciago destino (1896–1930)," p. 54).

The first sound films were screened in Spain on September 19, 1929, in Barcelona and on October 4 of the same year in Madrid. These films were, for the most part, shown silently due to their technological incompatibility with exhibition halls and their existing equipment. Only fragments of films were sonorized, such as Maurice Chevalier's singing in *Innocents of Paris/La canción de París*.[9] Nevertheless, as Pérez Perucha colorfully writes, "the arrival of sound cinema mercilessly liquidated Spain's fragile cinema" ("Narración de un aciago destino (1896–1930)," p. 105). Some final noteworthy films made during this period of crisis and decline are: *La hermana San Suplicio* (directed by Florián Rey and with the first appearance of future film star Imperio Argentina), *Una aventura de cine* (Juan de Orduña), *Es mi hombre* (Carlos Fernández Cuenca), all made in 1927; *Agustina de Aragón* (Florián Rey) in 1928; and in 1929, *El sexto sentido* (Nemesio M. Sobrevila) and *El gordo de Navidad* (Fernando Delgado). Luis Buñuel and Salvador Dalí's *Un chien andalou* was filmed in 1929 in France.

Florián Rey's classic melodrama *La aldea maldita* (1930) is the last film featured in this chapter. The film is considered to be the last great silent epic of Spanish cinema. It centers on Castilian peasants' strong ties to the land, misery, poverty, urban migration, and clashes between tradition and

modernity. The film probes questions of honor codes, sexuality, gender relations, emigration, and race, themes favored by the director and explored
further in his later films, such as the well-known *Nobleza baturra* (1935).
In *La aldea maldita* Florián Rey ties the moral "corruption" of women to
threats posed to crumbling patriarchal structures. The issue is problematized
through the central figure of the "fallen" mother. In addition to these socio-
moral issues, the film also has significant visual appeal and was influenced
by Soviet expressionism.[10] As Marsha Kinder notes, "the forces of change
are associated with the uniqueness of the cinematic spectacle" (*Blood Cinema*,
p. 45). The film effectively couples a strong conservative message with
striking visual beauty.

In sum, although the infrastructure of Spain's film industry nearly
collapsed, there were several figures that reappeared and surfaced from this
disintegration. Many of them were from the Madrid milieu including the
aforementioned Benito Perojo, a filmmaker who very successfully depicted
the urban middle class, Florián Rey, the director of *La aldea maldita*, and
Luis Buñuel, whose prolific career, as we will see in the next chapter, was
also marked by the silent screen.

1   *El ciego de aldea* (Ángel García Cardona, 1906)

Context[11]

Production credits[12]

Director: Ángel García Cardona
Production: Films Cuesta (Valencia); Joan María Codina
Cinematography: Ángel García Cardona
Screenplay: Antonio Cuesta
Genre: Drama, 35 mm, black and white, silent
Country: Spain
Runtime: 75 minutes

Synopsis

In Godella, a town in Valencia, a blind beggar and his granddaughter solicit
money in the street. First they encounter a group of sinister bandits who

refuse to help them, but then have better luck with a generous wealthy couple. In a horse-drawn carriage, the newlyweds pass by a dangerous area, where the same gang that refused to give the beggars money attacks the couple and kidnaps the woman. By chance, the blind man and his grand-daughter watch hidden as the bandits take the woman into a cave. When the gang leaves, the beggars free the woman. The granddaughter goes in search of the husband, whom she finds accompanied by the Civil Guard. Between them they come up with a plan to ambush the bandits, whom they eventually capture. The newlyweds thank the blind man and his grand-daughter for their generous help.

Film Scenes: Close Readings

Scene 1   The walk to the cave

In this scene we see the bandits take the woman, her hands and feet bound, inside the cave that serves as their hideout. The little girl and her blind grandfather are also in the scene, hidden in the foreground, while in the background we see the houses of the town. Each aspect of the scene recalls a theatrical staging: from the flat perspective of the horizon and the framing of the scene through a fixed shot, where the blind man and the girl appear on the left and the criminals on the right, to the characters' exaggerated gestures. Through its simple story, the scene shows that the technical resources of the new medium were precarious, and still catering to spectators who were accustomed to the theatrical conventions of the stage. Film was a new art for both the pioneering spectators and producers, and both had to adjust to novel ways of capturing and perceiving moving images on the screen.

Directors (Life and Works)

Ángel García Cardona and Antonio Cuesta[13]

Ángel García Cardona directed this film in collaboration with producer Antonio Cuesta, owner of the film production company Films Cuesta, which was first headquartered in Barcelona and then later moved to Valencia.

In 1899 García Cardona was a recognized and prestigious photographer in Valencia. Because of his interest in the new cinematic medium, that same year he expanded his studio by opening a developing and editing lab, along with a projection room, producing films that included "panoramic views" and documentary reports. In 1901 he dedicated himself full-time to making films, working for various producers and eventually associating himself in 1905 with impresario Antonio Cuesta, of Films Cuesta. This collaboration resulted in the release of the film *Batalla de las flores* in 1905, and one year later of *El ciego de aldea*, which coincided with a boom in movie-theater openings in cities like Valencia and Barcelona. The expansion of film venues indicates how film was gaining popularity as a new medium, not just of art, but of entertainment as well.

2 *Amor que mata* (Fructuós Gelabert, 1909)

Context

Production credits

Director: Fructuós Gelabert
Production: Films Barcelona
Cinematography: Fructuós Gelabert
Screenplay: Fructuós Gelabert
Genre: Dramatic comedy, 35 mm, black and white, silent
Country: Spain
Runtime: 14 minutes

Cast

Joaquín Carrasco, José Vives, Guerra (mother), M. Mestres (daughter), María Miró, P. Ortín, L. Mas, Martí, Metas

Synopsis

Jacobo is set to marry Miss Vélez, but a vengeful woman begins writing anonymous letters saying that they should not marry because Miss Vélez's mother is a "sinner." Upon reading the anonymous letter, Miss Vélez faints and falls gravely ill. News of Miss Vélez's sickness appears in the newspaper. After finding out what she has caused, the woman who sent the anonymous letter decides to go the Vélez house. Meanwhile, Jacobo is also worried about his fiancée's health, so he goes to her house to see her. Upon hearing her mother confess the truth, Miss Vélez suffers one final attack and dies.

Film Scenes: Close Readings

Scene 1   The fatal faint

Jacobo goes to his gravely ill fiancée's house. From her bedroom Miss Vélez hears her mother confess that the allegations of her sinning were true, which causes Miss Vélez to faint and die. At this moment the woman who sent the anonymous letters also enters the scene. Upon seeing Miss Vélez die, the woman exits, as Jacobo and the sinning mother embrace the victim. In this dramatic finale the actors' highly exaggerated gestures, especially the protagonist's final faint, show that the theatrical gestures of that time persisted into the cinematic mode of representation. In addition to the staging and the fixed take typical of early film, *Amor que mata* demonstrates other characteristic elements of theatrical works of the time, such as the social importance of morality and decency, and an emphasis on poetic justice. Love, sin, and romantic death were also popular themes of literature and plays of that era. As *Amor que mata* demonstrates, film's first steps did not stray very far from these tendencies.

Director (Life and Works)

Fructuós Gelabert (b. Barcelona 1874, d. Barcelona 1955)

Fructuós Gelabert, who made the first Spanish fiction film, *Riña en un café*, in August of 1897, is a multifaceted filmmaker; he was a camera operator, actor, screenwriter, impresario, and director. Following the conventions of filming segments of "real life" in the style of the Lumière brothers, he filmed *Salida de los trabajadores de la fábrica España industrial* in 1897. Among his other outstanding films are: *Procesión de las Hijas de María de la iglesia parroquial de Sants* (1902) and *Los guapos de la vaquería del Parque* (1905). At the same time he filmed documentary reports like *Visita a Barcelona de doña María Cristina y don Alfonso XIII*.

In 1902 Gelabert worked as a tech in the Sala Diorama, the first movie theater in Barcelona. The company that ran the theater, Empresa Diorama, later became the well-known producer Films Barcelona (1906–13). Gelabert was prolific; he made about 11 movies between 1898 and 1906, with titles like *Tierra baja* (1907), *La Dolores* (1910), *María Rosa* (1908) and *Amor que mata* (1909). Gelabert's production started to decline with the advent of sound film. After a period of crisis, his last success was *La puntaire* (1927). He died in Barcelona in 1955, having retired from filmmaking.

3   *Don Pedro el Cruel* (Ricardo Baños, Albert Marro, 1911)

Context

Production credits

Directors: Ricardo Baños; Albert Marro
Production: Hispano Films
Cinematography: Ricardo Baños
Screenplay: Not known
Genre: Historical film, 35 mm, black and white, silent
Country: Spain
Runtime: Not known

Synopsis

In the living room of his castle, King Pedro the Cruel receives a message that his three bastard brothers (as the film's script refers to them) are preparing to overthrow him. After an initial moment of sadness, he decides to come up with a plan to take revenge on his brothers. He sends a spy and soldiers to the forest near the castle to try to uncover his brothers' plan. The spy overhears a conversation that the three brothers have in their tent, and then races to the castle to inform the king. The king reacts by summoning Don Fadrique, one of his brothers, and imprisoning him. Their mother is left alone in the living room of the castle, crying due to the feud between her children and from the pain of betrayal.

Film Scenes: Close Readings

Scene 1   The spy in the tent

King Pedro's three bastard brothers converse in their tent, situated in the middle of the forest near the palace, as a spy very obviously sticks his head into the tent to listen. In the shot we see the brothers discussing the plan to overthrow their brother, and in the center we see the spy's face as he pays close attention to what he's witnessing. All of the characters' exaggerated gestures are in keeping with the obvious presence of the spy, whom they never seem to perceive, giving the scene a more theatrical than filmic feeling. It is important to remember that the facts represented in this pioneering film are actually part of the country's historical reality (the betrayal of King Pedro the Cruel by his three brothers), but the scene, with the aforementioned recourses, seems less like historical reality than a lyrical meditation on it.

Directors (Life and Works)

Ricardo Baños (b. Barcelona 1892, d. Barcelona 1939)
and Albert Marro[14]

Ricardo Baños is another multifaceted figure from the early days of the Spanish national film scene. He gained exposure to the art of cinema in Paris through Gaumont, a renowned French photography and, later, film production company. He worked in both France and Spain, finally settling down in Barcelona in 1904, where he became instrumental in the creation of the burgeoning Spanish film industry. After this first successful period, Baños met Albert Marro, another filmmaker of the period; together in 1906 they founded Hispano Films, the very successful production company that they managed until 1918. Their production centered on low-budget, highly successful films, which allowed them, in turn, to finance more experimental and creative films. Historical films and romantic dramas were prevalent; particularly noteworthy is *Don Juan Tenorio* (1910), the first filmic adaptation of a popular play by José de Zorilla, whose rights were bought by Charles Pathé's powerful French photography/film company.

Critical Commentary

El ciego de aldea, Amor que mata, and *Don Pedro el Cruel* are typical of Spain's emerging film culture. *El ciego de aldea,* directed by Ángel García Cardona, is representative of the productions of the Valencia company Films Cuesta; *Amor que mata* was filmed by Fructuós Gelabert, one of the most significant and innovative figures of the period and the director of Spain's first fiction film; and *Don Pedro el Cruel,* directed by Ricardo Baños and Albert Marro, illustrates the politics of production of the successful Hispano Films. These three films' themes reflect the diverse aesthetic, economic, and political aspects that characterize this early stage of film production and show the tendencies of so-called "primitive" cinematographic expression.

Each film illustrates recurrent traits of early silent cinema. *El ciego de aldea,* with its blind protagonist – a frequent figure in Spanish literature – displays early cinema's reliance on literary tropes and conventions. *Amor que mata* illustrates the prevalence of the adaptation of popular melodramas. Fructuós Gelabert was one of the most prolific and commercial directors and made other famous film adaptations such as *Tierra baja, María Rosa,* and the musical *La Dolores,* based on a celebrated *zarzuela. Don Pedro el Cruel* also illustrates how national history was a thematic source for film during this initial period.

These early films suggest that the politics of production took few risks; the priority at that time was commercial success, to the detriment of filmic creativity. Aesthetically, early Spanish film did not stray very far from the forms of its dramatic precursor, theater. Filmmakers relied on familiar genres and themes in an attempt to attract the theater-going audience. Filmmakers also used a theatrical model to construct scenes, which is reflected in the fixed framing, single takes, and static shots that characterize early silent films. Furthermore, film actors maintained theater's interpretive conventions, such as exaggerated and melodramatic gesturing. Given the cautious production policies, the cinematic production of this era is limited to films with few pretenses and low budgets, like comedies, fantasies, or documentaries. The three films analyzed in this section are also inscribed within a period of Spanish film history that several film historians define as a "prolonged pioneer phase," covering the years between 1897 and 1913 (Pérez Perucha, "Narración de un aciago destino (1896–1930)," p. 25). Aside from the slow passage from one artistic medium (theater) to another (film), cinematic production was also limited by Spain's political situation, its profound social crisis, and its archaic economic structures.

4   *La aldea maldita* (Florián Rey, 1930)

Context and Critical Commentary

Production credits

Director: Florián Rey
Production: Florián Rey; Pedro Larrañaga
Cinematography: Alberto Arroyo
Screenplay: Florián Rey
Score: Rafael Martínez
Genre: Melodrama, black and white, silent
Country: Spain
Runtime: 58 minutes

Cast

Pedro Larrañaga	Juan de Castilla
Carmen Viance	Acacia
Pilar G. Torres	Fuensantica
Ramón Meca	Uncle Lucas
Víctor Pastor	Abuelo (grandfather)
Antonio Mata	Gañán
Modesto Rivas	Administrator
Amelia Muñoz	Magdalena

Synopsis

A humble peasant family, including Juan de Castilla, a farm worker, his wife Acacia, their young son, and Juan's father Martín, lives in Luján, a small Castilian town. Due to bad weather, the town loses its crops and the majority of the inhabitants flee in hunger, looking for work in other places. Juan is taken to jail after an altercation with Uncle Lucas, the town loan shark. Magdalena, the family's neighbor, convinces Acacia to look for work in a nearby city, Segovia, where she becomes a prostitute. Martín, her father-in-law, prevents Acacia from taking her young child with her to the city. Later, after Juan is released from jail, he also moves to Segovia, where he finds a comfortable position as the overseer of a farm. There he reunites with Acacia, his wife, who is working in a tavern under dubious auspices. He drags her back to the lucrative farm at which he now lives with his father and his son, holding Acacia captive in the house in an effort to protect the family's honor. Juan also does not allow Acacia to have any contact with her son. Time passes, and Juan's father finally dies. Juan then throws Acacia out of the house in the dead of winter. She wanders aimlessly through the town, physically sick and deranged from the loss of her child, and ends up in a mental hospital. More time passes and the couple reunite in Luján, the cursed town of the title, where Acacia, finally forgiven by Juan, returns to be with her son.

Critical commentary

Considered a masterpiece of Florián Rey, the director, and Spain's final era of silent film, *La aldea maldita* is an "involuntary document of the customs, female condition, and moral conservatism of agrarian Spain" (Gubern, "1930–1936 (II República)," p. 94). The film explores the themes of urban migration, poverty, and the clash between tradition and modernity. In spite of its conservative focus on certain aspects like honor, the subordination of women, or the patriarchal family, the film stands out for its striking visual style, influenced by Russian expressionism, with its close-ups of peasants' faces and its narrative and aesthetic intensity. The director magisterially captures the collective drama of migrant peasants plagued by the universal tragedies of hunger and misery.

La aldea maldita juxtaposes the continued presence of Spain's outdated social and cultural structures with the country's budding modernization at the advent of the Second Republican regime, one of the most progressive of the era. The sinful wife's punishment can thus be seen as illustrative of the oppressiveness of the tyrannical honor system that sustained patriarchal family structures in Spain. This thematic tendency is reminiscent of sixteenth- and seventeenth-century Spanish Golden Age theater, which is rife with similar tragedies of honor. Through its melodramatic overtones Florián Rey's film probes the implications of the persistence of this honor system. It also vividly evokes certain idiosyncratic Spanish elements, like the harshness of the rural space, the sober environment, and the peasants' austere existence.

The director masterfully utilizes the visual resources of the new medium, making dramatic use of light and shadows, and varying his shot composition by juxtaposing extreme, personalized close-ups of human faces with harsh landscapes, the movement of the crowd in the scene showing the peasants' mass exodus, and the bustling, modern city street scenes. These innovative techniques made *La aldea maldita* one of the first masterpieces of early Spanish cinema, and strongly influenced the burgeoning art form. Furthermore, the tragedy of rural migration that *La aldea maldita* introduced to the film screen became an essential reference for later Spanish film production.

Film Scenes: Close Readings

Scene 1   *The exodus of the carts*

The inhabitants of Luján, the cursed town, decide to abandon their homes when faced with the threat of starvation after a violent storm destroys all of their crops. Florián Rey's noteworthy establishing shot, which captures the village as hundreds of carts descend a serpentine path down the hill as they leave the town, is juxtaposed with alternating close-up shots of the peasants' faces. The aesthetic composition of this sequence of collective emigration communicates the intensity and drama of the moment, just as it shows the filmmaker's talent for using long shots that can encompass a large quantity of actors. The mass migration depicted on screen captures a historical moment that reflects the profound economic crisis Spain was experiencing at the time, in which agricultural devastation in particular provoked the abandonment of the towns and the growth of the urban population. This shot of the exodus of the carts also demonstrates how Rey, through his mastery of the new medium, was able to break with other directors' dependence on theatrical techniques and create a more specialized filmic language.

Scene 2 *The city on the other side of the sierra*

In order to convince Acacia to leave the town, Magdalena tells her "you doubt, because you don't know what's on the other side of the sierra." This statement is illustrated by consecutive shots of bustling city streets, the accelerated tempo of cars in motion, people walking, and the architecture of the city. The city's modernity is contrasted with the rural Castilian environment, sober and oppressive, that predominates the rest of the film. This "other side of the sierra" is understood as the symbolic border that separates two Spains: the rural, anchored in the archaic atavism of honor, patriarchy, and the fight for daily subsistence; and the urban, which is modern, vital, anonymous, and presented as the hope for the future. Rey's intricate and complex montage strategies show his mastery of filmic language, not only in terms of camera work, but also in respect of the conceptual production of meaning; the city symbolizes a utopian modern space that gives hope to those who are trying to escape the oppression of the cursed town.

Figure 1.1 The city on the other side of the sierra (*La aldea maldita*, 1930)

Scene 3   The Calderonian shadow[15]

When Juan discovers Acacia working in a tavern, he forces her to return with him to the cursed town, but only after making her change into the clothes she used to wear when she lived there. Acacia appears scared and ashamed as she emerges from behind the dressing curtains in her peasant clothes, as a threatening shadow – Juan's judgmental profile – looms to the right of the screen. Rey seems to suggest that the silhouette that sub-jugates Acacia is symbolic of the suppression of the peasant woman before the patriarchal power exercised in Spain's rural atmosphere. The codes of honor and morality alluded to in this scene keep the woman in a position of absolute submission before the patriarchal figure. Rey's expressionistic looming shadow illustrates his command of visual cinematic language, but also situates the film within Spain's historical and artist context, recalling Calderonian dramas with their exploration of themes of honor, jealousy, love, forgiveness, moral decline, and the rigidity of class structures.

The scene thus critiques the rural Spanish system of values by creat-ing empathy for Acacia's fragility and her forced submission to Juan. The actors evoke feeling in the spectators without resorting to the exaggerated gesticulation that is so typical of the heavily theater-influenced early films. In this way, Spanish film begins to develop its own language.

Director (Life and Works)

Florián Rey (Antonio Martínez de Castillo) (b. La Almunia de Doña Godina, Zaragoza, 1894, d. Alicante 1962)

Florián Rey, whose real name was Antonio Martínez de Castillo, was born in 1894 in the small village of La Almunia de Doña Godina, in Zaragoza. After abandoning a career in law in 1910, he began to work as a journalist for various daily papers in Zaragoza and Madrid, where he started using the pseudonym that would accompany him throughout the rest of his career. His first contact with film was as an actor. After a brief involvement in Madrid's theater scene, he got a role in the film *La inaccesible* (José Buchs, 1920). Soon thereafter, he ventured into filmmaking and directed his first film, *La revoltosa* (1924), an adaptation of a popular *zarzuela* that quickly became a success. The following year he released another *zarzuela* adapta-tion called *Gigantes y cabezudos*.

In 1927 Rey introduced the celebrated singer Imperio Argentina to the screen in his film *La hermana San Sulpicio*, of which he released a sound version in 1934. The next year Imperio Argentina and Florián Rey were married, and together they contributed to the success of the production company CIFESA (Compañía Industrial Film Española S.A.), which made numerous commercially successful films in that era by teaming up popular actors and singers with successful directors of the time.

In 1930 Rey directed *La aldea maldita*, a masterpiece of Spanish silent film, and the first filmic work to be screened internationally. In 1933 he released his first sound film, *Sierra de Ronda*, which sparked a trend of commercial films based on popular culture themes that would last throughout the Second Republic (1931–6). After directing hit titles like *Nobleza baturra* (1935) and *Morena clara* (1936), starring Imperio Argentina, Rey then ventured into *costumbrista*[16] cinema based on folklore and popular Spanish myths. These works formed part of the so-called Golden Age of Spanish cinema that even managed to compete with Hollywood movies in terms of garnering a public following.

After the start of the Spanish Civil War, Florián Rey and Imperio Argentina filmed two movies in Berlin: *Carmen, la de Triana* (1938) and *La canción de Aixa* (1939), which were also extremely popular. However, 1939 also saw the couple's divorce and the beginning of Rey's decline as a director. Upon returning to Spain, Rey released what would be his last big hit, *La Dolores* (1940), starring the celebrated couplet singer Concha Piquer. His final successes were *Brindis a Manolete* (1948) and *Cuentos de La Alhambra* (1950). He made his last film, *Polvorilla*, in 1956 and died shortly thereafter, in 1962, in Alicante.

2

Surrealism (1924–1930) and the Advent of Sound (the Second Republic: 1931–1936)

1 *Un chien andalou* (Luis Buñuel, 1929)
2 *Tierra sin pan* (Luis Buñuel, 1933)

Historical and Political Overview of the Period

Transcending numerous geographical, chronological, and political boundaries, *Un chien andalou* (1929), *L'Âge d'or* (1930), and *Tierra sin pan* (1933), directed by Luis Buñuel, reflect surrealist tendencies and the period of transition from late silent cinema to sound films.[17] Both Spanish and French, yet really neither one nor the other, these films resist easy classification and challenge the very notions of national cinema and national specificity. Aesthetic and economic hybrids, they were filmed in collaboration with various other important Spanish and foreign surrealists and avant-garde figures: Salvador Dalí, Max Ernst, Jean Aurenche, Pierre Prévert, Francisco Cossío, Jaume Miravitlles, Ramón Acín, Rafael Sánchez Ventural, Eli Lotar, and Pierre Unik among others. This diversity of personalities coincides with the complexity of the period. The films from this era contextualize the complex political panorama of the times, including the power shift from the military dictatorship and monarchy to the proclamation of the Second Republic; the relationship between Buñuel's cinema, the Spanish avant-garde, and the surrealist movement in France; and the transition from silent to sound films.

All three films reflect a series of tumultuous social transitions that occurred during this period. While Luis Buñuel and Salvador Dalí were writing the script for *Un chien andalou* in Cadaques (Catalonia) and filming in Paris in 1929, Spain was experiencing an extremely tense political moment. The repressive final year of Miguel Primo de Rivera's dictatorship resonates in this film, which is recognized as an exemplary embodiment of oppressive mechanisms and their (im)possible articulations (what we could consider a mise-en-scène of Freudian theories). The second film, *L'Âge d'or*, was made in 1930, the year of social unrest and civil uprisings that culminated in the fall of Primo de Rivera. *L'Âge d'or* focuses on violence, corruption, and disorder, echoing the great social upheaval that was taking place. This film, known for its attack on powerful institutions such as the church and the monarchy in general, was actually prophetic of the very fall of the Spanish monarchy. Only a year after it was filmed the general elections that resulted in the abdication of Alfonso XIII and the proclamation of the Second Republic (1931–6) were held. Finally, *Tierra sin pan*, filmed in 1933, two years after the proclamation of the Second Republic, exposes the government's frailty and instability. In addition to capturing and echoing the Spanish reality of those times, the films were also symptomatic of wider political turmoil – volatile social tensions in Europe that were intensified by the outbreak of the Russian Revolution, Hitler's ascent to power in 1933, threats of totalitarianism, and the global crisis of capitalism and economic collapse illustrated by the Wall Street Crash in 1929.

Luis Buñuel's cinematic career and the history of all three films are deeply connected to Madrid's avant-garde milieu. This scene served as Buñuel's initiation into film culture and criticism. Buñuel's studies at Madrid's prestigious college the Residencia de Estudiantes (1917–24) exposed him to the cultural elite of the capital and to the literary avant-garde's interest in cinema as a new form of creative expression. His 1925 departure for Paris marked the beginning of his transnational projects and his nomadic existence, as he alternated between Madrid and Paris from then on. Given that they originated in this complex cultural context, it is not surprising that Buñuel's films were cinematic and aesthetic hybrids.

Un chien andalou, *L'Âge d'or*, and *Tierra sin pan* can also be read as a dramatization of Buñuel's own struggles with the surrealist group and its postures, with which he was associated. *Un chien andalou* can be seen as an attempt to gain membership in the surrealist movement and was "created with half an eye to getting [Luis Buñuel and Salvador Dalí] into the exclusive, explosive fraternity they craved" (Hammond, "Lost and Found: Buñuel, *L'Âge d'or* and Surrealism," p. 13). *L'Âge d'or*, despite being considered the quintessential piece of surrealist cinema, reveals its author's doubts and tensions with the movement, exemplified by Buñuel's absence from the film's screening and his lack of involvement in the scandals it ended up provoking.[18] Finally, *Tierra sin pan*, filmed in 1933, was preceded by Buñuel's letter of resignation from the surrealist movement, written to its founder André Breton on May 6, 1932.

Buñuel's first film, *Un chien andalou*, was made in 1929 in collaboration with Dalí at the very end of the industry's transition to sound. It is important to emphasize that the history and production of *Un chien andalou*, *L'Âge d'or*, and *Tierra sin pan* is inseparable from Spanish cinema's silent-to-sound trajectory. This trajectory began with the quite common but often disastrous practice of adding sound to silent films. While Buñuel's "sonorization" of *Un chien andalou* with Argentine tangos and fragments from Wagner's *Tristan und Isolde* was successful, other Spanish directors' attempts at sonorizing were not as compelling. *L'Âge d'or* holds an equally prominent place in the history of sound. It was a state-of-the-art sound film and Buñuel's assistant directors Jacques Brunius and Claude Heyman were hired precisely for their expertise in nascent sound cinema.[19] The film's experimental form is tied to its experiments with sound, including incongruity between sound and image, paradoxical use of intertitle, disorienting sound, contrapuntal sound/image relation, and conceptual experimentation. *Tierra sin pan* is as important in sound cinema development as its predecessors. As several critics have noted, its disturbing, ironic voice-over, co-written with Pierre Unik, is a brilliant technical exercise and social critique that fuses ethnographic documentary with surrealism. In the film analysis section that follows, we offer a close reading of *Un chien andalou* and *Tierra sin pan*, two films that are highly representative of this period.

While Buñuel creatively exploited the medium's revolutionary new feature and "responded as a modernist to the challenge posed by sound," most other Spanish directors resigned themselves to simply continuing shooting silent films that were later sonorized (Kinder, *Blood Cinema*, p. 29). Partially due to this unimaginative, unsuccessful, and mostly catastrophic practice, Spanish cinema production rapidly declined and was faced with numerous challenges. *El misterio de la Puerta del Sol* (Francisco Elías, 1929), technically Spain's first sound film, illustrates the problematic transition to sound. In addition to its own struggles with sound technology, unequipped movie houses hampered its distribution, and the film was practically unseen by the public at large. The same challenges that confronted *El misterio de la Puerta del Sol* plagued other Spanish films of the period and were eventually addressed at the October 1931 Congreso Hispanoamericano de Cinematografía (Hispanic American Film Congress). The congress focused on Spanish cinema's technological inadequacies and raised debates about foreign domination and its effect on the future of the Spanish film industry. The traumatic transition to sound left a few mostly unsatisfactory "alternatives": moving Spanish production to foreign studios (German, French, English); a posteriori sonorization of the silent films directed in Spain; or finally, the option of Spanish cinematographers and professionals moving abroad.[20] Given the situation, it is not surprising that during this period Spanish directors often worked in foreign studios and industries – Warner Brothers in Madrid, Paramount in Joinville (Paris), and Hollywood in the US.[21] Finally, in 1932 Francisco Elías founded the first sound studio in Spain, Studio Orphea in Barcelona. Therefore, the true beginning of sound film production corresponds to the years of the Second Republic (1931–6). Between 1932 and 1936, 109 sound films were produced in Spain.[22]

However, the Republic's progressive and culturally innovative impulses did not prompt a radical change in cinematic practices and expression. Films largely based on conservative cultural models inherited from the previous period continued to dominate the big screen. The persistence of *españoladas*, which painted a picturesque, pre-modern, underdeveloped, and folkloric Spain of gypsies and *toreros*, can be partially explained, Román Gubern argues, through the structure of a cultural market of the times that favored "a native cinema dominated by ruralism, religious conservativism, and an aesthetic autocracy" (Gubern, "1930–1936 (II República)," p. 91).[23] While changes in the film industry did not quite live up to the possibilities opened up by the socio-political transformation taking place at the time, there were directors and producers that took advantage of the radically different cultural climate.

The history of filmmaking under the Second Republic accommodated various ideological tendencies. The two most important production companies of this period, CIFESA (Compañía Industrial Film Española S.A.) and Filmófono, were illustrative of the coexistence of aesthetic, ideological, and cultural differences. CIFESA, founded by Manuel Casanova in 1932 in Valencia, reflected his own conventional and religious cultural milieu. CIFESA was representative of conservative tendencies and was anchored to the right of the political spectrum. Nonetheless, the films it produced revealed tensions between the company's ideological leanings and the works of its directors, typified by Benito Perojo and his urban cosmopolitan comedies.

Ricardo Urgoiti, the founder of Filmófono, CIFESA's main competitor, was an heir to a Basque newspaper family that belonged to the progressive, liberal, laic tradition. Urgoiti's liberal leanings were nevertheless counter-balanced by the production of escapist films geared toward a mass audience. Both companies were very successful. CIFESA's clever use of a Hollywood strategy, *acaparamiento de talentos*, (monopoly over the most prominent directors and stars), resulted in the most commercially successful films of the era. CIFESA's film team counted on such prominent names as Florián Rey, Benito Perojo, Imperio Argentina, and Miguel Ligero among others. Filmófono produced fewer films but had significant popular and commercial success.[24] This early sound period had its golden age in the 1935–6 season, just before the beginning of the Spanish Civil War. The following films were among the most popular: *Don Quintín el amargao* (1935), *Nobleza baturra* (1935), *La verbena de la Paloma* (1935), *La hija de Juan Simón* (1935), *Morena Clara* (1936), and *El bailarín y el trabajador* (1936). This golden film age was also tied to the emergence of a star system featuring the immensely popular Imperio Argentina, Rosita Díaz Gimeno, Antoñita Colomé, Alady, and Miguel Ligero. Furthermore, as Marvin D'Lugo remarks, "it was possible to speak of a boom in national cinema in Spain, spurred in part by the extraordinary support of Spanish films by the general populace" (*A Guide to the Cinema of Spain*, p. 6). Madrid audiences had finally embraced filmgoing with the same intensity that was once reserved for other popular forms of entertainment.

The Republican period also saw the emergence of Spain's first woman director, Rosario Pi (b. Barcelona 1899, d. Madrid 1968).[25] A co-founder of Star Films-Barcelona, she made her directorial debut with *El gato montés* (1935), an adaptation of Manuel Penella's popular *zarzuela* (a light, comic opera). Her second feature film, *Molinos de viento*, was shot at the very beginning of the Civil War in 1936 during the bombings of Barcelona. These films have noted technological shortcomings that are partially the result of precarious filming conditions during the rapidly intensifying conflict. This moment also signals the disintegration of the Spanish film industry and its definitive separation into two ideologically dichotomous cinemas: National versus Republican.

One could argue that half a decade earlier in 1930, Buñuel had already foreseen this catastrophic event, which not only divided Spain but also show-cased the global economic and political divisions that culminated in World War II. Paul Hammond reads *L'Âge d'or* as symptomatic "of a polarisation that would determine the political landscape prior to World War II: the struggle between paired totalitarianism, Stalinism and fascism" ("Lost and Found: Buñuel, *L'Âge d'or* and Surrealism," p. 20). Buñuel's prophetic voice leads us to the next segment of Spanish (film) history – the Civil War that lasted from 1936 to 1939.

1   *Un chien andalou* (Luis Buñuel, 1929)

Context and Critical Commentary

Production credits

Director: Luis Buñuel
Production: Pierre Schilzneck; María Portolés, Luis Buñuel's mother
Cinematography: Albert Duverger
Screenplay: Luis Buñuel; Salvador Dalí
Score: Fragments of Wagner's *Tristan und Isolde*; popular Argentine tango
Genre: Drama, black and white, original version silent; soundtrack added in 1960
Country: France
Runtime: 17 minutes

Cast

Pierre Batcheff	Bicyclist
Luis Buñuel	Young man with razor
Salvador Dalí	Seminary student
Simone Mareuil	The woman
Fano Mesan	Androgynous woman
Jaume Miravitlles	Seminary student

Synopsis

This fractured, non-linear film begins with the title, "Once upon a time . . ." A young man sharpens his shaving razor on a balcony in the moonlight. A cloud then shades him as he slices a woman's eye with the razor. An intertitle then reads, "Eight years later." A bicyclist has an accident in the street. The young woman from the previous scene helps him up and kisses him. They go up to an apartment and begin a sexual encounter, when an incident on the street outside interrupts them. Someone plays with a severed hand that appears on the floor. Later, a police officer picks up the hand and gives it to a woman, who then puts it in a box. Directly following that incident, the woman is hit by a car. The bicyclist and the young woman continue their amorous pursuits in the apartment. Various typically surrealist dream sequences then occur, including the celebrated scene featuring bulls and pianos, discussed in the scene analysis below. Another intertitle reads, "Around 3 o'clock in the morning . . ." A character then enters the apartment, where he finds the couple and chastises the bicyclist by forcing him to carry books like a student. The books turn into pistols, which then kill the bicyclist. The young woman goes to a beach and there she meets another man. In the final scene another intertitle indicates that it is spring. Finally, the bodies of the young woman and her new companion appear half-buried and devoured by insects.

Critical Commentary

Un chien andalou *would not exist had surrealism not existed.*[26]

Although more than 70 years have passed since this film's release, Buñuel's images continue to shock the public to this day. With little experience and a very limited budget (half of the money was provided by his mother), Luis Buñuel made his first film, which became a surrealist masterpiece and the movement's cinematic manifesto. Dalí and Buñuel collaborated on the screenplay, written in only six days and based on images from dreams they both had; Buñuel's was a cloud slicing the moon as a knife cuts part of an eye, and Dalí's was a hand full of ants. They consciously decided to avoid representing any ideas or images that could lend themselves to a rational plot explanation. The movie's scenes, surrealist in their representation of the unconscious dream process, were filmed in only two weeks. The release was an absolute public and critical success, motivating Buñuel to begin filming his second surrealist work, the feature-length *L'Âge d'or*, and consecrating him as a surrealist filmmaker par excellence. In 1960 the soundtrack was added to *Un chien andalou* under Buñuel's supervision, putting the final touch on the film that was released more than 30 years earlier, in 1929.

Film Scenes: Close Readings

Scene 1   *The sliced eye*

The slicing of the woman's eye with a razor that opens *Un chien andalou* could be interpreted as an aperture to the surrealist perspective, suggesting an allegorical reading of the movement's artistic postures. The conventional way of seeing is problematized through the cutting of the eye, which encourages an exploration of the latent contents of the irrational world and the unconscious. The man with the razor is played by Buñuel himself. It is noteworthy that the director actually slices the eye, claiming artistic agency, inserting himself into the action of the film, and visually connecting the director to the intentionality of the gesture. With this radical act Buñuel demonstrates, as Jenaro Talens suggests, that "the question is not so much to show the world but to analyze how this world is looked at (that is, constituted) by the cinematographic apparatus" (Talens, *The Branded Eye: Buñuel's Un chien andalou*, p. xvi). The surprising and visually graphic mutilation of the eye enacts a form of physical aggression not just on the eye, but on the spectator as well. Thus, in the spirit of surrealism, this gesture compels the spectator to be an active subject when faced with a work of art.

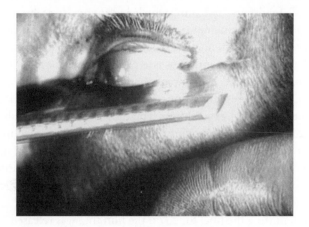

Figure 2.1   The sliced eye (*Un chien andalou*, 1929)

Scene 2   Seduction

This scene can be considered a mise-en-scène of desire and its impulses, made visible in the lover's unabashed chasing of the object of his passion – the woman. The seduction also reveals a power struggle. The spectator sees the close-up of the male hands ripping the dress and caressing the parts of a visually fragmented female body: hair, breasts, waist, and buttocks. Furthermore, this scene alternates superimposed takes of a "dressed" body with those of a "naked" body, thus metaphorically advocating the "undressing" of the body from that which constricts and alienates it from its "liberated" state.

This scene also manifests a nearly endless frustration of desire, as the body has to be repeatedly revealed through the removal of yet another layer of clothing. The other interruption, from the disturbance on the street, also points to the structural impossibility of desire's fulfillment. Finally, this scene reflects the tumultuous relationship between surrealism and its representation of women, both venerated and objectified in the surrealist's quest for aesthetic expression. The fragmented female body conceptually sustains the surrealist work of art, where the intersection of art and femininity (often fragmented) is inevitable. There are various instances that present the female body as the site through which an avant-garde revolution of thought is enacted; however, this very transgression objectifies the female body, putting it on the front lines of the surrealist's conceptual and ideological battleground.

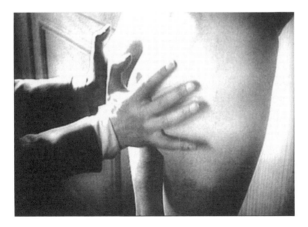

Figure 2.2   Seduction (*Un chien andalou*, 1929)

Scene 3   Seduction interrupted: bearing burdens

In this scene, which follows the "Seduction" scene analyzed above, the protagonist, a prisoner of his own desire, displaces his impulse to pursue the woman onto the surprising act of dragging heavy burdens (corks, melons, priests, donkeys, and pianos). Various critical articles have interpreted these images as representations of the burdens of the protagonist's childhood, tradition, religion, and education. According to Phillip Drummond, this interpretation is "too transparent," resulting in "overly literal" readings ("Textual Space in *Un chien andalou*: Donkeys and Pianos"). Instead, analyzing the scene's incongruence offers a more fruitful reading. The scene brings together vital elements of the surrealist project: narrative disruption; the presence of dream matter; the element of surprise in the narration; incongruence; absence of a defining logical thread; and a break with the traditional concept of spatial and temporal borders. In formal terms, the editing also follows surrealist principles: movement, camera angles, and different takes correspond arbitrarily to each other, depriving the viewer of spatial and narrative referents. The formal and thematic incongruence reaches its climax when, in the end of the scene, the "seduced" protagonist escapes through a window that brings her back to the identical spot from where she had fled.[27]

2   *Tierra sin pan* (Luis Buñuel, 1933)

Context and Critical Commentary

Production credits

Director: Luis Buñuel
Production: Luis Buñuel; Ramón Acín
Cinematography: Eli Lotar
Screenplay: Luis Buñuel; Pierre Unik; Julio Acín
Score: Johannes Brahms (Symphony no. 4)
Genre: Documentary drama, black and white, voice-over
Country: Spain
Runtime: 30 minutes

Cast

Anonymous characters from the different rural zones of the region of Las Hurdes, in the autonomous community of Extremadura, western Spain.

Synopsis

An establishing shot shows a map of Europe and then slowly zooms in on Spain and the area of Las Hurdes, while a voice-over indicates that there are some places where civilization is at a standstill. This voice-over narration comments on the images and scenes of daily life in Las Hurdes throughout the documentary. The camera then shows the streets and houses of the town of La Alberca, where the inhabitants congregate in the plaza to celebrate a traditional festival in which some of the townspeople decapitate chickens while riding horseback. Various shots then show the landscape of the towns in the region and single out an old convent. The camera pans over a river stream where it settles on children drinking and washing themselves, a woman washing dishes, pigs splashing, and children soaking stale bread to eat. These same children, dirty and barefoot, then enter a school where they write about respect for private property while the voice-over points out the absurdity of the image. Various sequences then show people sick with some of the abundant illnesses in the area, in addition to people with development disabilities and dwarfism. In a series of images, we see a swarm of bees as it attacks and kills the donkey that is transporting their hive; the misery of the townspeople contrasted with the wealth of the town's churches; a goat falling as it is killed by a gunshot; and the cadaver of an anonymous baby transported several miles away for its burial. Finally, one night an old woman laments in the street that one of its inhabitants has died. The narrator concludes the film by saying that after two months in Las Hurdes the film crew abandoned the region.

Critical commentary

Tierra sin pan, a "cinematographic essay of human geography," as the film's opening credits indicate, was filmed in 1933. It is structured as a film-collage, or a montage of images and narration that reveal the harsh reality and daily misery of the anonymous inhabitants of Las Hurdes, in Spain's Extremadura region. *Tierra sin pan* is not a purely ethnographic film, but a hybrid work that combines Buñuel's particular, idiosyncratic surrealist montage with testimonial documentary about the lives of the people of Las Hurdes.

The intellectual fascination with the zone of Las Hurdes goes back to the beginning of the twentieth century. From 1904 to 1908, and later in 1926, a cultural magazine entitled *Las Hurdes* was published monthly. The interest in the region culminated in the celebration of a conference for scholars with an interest in Las Hurdes (Congreso de Jurdanófilos), which featured various reformist intellectuals of the time who were involved in a progressive social agenda. But it was in 1922 that the zone came into the public light when the Spanish press widely covered a visit King Alfonso XIII made to the region. Doctor Marañón, a prestigious Spanish doctor and intellectual figure, accompanied the king on his trip and published a memoir of the trip. A film was even made about the royal visit, and although its primary purpose was to promote the figure of the king, it showed scenes of what life was like in Las Hurdes at that time. In 1927 Maurice Legendre, a Frenchman, published his book *Las Hurdes: étude de geographie humaine*, which intrigued intellectuals and scholars of the time. Inspired by this publication, various members of the Parisian October Group, consisting of writers with communist leanings, decided to make a film about Las Hurdes. Writer Yves Allegret and photographer Eli Lotar traveled from France to Las Hurdes to hunt out scene locations. However, when they arrived the authorities detained Allegret and Lotar for their political beliefs, and the two left once they were released. When Allegret returned to Paris, he told Buñuel about their aborted project, prompting Buñuel to make his own film about the remote region in 1933.

Tierra sin pan, noteworthy for its abundant winks to surrealism and the intentionality of its montage, is a complex work of art rather than a simple geographical documentary. Buñuel manipulates and constructs the reality of the film, as in the famous scenes of the shooting of the goat or the killing of the donkey by a swarm of bees. The soundtrack is as manipulated and transgressive. Buñuel juxtaposes the dry, distant voice-over with the dreadful content of what is actually being described; the lack of empathy in the voice clashes with the poverty-stricken milieu and is designed to provoke an emotional reaction in the spectators.

Buñuel himself supervised the recording of the voice-over, whose cold and distant reading sounds as if, instead of describing a trip to misery, it is narrating an excursion to an exotic place, coded in the tone of a documentary travelogue. This Brechtian technique of reinforcing the distance between the image and the narration intensifies the rawness of what we see on screen, and the spectator thus tunes in to the desperation of these anonymous subjects. The film also employs surrealist iconography and cinematic techniques, such as experimentation with close-ups, fades, the evocative juxtaposition of images, and the dislocation of sound from image.

With this film Buñuel denounces the endemic problems of Spanish society – the educational system, the power of the church, the economic crisis – and advocates for the disentitlement of private property belonging to the aristocracy and the Catholic church; the restructuring of the agricultural system; the push for public medicine; and the development of a more solid economic and social infrastructure – the very same issues that the Republican regime in power was facing. Without a doubt, in *Tierra sin pan* Buñuel makes a case for the modernization of Spain, a goal that was also defended by the Republic, and in this way shows the commitment of the Spanish avant-garde and progressive groups to the concrete social reality of the moment. Perhaps for this reason, *Tierra sin pan* was censored during the second, more conservative term of the Republican government under the presidency of Alejandro Lerroux. Buñuel would have to wait until 1936 to show this film in Paris and London, with the narration recorded in both French and English. Consequently, there are different versions of the film: the original in Spanish; the French version, which was sonorized in 1965 under Buñuel's supervision; the English version with some scenes censored; and finally, another Spanish version from 1966, which was dubbed by the actor Francisco Rabal and includes scenes that had been censored in the original version. In this last copy, however, the actor's narration loses the distance and coldness that Buñuel had originally scripted to provoke the viewer. The screening of *Tierra sin pan* was followed by the onset of the Spanish Civil War, and Buñuel's exile to Mexico; 13 years passed before he made another film.

Film Scenes: Close Readings

Scene 1   *The Buñuelian composition: the donkey and the goat*

In *Tierra sin pan* not only are the images that capture the daily reality of the people of Las Hurdes remarkable, but so are the sequences that Buñuel intentionally constructed to make them fit with the film's objective: to provoke the spectator with visualizations of misery and hopelessness. This intentionality implies that not only was the film's narration meticulously scripted, but the visual aspects and events that are presented as non-fiction were carefully constructed as well.

The scene of the goat falling down the mountain did not occur as explained by the narrator; Buñuel himself shot the animal, which the viewer can see through the gun smoke that appears on the right side of the screen. Nor is the scene in which a swarm of bees kills a donkey spontaneous. The crew planned two separate shots to film the scene in which vultures pick at the dead donkey, and actually transported the dead animal to their chosen site.

These sequences – the goat falling and the dead donkey, among others – show how in *Tierra sin pan* reality is altered to fit a scripted narrative. These scenes, which are not a simple reproduction of "reality," together with the film's unsettling voice-over, create an exceptional fusion of ethnographic documentary with surrealism. Lastly, this surrealist manipulation of reality is emphasized through the association between the dead donkey of *Tierra sin pan* and the donkey head that sits on top of a piano in Buñuel's surrealist masterpiece, *Un chien andalou*.

Scene 2   The denunciation: "respect other people's property"

In this scene depicting education in Las Hurdes, not only are the visual shots relevant, but the voice-over is as well, as it underscores what we see on screen. After a scene in which children soak their stale bread in a river where pigs are also bathing, the children enter the village's humble school. Dirty and barefoot, they sit at their decrepit desks while the narrator says, "these children, barefoot and with ragged clothes, receive the same schooling as the rest of the children in the world." The message of this line highlights the incongruity between the misery of the children of Las Hurdes and the educational system, which is anachronistic and alienated from the reality and social context in which these children actually live. The shots of their bare and dirty feet are juxtaposed with the close-ups of their faces, serious and prematurely old, while the narrator describes how "these hungry children are taught, as they are everywhere else, that the sum of the angles of a triangle . . ." Then in perfect handwriting a child writes on the chalkboard, "respect other people's property," which is meaningless within the framework of their absolute poverty.

In this sequence Buñuel denounces one of the endemic problems of Spanish society that the Republican regime of the time attempted to resolve: public education. In 1933, the year Buñuel filmed *Tierra sin pan*, the Spanish Republic that was installed two years earlier was living through a moment of crisis and contradiction; despite its progressive inspiration, the regime took a conservative turn with Alejandro Lerroux's period of centre-right rule (1933–5). Perhaps for this reason, in *Tierra sin pan* Buñuel denounced the persistence of the atavistic educational system and old ideological structures, and demonstrated the need for a pedagogical renovation of public education, one of the Republic's main objectives. The writing of the sentence about respecting other people's property is paradoxical in a situation like that of the children of Las Hurdes, where the images on screen lay bare the misery and scarcity they suffer. The empathy that the Hurdanos' poverty evokes from the viewer is heightened by this perfectly written yet absurd sentence. In addition to the outdated educational system, the film critiques Spanish society's other unjust structures or systems, such as the ownership of private property and land being almost exclusively in the hands of the aristocracy and the church. Thus, the ties between the socialist agenda of the times and the film's objectives are explicit; moreover, some members of the film crew, like Pierre Unik or Buñuel himself, were linked to the Communist Party and advocated its political and social ideals. Finally, at the time of its completion, a photo essay of the film was published in the communist-oriented magazine *Octubre*, edited by poet Rafael Alberti.

Scene 3   *The convent of Batuecas: the surreal and the subconscious*

In this scene we see a wide shot of the abandoned convent of Las Batuecas while the narrator emphasizes that "only one monk, surrounded by various servants, actually lives there." Then the camera juxtaposes multiple close-ups: the church steeple, a servant's body, and the Virgin carved on the front of the building; and shows a panorama of the convent in ruins along with the suggestive penetration of the arc of one of its walls. The scene's Freudian elements and surrealist aesthetic foreground Buñuel's complex scrutiny of religion, power, and sexuality. Buñuel appeals to the subconscious as a means of linking the otherwise disconnected elements of the scene. Thus, the way the scene is edited suggests a critique of the power of the Catholic church, a key element of Buñuel's political and surrealist engagement. Through the visual parallel between the church steeple, whose phallic symbolism stands out over the flat landscape, and the penetration of the arc as a suggestion of femininity or the female, the filmmaker constructs an unconscious association characteristic of surrealism. Through this symbolic linkage, the film denounces not only the institutional power of the church over the town's inhabitants, but also the outdated persistence of Catholic doctrine with respect to chastity and sexual relations, and the anachronistic iconicity of feminine virginity.

Some of the technical aspects that stand out most in this scene are the fades, the associative juxtaposition of shots, and the collage of images that illustrate Buñuel's surrealist stylistic tendencies. The montage technique utilized in this scene is also reminiscent of Buñuel's avant-garde period, intensified by the presence of his surrealist iconography and subjects: the obsessive focus on death, the fascination with repressed drives and desires, the seductiveness of violence, and the sinister power of the church. All of these elements inscribe the film in the ambiguous, hybrid space between an ethnographic documentary and a disturbing surrealist aesthetic exercise.

Director (Life and Works)

Luis Buñuel (b. Calanda 1900, d. Mexico City 1983)

Luis Buñuel Portolés was born on February 22, 1900, in Calanda (Teruel, Spain). He was the oldest of seven children in a wealthy bourgeois family living in Zaragoza. In 1917 he moved to Madrid to begin his higher education. Buñuel went to the prestigious Residencia de Estudiantes, where he met Salvador Dalí and Federico García Lorca, among other artists and intellectuals who would also become powerful cultural figures in Spain. Forced by his father, Buñuel applied to study agricultural engineering, but was not accepted. Instead, he registered for courses in entomology, and also studied philosophy and literature. Ultimately, he graduated in 1924 with a major in history. His attraction to the sciences, principally entomology, influenced his films, the early surrealist works in particular.

In 1924 Buñuel moved to Paris and enrolled in the Film Academy, which was run by Camilla Bardoux, Alex Allen, and Jean Epstein, for whom he worked as an assistant director. Epstein fired Buñuel in 1927 because he refused to work with Abel Gance, a well-known director of large-scale productions such as *Napoleón*, whose style Buñuel did not appreciate. In 1928 Buñuel joined the group of Parisian surrealists, whom he met through his circle of friends from the Residencia de Estudiantes in Madrid. His exploration of surrealist aesthetics and cinema, led to the making of his first film, *Un chien andalou* (1929), co-written with Salvador Dalí. The film received unanticipated public and critical acclaim. The following year Buñuel released *L'Âge d'or*, initially written in collaboration with Dalí, but ultimately finished solely by Buñuel. Because of its anticlericalism and critique of established bourgeois society, the film was censored only a few months after its release.

Buñuel then returned to Spain to make *Las Hurdes* (1932), whose title later became *Tierra sin pan* (*Land Without Bread*). The majority of critics agree that this work could be labeled a "documentary parody" because of its fusion of ethnography and surrealism through a dissociative process of montage, image, and sound that provoke a more intense engagement with the spectator. In this way, Buñuel continued to employ the unconscious associations characteristic of surrealism that he had already used in his two earlier films. The movie was doubly censored in Spain by both the Republican government (1931–6) and the Franco regime (1939–75), which alleged that the images were excessively harsh in their exposition of the abject poverty and misery of the region.

In the mid-1930s Buñuel worked for Ricardo María Urgoiti at Filmófono, where he produced and partially directed four early Spanish sound films: *Don Quintín el amargao* and *La hija de Juan Simón* in 1935 and *¿Quién me quiere a mí?* and *¡Centinela alerta!* in 1936. That same year the Civil War broke out, and Buñuel, a Republican sympathizer, went into exile in the United States, living in Los Angeles and New York from 1938 to 1945. While in the United States, he worked on political documentaries as an adviser and film editor at the Museum of Modern Art in New York as well as for major Hollywood studios, supervising Spanish-language versions of films for MGM and dubbing for Warner Brothers.

In 1946 he moved to Mexico, where he filmed *Gran casino*. He became a Mexican citizen, along with his wife, Jeanne Rucar, and their two children. In this context Buñuel's personal nomadism was transposed to what Marsha Kinder termed a "nomadic discourse" ("The Nomadic Discourse of Luis Buñuel: A Rambling Overview"), potentiated by his exile and displacement. Buñuel's films, reflecting his existence in such diverse and complex cultural milieus, are cinematic and aesthetic hybrids.

In 1950 Buñuel filmed *Los olvidados*, his Mexican masterpiece on poverty-stricken, marginalized street children, and won the award for Best Director at the Cannes Film Festival. It is during this "Mexican phase" that Buñuel gained international recognition for his work. These films, *Nazarín* (1958), *Viridiana* (1961), which obtained the Palme d'Or at Cannes, and *El ángel exterminador* (1962), are characterized by their biting social commentary, and are universally acknowledged as Buñuel's tours de force. It is important to highlight that Buñuel returned to Spain to film *Viridiana*, at which point the Franco regime attempted to use the film and its director, a world-renowned figure and an icon of the Spanish avant-garde, as a self-promoting cultural and political tool. However, *Viridiana*'s transgressive and sacrilegious content earned it the Vatican's condemnation, and the Franco government prohibited the film from being shown in Spanish theaters. It was finally screened in Spain in 1977, two years after the dictator's death.

Buñuel's following films include *Simón del desierto* (1965), *Belle de jour* (1966), *La Vía Láctea* (1969), and *Tristana* (1970). He then made two of his most significant works: *Le Charme discret de la bourgeoisie* (1972), which won the Oscar for Best Foreign Film, and *Cet obscur objet du désir* (1977), his final film. He retired from filmmaking completely and in 1982 published a memoir, *Mi último suspiro* (*My Last Breath*). Luis Buñuel died at his home in Mexico City on July 30, 1983.

3

Spanish Civil War (1936–1939)

1 *Suspiros de España* (Benito Perojo, 1938)
2 *Canciones para después de una guerra* (Basilio Martín Patino, 1971) (documentary footage 1939–54)

Historical and Political Overview of the Period

Social tensions and political instability, in part due to the discontent of conservative sectors and the monarchy, which rejected the Second Republic (1931–6), culminated in a military uprising led by General Francisco Franco on July 17, 1936, against the democratically elected Popular Front government. The Popular Front was an electoral coalition of left-wing political organizations that had won the previous election with the support of the progressive middle class, industrial workers, unionists, peasants, and activists, as well as the regional governments of Catalonia and the Basque provinces. On the opposing side, the church and the landowning and industrial elites backed the military, led by General Francisco Franco. The Falange, the Spanish fascist party, and various right-wing paramilitary groups were also opposed to the Republic. The military conflict intensified into a full-scale, three-year-long civil war that divided the national territory of Spain into two spheres: Republican and Nationalist.

Since the Popular Front government had strongholds and support in the eastern part of Spain, as well as Barcelona and Madrid, the two most important film industry centers remained in Republican hands. The Nationalists were in a much weaker position in the beginning of the war, left with only the crews from two movies that were being filmed on their territory at the time: Fernando Delgado's *El genio alegre* (Córdoba) and Tomás Cola's *Asilio naval* (Cádiz). The Spanish Civil War thus divided both the nation and national cinematography. Nevertheless, the Nationalist disadvantage was soon equalized through the use of the film industry infrastructure of the Axis forces (Germany and Italy) as well as Portugal.

Spain's two cinemas differed significantly. Class distinctions, ideological discrepancies, and religious struggle at the heart of the wartime conflict impacted film production as well. The conflict centered on contested notions of national history in which Nationalist Christian values opposed those of the atheist and materialist Republic. The Nationalists sought political legitimacy through their reclaiming of national culture and tradition, exemplified by their focus on the carefully chosen periods of Spain's allegedly glorious history: the Christian *reconquista* (the reconquest of land lost to the Moors between the eighth and fifteenth centuries), the subsequent reign of the Catholic Monarchs Fernando and Isabel la Católica, the military monarchy of sixteenth-century Castile, and the powerful Spanish Empire. This use of the past worked as an immensely effective unifying trope.

In contrast, the Republicans sought political legitimacy through their plea for democracy against (inter)national fascism and against Franco's troops as illegitimate usurpers of the political order. Winning the military conflict at home and securing political legitimization abroad was a principal aim of both Republicans and Nationalists. It is therefore not surprising that documentaries, propaganda films, and newsreel shorts became the dominant genres of wartime cinematographic production. As Fernando Mantilla poignantly encapsulates it, "we slung a gun over one shoulder and a camera over the other."[28] Feature films were still produced, but their numbers radically declined, especially in comparison to the commercial and artistic vitality of the previous Golden Age of Spanish cinema (1935–6).

What follows is a brief outline of wartime film production. In the Republican camp we can distinguish at least three distinct types of production: anarchist, communist, and governmental. In contrast to the Republicans' exacerbated political polarization, the Nationalists developed more centralized military and cultural initiatives.

Anarchist production

Anarchist cinematographic activities were influenced by the desire for the radical transformation of society, and their belief in this new society was inseparable from the development of innovative forms of creative expression. The Confederación Nacional del Trabajo (CNT, or National Confederation of Labor), the most powerful anarchist organization, held the monopoly of film production and exhibition during the early years of the Spanish Civil War, especially in Barcelona. Necessary resources, such as film equipment and movie theaters, were nationalized and collectivized. This collectivization mirrored the wider political situation, in which the representatives of the working-class parties and unions established their own people's organizations, challenging the authority of the regional and central institutions and governments.

Anarchist production can be divided into two aesthetically and ideologically distinct periods. Their initial fervent cinematographic activities reflected utopian visions of culture, the future, and politics that translated into captivating film works. The emphasis on visual experimentation and improvisation was meant to revolutionize both society and the cinema. Some of the most notable anarchist films were Antonio Sau's *Aurora de esperanza* and Pedro Puche's *Barrios bajos*, both made in 1937. There were also many short films with telling titles that were indicative of their directors', or creators' political beliefs, such as *Reportaje del movimiento revolucionario* (*Report on the Revolutionary Movement*), *La toma de Siétamo* (*The Taking of Siétamo*), *La batalla de Farlete* (*The Battle of Farlete*), *Bajo el signo libertario* (*Under the Libertarian Sign*), *20 de noviembre* (*The 20th of November*), *El acero libertario* (*Libertarian Steel*), and *En la brecha* (*In the Breach*).[29] While this first wave of anarchist films integrated inquisitiveness about the new medium with revolutionary commitment, in the second wave (from August 1937 onward), political zeal faded and production was geared toward more commercial genres, such as comedy. Typical of this later commercial trend were *Nuestro culpable* (1938) by Fernando Mignoni and *¡No quiero . . . no quiero!* (1940) by Francisco Elías. Popular yet criticized, these entertaining comedies were seen as irrelevant and improper within the devastating social and political context.

Communist and Marxist production

The social and cultural utopian ideals that characterized the first wave of anarchist film production differed radically from the political pragmatism of the communists. The Communist Party's military objectives were centralizing and unifying, and their cinematic production mirrored these goals. Unity and a monolithic political message on the front line found a forum in the cultural arena, with *mando único*, or "unified command," on the battlefield and a corresponding *mando único* in the production sector (Gubern, "El cine sonoro (1930–1939)," p. 169).

The goals of the most important and visible communist film production company, Film Popular, were summed up in its motto: "firma comercial antifascista y al servicio de la República" ("an antifascist commercial company at the service of the Republic"). Its newsreel, *España al día*, and its international versions aired abroad – *Nouvelles d'Espagne* and *Spain Today* – underscore the importance of the dissemination of news and propaganda in a time of war. The titles of other short films are illustrative of the documentary activities of the times: *La mujer y la guerra* (*Women and War*, 1938), A. M. Sol (Sollin); *Industrias de guerra* (*War Industries*, 1937), Antonio del Amo; *Sanidad* (*Sanitation*, 1937), Rafael Gil; *Nueva era en el campo* (*A New Era in the Field*, 1937), Fernando Mantilla; *Tesoro artístico nacional* (*Artistic National Treasure*, 1937), Angel Villatoro.[30] Didactic in tone, the films emphasized culture as a weapon of mobilization, cinema at the service of revolution, the importance of education, gender equality, and the significance of the class struggle. Communist/Marxist cinematographic working groups proliferated and were instrumental in disseminating the party's political message and cultural goals. The working groups included, for example, 46 División de "El campesino" and 13 Regimiento de Milicias Populares "Pasionaria." The following organizations also participated in film production: Socorro Rojo Internacional, Alianza de Intelectuales Antifascistas para la Defensa de la Cultura, and Juventudes Socialistas Unificadas.

Republican government production

The legitimization of the Republican government in Spain was tied to gaining political sympathy abroad. Film production was seen as instrumental in influencing international public opinion that would in turn prompt financial and military aid from foreign powers. The emphasis was on seeking support for a democratically elected government that had been overthrown by illegitimate military usurpation. The conflict was also delineated in broader terms as a battle between democracy and the rapidly spreading menace of international fascism.

Among the most notable government productions were: *España 1936* (*Spain 1936*); *España leal en armas* (*Spain Loyal in Arms*); and *Sierra de Teruel* (*Sierra of Teruel*). The most famous film, *Sierra de Teruel/L'Espoir*, was directed by the celebrated French writer André Malraux in 1939 and co-written with Max Aub. Malraux's activities are illustrative of the impact of the foreign presence and its cinematographic activities within Republican

Spain. Other important foreign filmmakers in Spain were Joris Ivens (Dutch), Ernest Hemingway (North American), Roman Karmen (Russian), and Ivor Montagu, Thorold Dickinson, and Norman McLaren (British).

Sierra de Teruel/L'Espoir is an exemplary film for many reasons. For one, it is indicative of the importance placed on gaining support for the Republic from the broad international community. However, to reach this goal, the film had to downplay what were potentially its most radical elements. The director's leftist, revolutionary commitment is therefore sacrificed to a pragmatic aim. According to Román Gubern, *Sierra de Teruel* underplays the disorganization and anarchism of the Republican forces, the atrocities and violence of the conflict, and the religious dispute at the core of the war. Instead, the film emphasizes injustice, the celebration of Republican fraternity, the suffering the Republicans faced due to a lack of material and military means to continue fighting for the right cause, and the general human condition during times of war. Furthermore, as Gubern points out, the nationalities of the foreign volunteers shown in the film are carefully chosen for political reasons, highlighting the participation of Belgian, Arab, German, and Italian volunteers while omitting Anglo-Americans. Republican combatants' political affiliations are deliberately selected as well. While they share a general antifascist spirit (independent, pacifist, socialist) they are never explicitly linked to communism or anarchism (Gubern, "El cine sonoro (1930–1939)," p. 174).

Facing losing the war, *Sierra de Teruel/L'Espoir* was the Republic's last feeble political and economic attempt to rally Western democracies to its cause. However, the ideological concessions they made in an attempt to appeal to the international community were futile. Unfortunately, the film was ill timed. Despite its original intentions, *Sierra de Teruel/L'Espoir* became a testimony to the loss of the war. Filming began in July of 1938 but was not completed before Franco and the Nationalists claimed victory. The crew was forced to leave Barcelona in the beginning of 1939 when the city fell into Nationalist hands. The film was finally finished in Paris after the war ended, thus having its goals rendered obsolete, but becoming one of the most powerful visual testimonies of the defeated side.[31]

Nationalist production

The Nationalists' loss of two major centers of peninsular film production, Barcelona and Madrid, was compensated for by access to film studios and technology in Portugal, Italy, and above all, Germany. On the war front the Nationalists depended on the Axis powers for military and financial aid. This dependence was mirrored on the cultural front by the Nationalist reliance on Axis cinematographic infrastructure. Despite their access to solid propagandistic machinery and support, the Nationalists, curiously enough, did not show an interest in cinema and its mass media capabilities in the first years of the war. This lack of interest is seen in the belated formation of the first official cinematographic institutions and organizations. The Departamento Nacional de Cinematografía (National Department of Cinematography), formed as late as 1938, illustrates the extent to which the Nationalists underestimated the propagandistic potential of the medium. Once involved, they were not as efficient as their Republican counterparts, who had already saturated screens across the globe with their own documentaries from the Spanish Civil War. Nevertheless, the National Department of Cinematography, under the director of propaganda Dionisio Ridruejo and his exceptional crew, produced some well-known shorts as well as the outstanding newsreel *Noticiario Español*, the Nationalist counterpart to films like *España al día*. Among some of the most notable documentaries were *La gran victoria de Teruel* (*The Great Victory of Teruel*), *España heroica* (*Heroic Spain*), and *Marcha triunfal* (*Triumphal March*). *España heroica/Helden in Spanien* (1937), directed by Joaquín Reig, can be interpreted as a Nationalist replica of Republican propagandistic documentaries like *España 1936*.

Significantly, CIFESA (Compañía Industrial Film Española S.A.), one of the most important production companies from the years of the Republic, continued its activities during the Spanish Civil War. Faithful to its conservative political beliefs, the company produced 17 important shorts in 1936 and 1937: *Hacia una nueva España* (*Toward a New Spain*), *Bilbao para España* (*Bilbao for Spain*), *Asturias para España* (*Asturias for Spain*), *Sevilla rescatada* (*Seville Rescued*), *Santander para España* (*Santander for Spain*), *Brigadas Navarras* (*Brigades from Navarra*), *La gran victoria de Teruel* (*The Great Victory of Teruel*), *Entierro del general Mola* (*The Burial of General Mola*). Besides its engagements at home, CIFESA was also involved with German–Spanish co-productions.

One of the most significant wartime co-production companies was Hispano-Film Produktion, which produced five feature films in Berlin, made by CIFESA veterans Florián Rey and Benito Perojo. Florián Rey made two movies, *Carmen, la de Triana* (*Carmen, the Girl from Triana*, 1938) and *La canción de Aixa* (*Song of Aixa*, 1938), both starring the immensely popular Imperio Argentina, his wife at the time. Benito Perojo filmed the other three, featuring his new female star Estrellita Castro: *El barbero de Sevilla* (*The Barber of Seville*, 1938), *Suspiros de España* (*Sighs of Spain*, 1938), and *Mariquilla Terremoto* (*Mariquilla the Earthquake*, 1939).

These films resulted from the intersection of both countries' political and economic interests; Spain needed Germany's industrial infrastructure to continue its own feature film production, not to mention its ideological, propagandistic, and military support. Germany was interested in having access to Spanish crews and materials for documenting its own military trials and maneuvers in Spain (Condor Legion), in addition to the economic benefits of the significant Hispanic film market in Latin America. Thus "colonized," Spain provided directors, actors, and quintessentially "Spanish" themes while the Germans controlled the financing, equipment, studio production, and distribution.

Hispano-Film Produktion films were shot both in Berlin studios and on location in Spain (Seville). The thematic choices, mostly drawn from *españoladas*, were seen as beneficial to both countries.[32] For Germany, exalting the cliché of Spanishness was a solid and successful marketing ploy. For Spain, these films offered the chance to reclaim cultural pre-eminence in Latin America through the concept of *hispanidad*.[33] Given the socio-political context and economic interests of Hispano-Film Produktion, it is not surprising that the tropes and images that saturated these films were flamenco, guitars, Andalusian patios, polka-dot dresses, clichéd bravery, and other folkloric elements.

The first film featured in this Spanish Civil War section, Benito Perojo's *Suspiros de España*, is representative of this context. Although Perojo's prolific and diverse career, spanning six countries and as many decades, can't simply be reduced to these Berlin activities, his early films are nevertheless representative of Spain's cinematographic collaboration with the Axis powers. This film is named after a popular pasodoble. Gubern notes that the film's success was precisely tied to "the exaltation of a pan-hispanism and fatherland that was distant, but not lost" (Gubern, *Benito Perojo: Pionerismo y supervivencia*, p. 306). The film's nostalgic tone and explicit allusions to the native soil, seen in the title itself, acquired even more significance during the Spanish Civil War period.

The second film in this section, Basilio Martín Patino's *Canciones para después de una guerra*, is not from this period, but we have included it for its invaluable documentary footage of the Spanish Civil war and the postwar period that follows (1939–54). Filmed in 1971 and authorized for release only in 1976, it is the first of Martín Patino's celebrated "trilogy of remembrance" (see "Director (Life and Works)" below). The film engages intensely with the Spanish past, focusing on collective and popular historical memory through its resourceful use of (post)war newsreel footage and other archival materials such as advertisements, popular film, and songs from the period. As Jo Labanyi has argued, the visual fragments are "lifted out of context and reorganized into a new constellation releasing alternative meanings" ("History and Hauntology; or, What Does One Do with the Ghosts of the Past? Reflections on Spanish Film and Fiction of the Post-Franco Period," p. 71). Furthermore, this archival footage is interwoven and overlaps with voice-overs of personal (post)war testimonies. What emerges from these fragments is a visual and material sense of the era, the issues underlying the violent conflict, and the respective agendas and beliefs of the warring sides. Martín Patino emphasizes the conflict by manipulating the film negative to depict Nationalists through blue filters and Republicans, anarchists, and communists through red ones.

Canciones para después de una guerra is also significant because Martín Patino's strategies of representation can be read as a postmodern rendition of some of the filmmaking conventions that were employed during the Spanish Civil War. Through his use of light, color, and sound Martín Patino shows that the nature of memory is intrinsically tied to the nature of representation and cinematic language. Martín Patino's film is an elaborate exercise of montage and sound manipulation as he overlaps the past "remembered" with a reconstructed present. The documentary, ravaged by the effects of history, gives us a glimpse into the mediated, re-created, and reconstructed past. In sum, through its very form, with its spectral voices and haunting images, Martín Patino's film presents the contemporary spectator with the ghostly and traumatic history of the Spanish Civil War.[34]

1   *Suspiros de España* (Benito Perojo, 1938)

Context and Critical Commentary

Production credits

Director: Benito Perojo
Production: Hispano-Film Produktion

Cinematography: Georg Bruckbauer
Screenplay: Benito Perojo, Roberto de Ribón
Score: Juan Mostazo and Walter Sieber
Genre: Comedy, black and white
Country: Spain/Germany
Runtime: 90 minutes

Cast

Estrellita Castro	Sole
Concha Catalá	Dolores
José Escandel	Artistic agent
Pedro Fernández Cuenca	Businessman
Fortunato García	Hotel manager
Miguel Ligero	Relámpago ("Lightning Bolt")
Manuel Pérez	Bellboy
Roberto Rey	Carlos
Alberto Romea	Freddy

Synopsis

Sole and her mother Dolores work in the public laundry in Seville, sharing the work of washing the clothes and maintaining their modest house. They live next door to Sole's roguish uncle, Relámpago ("Lighting Bolt"), who is always trying to get them to evade work and survive on as little as possible. While the whole family is at home doing different things, on the other side of the city, Carlos, the ambitious manager of one of the great cabarets in Havana, is in a hotel room. He has traveled to Seville to find an artist who won a local talent show, with the intention of taking her to Havana to perform in the cabaret Perroquet.

Sole comes to the hotel to return an article of clothing to Carlos, who then realizes that she is the singer he was searching for. As he tries to explain this to her, Sole quickly leaves the hotel. Relámpago, who is also at the hotel, befriends Carlos by telling him that Sole is his goddaughter, and promises to lead him to Sole. When Carlos and Sole meet again he offers her a contract in his cabaret, but she feels ambivalent about leaving Seville. Nevertheless, during one of Dolores and Relámpago's arguments,

Sole leaves the house and departs for Cuba. However, to Sole's surprise, in one of the boat's cabins she runs into Dolores and Relámpago, who don't want her to go to Cuba without them. To complicate matters further, Carlos refuses to allow Sole's family to travel with her in a first-class cabin, so she breaks her commitment to him, refusing to abandon them for artistic fame. When Carlos arrives in Havana, his boss scolds him for his conduct and incompetence. Once in the city, another entertainment company offers Sole a contract, but she refuses because she realizes she is in love with Carlos.

Critical commentary

Suspiros de España is emblematic of the tendency of Perojo's film productions in Berlin to exalt Spanishness through folkloric tropes. Each of the film's characters, especially Sole and Relámpago, embodies stereotypical aspects of Spanish culture. Sole, the protagonist, represents an "archetypal" Spanishness reflected in the songs that she interprets, her costumes, and her popular vernacular. As Terenci Moix points out, Estrellita Castro, the actress who played Sole, "stood out for her use and abuse of vernacular humor, street smarts, and her employment of *castizo*[35] recourses in both her acting style and the themes of the songs in her films. She exaggerated the ethnic aspects of her characters and stubbornly insisted on the superiority of the local" (*Suspiros de España: la copla y el cine de nuestro recuerdo*, p. 82). On the other hand Sole's godfather, Relámpago, also represents the idea of Spanishness, though from a different perspective; he embodies the picaresque spirit of the lower class, traditionally stereotyped in Spanish culture. Furthermore, the film's characters constantly celebrate their loyalty and love for their country, exemplifying *Suspiros de España*'s exaltation of Spain, the far-away, but not lost, country. The sentiment of nostalgia for Spain is reinforced through the film's central musical piece performed by Sole, the traditional pasodoble "Suspiros de España."

In sum, these Berlin films tended to highlight *castizo* features and recycled tried-and-tested elements of folkloric musicals by exploiting the celebrity of Spain's star actors. Benito Perojo's *Suspiros de España* reflects a struggle over the redefinition of Spanish identity, an inevitable enterprise in an era of wartime national exaltation. By the end of the Civil War and with the triumph of Franco, filmmaking was further reduced to propagandistic folkloric and *costumbrista*[36] topics at the service of legitimizing the war – all under the watch of fierce censorship that imposed its control on all cultural production. Thus, in *Suspiros de España* we can discern several elements that would later become some of the principal characteristics of cinematic production during the first years of the Franco regime.

Film Scenes: Close Readings

Scene 1   The "communion" of the social classes

Narrated in a humorous and comical way, the first scenes in *Suspiros de España* illustrate the differences between social classes that coexisted in Spain during this period. Carlos, the ambitious talent scout who discovered Sole, invites her godfather Relámpago to celebrate her imminent fame. The difference in social class that separates Carlos and Relámpago seems to dissipate through the sense of bonding created by their communal enjoyment of *jerez* (a Spanish sherry), the guitar, and flamenco. In accordance with the film's broader ideological aim, the exaltation of the fatherland, coded through these folkloric elements, supposedly transcends class boundaries. Both Carlos and Relámpago are happy to have found in Sole a future star who can bring them prosperity. At the end of the scene, however, the characters' newfound brotherhood is broken once each returns to his own social world. Carlos stays in his luxurious hotel room while Sole's picaresque godfather is forced to return to his modest household, but not before slipping something into his pocket without Carlos noticing.

Scene 2   Sole's universe

In this scene a banal brawl turns into an intense fight in which Sole's mother and godfather struggle for control and power over the house. The scuffle has the classic comedic elements of simple and predictable humor, depicting a slapstick representation of the customs and nature of the working class. What results is an exaltation of the simplicity of the village and the richness of its customs, while at the same time the viewer perceives a strong critique of the characters' inability to develop and incorporate the "civilizing" values of modernity. It is this very fight that propels Sole to abandon Seville because she feels that her limited cultural context will never change. However, once embarked on her overseas journey, she continues to experience the limits of her socio-economic background. In order for Sole's family to travel with her, she has to change her ticket from first to third class, relegating the family to its original poverty-determined "place." Thus, as in the "communion" scene, the promise of social mobility is truncated.

Scene 3 Couplets of nostalgia

Dolores, Relámpago, and Sole's voyage to Havana, in the company of a group of people who are emigrating from Spain to Cuba, is tied to larger issues at the core of the film: Spanish migration abroad and the idealization of the nation left behind. In this scene the three protagonists focus on the shrinking horizon, a symbol of the increasing distance from the country they have left in search for a better life in the Americas. In each of their faces we can perceive nostalgia for their country, which is reinforced by the couplets that they each sing. The most noteworthy song is the one that Sole sings: "mothers never abandon their children, Spain comes with us and will live in our hearts as a memory and a hope, a song and a sigh." Within this framework it is important to emphasize that Sole is played by Estrellita Castro, who was popularly known as "the star of the gypsies;"

Figure 3.1 Couplets of nostalgia (*Suspiros de España*, 1938)

gypsies being coded as an equivalent of Spanishness itself, especially for foreign spectators. This problematic racial coding, erasure, and stereotyping are especially significant within the context of Spanish and German wartime film co-productions that relied on such reductive representations for the commercial success of their films. Sole's performance of "Suspiros de España" ("Sighs of Spain") defines the characters' spirits as well as represents a folkloric national exaltation of Spanishness. For Sole, Spain is the motherland engraved on her heart, even if she is a world away. The feeling of nostalgia also intensifies for Dolores and for Sole's uncle Relámpago, as they drift further away from Spain while listening to Sole's "Suspiros de España." The strategic and ideological use of Spanishness that this scene reflects – music, dance, and dress – as well as the construction of homeland, are incarnated in Sole, who will later commercialize this image through her successful artistic career.

Director (Life and Works)

Benito Perojo (b. Madrid 1894, d. Madrid 1974)

Benito Perojo was born in Madrid into a bourgeois family. His father was a journalist and politician of Cuban origin. Perojo majored in electrical engineering at the University of London, where he came into contact with new technology that he would later use in his filmmaking. His first works date back to 1913, when he made silent documentaries such as *Cómo se hace un periódico*. In 1915, influenced by the success of a film character, Charlot, played by Charles Chaplin, Perojo created an aesthetically similar character named El Peladilla. With this character, Perojo became extremely popular and filmed various comic shorts such as *Donde las dan, las toman* and *Clarita y Peladilla en el fútbol*, both in 1915.

Following the popularity of his early films, Perojo began his sound film period, which consecrated him as a director of folkloric musicals and earned him public acclaim. Along with the director Florián Rey, Perojo was considered to be the most commercial pre-Civil War filmmaker. Despite this success, his work was not always highly regarded by critics; some defined his particular style of making simple and commercial films based on patriotic folkloricism as *perojism*. These films were musicals made strictly for entertainment, with simple plots and traditional Spanish folkloric songs. Among these productions *El negro que tenía el alma blanca* (1926, later remade as a sound film), *Los hijos de la noche* (1934), *Malvaloca* (1927), and *La verbena de la Paloma* (1935, filmed in Berlin), stand out. In 1938 *Suspiros de España* debuted, with the famous folkloric singer Estrellita Castro. Following the popular success of these films, Perojo made a series of films in Argentina between 1942 and 1948, mostly starring the actress and singer Imperio Argentina, who thereafter became the diva of Spanish folkloric films like *Goyescas* (1942), *La casta Susana* (1944), *Los majos de Cádiz* (1946), and *Lo que fue de la Dolores* (1947).

In 1948 Perojo returned to Spain and founded his production company Producciones Benito Perojo, which completely occupied his time and led him to retire from directing. With his company Perojo financed films along the lines of those that he had directed earlier – commercial comedies for pure entertainment. In 1954 he produce a comedy, *Novio a la vista*, directed by Luis García Berlanga, and *Morena Clara*, by Luis Lucia. Perojo went on to produce the majority of Luis Lucia's musicals, which brought child stars like Marisol and Rocío Dúrcal into the limelight with movies such as *Un rayo de luz* (1960) and *Ha llegado un ángel* (1961). He also produced a new version of *La verbena de la Paloma*, directed by José Luis Sáenz de Heredia in 1963. In 1971 Benito Perojo produced another of Luis Lucia's films, *La orilla*, which was his last production. He died in Madrid in 1974.

2   Canciones para después de una guerra (Basilio Martín Patino, 1971)

Context and Critical Commentary

Production credits

Director: Basilio Martín Patino
Production: Julio Pérez Tabernero
Cinematography: José Luis Alcaine
Screenplay: Basilio Martín Patino
Score: Classics from the era, selected by Manuel Parada
Genre: Documentary
Country: Spain
Runtime: 115 minutes

Songs

Cara al sol	Falange hymn
Ya hemos pasado	Celia Gámez
Legionario	Popular
Échale guindas al pavo	Imperio Argentina
La hija de Don Juan Alba	Niño de Utrera
La morena de mi copla	Estrellita Castro
Noticiero y discurso	Don Ramón Serrano Suñer
La bien pagá	Miguel de Molina
Mírame	Celia Gámez
Yo te diré	Isa Pereira
Tatuaje	Conchita Piquer
La gallina papanatas	Popular
Mi vaca lechera	Juan Torre Groso
Raska-yu	Bonet de San Pedro
Total para qué	Don Liñán
Mi casita de papel	Antoñita Rusel
Santa Marta	Tomás Ríos
Viajera	Lolita Garrido
Una, dos, patatín, patatín	Antonio Machín
La despedida	Antonio Machín
Amar y vivir	Antonio Machín
María Dolores	Jorge Sepúlveda
La Chunga	Pepe Blanco
Himno a la Virgen de Fátima	Popular
Sitio de Zaragoza	Popular
Montañas nevadas	Popular
Lerele	Lola Flores
Coplillas de las divisas	Lolita Sevilla
Limosna de amor	García Guirao

Synopsis

Canciones para después de una guerra depicts postwar Spain and its evolution through the 1950s. It is a montage of images and sounds from the period between 1939 and 1953, with some fragments that correspond chronologically to the Spanish Civil War. The first scene of the film shows the triumphal entrance of Franco's army into Madrid following the Spanish Civil War, which marked the beginning of the dictatorship. We also see ritualized spectacles of power in the spirit of the fascist aesthetization of politics, such as parades, Franco speaking to the masses, and huge demonstrations, as well as scenes of daily life and postwar misery. Accompanying the screen images are popular songs of the time and the sporadic interventions of voice-overs that testify to and remember the years of dictatorial repression. The film's message is furthermore constructed through the director's inventive use of archival material such as newsreel footage, clips of NO-DO,[37] photos, newspaper and magazine articles, comics from the era, advertisements, and popular films. The film ends with images of the return of the *Semiramis* (1954), the ship chartered by the Red Cross that carried the surviving members of the Spanish Blue Division[38] from the war on the Eastern Front, and a close-up of then-prince Juan Carlos.

Critical commentary

Canciones para después de una guerra, made in 1971 and practically in hiding (Martín Patino compiled the archival material in Berlin), had a number of problems with the Franco regime's censorship, which eventually prevented its release altogether. The public didn't see the film until 1976, after Franco's death. It is also important to note that the government took Martín Patino's idea and funded the production of a similar film: *Canciones de nuestra vida* (Eduardo Manzanares, 1975), though it obviously obliterated a central element of *Canciones para después de una guerra*: the harsh critique of the Franco dictatorship.

   Canciones para después de una guerra engages intensely with the Spanish past, recuperating collective and popular historical memory. It also reveals what Manuel Vázquez Montalbán termed the *crónica sentimental de la España franquista* ("sentimental chronicle of Francoist Spain"; Vázquez Montalbán, *Crónica sentimental de España*), through an inventive use of archival material, advertisements, popular films and songs, and voice-overs of personal testimony.

   The film is celebrated for its creative and elaborate use of montage, a technique that Martín Patino, a prominent directorial voice from the 1960s and New Spanish Cinema, mastered through his experience of directing commercials. The film centers on the beginning of the dictatorship and the repressive and miserable early postwar years. The severe economic crisis in Spain caused by the destruction of so many factories and agricultural crops during the Civil War, in addition to the general crisis that World War II provoked, also contributed to these grueling years. This period, referred to as the *años de hambre* or "years of hunger," was also when the foundations of the Francoist ideology began to take root, with its exaltation of the fatherland, uncritical celebration of "Spanishness," promotion of the military ethos, and repressive assertion of order and social control.[39]

Clips of documentary reports from the era, scenes from popular films, newspaper photos, commercials, comics, and scenes from NO-DO fuse with the sounds of popular songs of the time. The strategic and premeditated composition of these elements sought to impact the spectator and provoke a reflection on the postwar reality, evoked through the testimony of the film's anonymous narrators. Thus, a personal, subjective, and authorial dimension is inscribed into the national narrative. The harshness of the postwar images mixes with the lyrics of the popular music from the era, while a narrator reminds the viewer about the affective and cultural importance of these songs: "they were songs to bring ourselves out of the darkness, the fear; songs to help us with the need to dream." The enjoyment of popular culture functioned as a survival strategy against wartime and dictatorial repression, and Martín Patino's concern with history, representation, and politics is tinted by a subjective, humanist aspect.

Canciones para después de una guerra is an outstanding and visually innovative documentary that denounces the repression and social control of the Franco regime, at the same time that it reclaims the testimony of the popular memory to the detriment of the officially endorsed memory of the postwar years. This critique of the dictatorial regime's manipulation of memory is quite explicit, revealed in a sequence of mass fascist demonstrations while the voice-over counters that "things were not as they seemed." Martín Patino not only documented a period in Spanish history, but also constructed a visual form of resistance to the repression of the Franco regime through the reclaiming of popular culture as a source of historical analysis.

Film Scenes: Close Readings

Scene 1   "Spain's salvation"

The first scene of *Canciones para después de una guerra* shows the Nationalist army's triumphal entrance into Madrid following the Spanish Civil War.

With the musical accompaniment of the Falange hymn "Cara al sol" ("Face to the Sun") and the gesture of the raised arm, a fascist salute with which Spanish people welcomed General Francisco Franco's victory, Martín Patino presents testimony of Spain's fascist past to the contemporary viewer. Archival images taken from Nationalist propagandistic footage show the entrance of the tanks into newly "liberated" Madrid. The camera shows close-ups of the radiant faces of people of all ages who appear to welcome the triumph of the new regime. We see numerous shots of smiling old women, mothers with children in their arms, boys and girls of various ages, adolescents, and adults, all saluting and welcoming the general and his troops. The Falangist hymn reinforces the public exhilaration seen on screen. The song's lyrics communicate a metaphor of renewal, praising the new regime that will supposedly return "the spring that was lost" during the Spanish Civil War.

One of the most significant aspects of this scene is Martín Patino's montage and symbolic use of color; tinting images with yellow or blue filters (representing Franco and the Nationalists), or red (signifying the left and the Republicans). The blue used to denote the Nationalists is also the color of the allies of the fascist Axis (Germany, Italy, and Japan), while the color chosen to represent the Republicans, red, has historically been associated with Marxism and socialism. In using these ideologically charged filters, Martín Patino manipulates the images as a way to show the ideological differences between the two main factions involved in the Spanish Civil

Figure 3.2   "Spain's salvation" (*Canciones para después de una guerra*, 1971)

War. Throughout the entire film the colors alternate, visually marking the discredited Republican past against the beginning of Franco's new regime and all its supposed promises of a brighter future. Therefore, by highlighting these ideologically charged images, the film confronts the viewer with the manipulation of information and historical events that were distorted after the war. This film shows how the new regime attempted to rewrite history and obliterate Spain's Republican past. The chromatic alternation and Martín Patino's own visual manipulations emphasize the importance of propaganda and montage, while pointing to the deceptiveness of the images and information that the Francoist government apparatuses diffused daily as the "official history."

Scene 2   *"They shall not prevail"* (No pasarán)

The song "Ya hemos pasado" ("We've Prevailed"), sung by Celia Gámez, accompanies the scenes that follow the Franco troops' triumphant occupation of Madrid. The scene opens with montaged and re-filtered images of Marxist symbols like the raised fist, as the song glaringly mocks the famous Republican motto "They shall not prevail" (*No pasarán*) attributed to Dolores Ibárruri, the leader of the Spanish Communist Party, who was also know as "La Pasionaria." The use of Celia Gámez's voice, a popular Spanish singer of the era, denotes how profoundly important it was for the regime to find well-known figures to help legitimize its rule. Gámez became one of the Nationalists' cultural and artistic representatives who helped to diffuse the ideas of Franco's incipient regime. "Ya hemos pasado" (literally, "We have entered") confirms and glorifies the Nationalists' triumph. Gámez's aural exaltation of Franco is accompanied by Martín Patino's visual manipulation of images that underline the song's true meaning: the demonization of Republican ideals and the veneration of the Nationalists. First, the red filter tints Republican images such as pistols in hands, statues of Lenin, and apparent chaos in the streets. As the voice of Celia Gámez begins to glorify the new regime, the scenes and color filter also change. Through the blue filter we then see the images representing the new regime: the supposedly restored order, the distribution of bread, and the celebration of the reunification of families separated by war. The effect produced by the representation of the Franco establishment's values, through the film's audio and visual elements, illustrates how the history told by the triumphant regime could become the official history. As Martín Patino shows, cultural production was a fundamental part of the Franco regime's apparatus of legitimization.

Scene 3   *Poorly paid postwar Spain*

Through the images in this scene Martín Patino experiments with the juxtaposition of visual effects and the soundtrack in order to confront the viewer with the fissures that the Civil War and the dictatorship left in Spanish society. The different shots show the faces of needy and hungry people, the true losers of the war. Martín Patino's montage shows society's most vulnerable members: children, the elderly, widows, and single mothers. Their faces are disquieting when accompanied by the famous song "La bien pagá" ("The Well-Paid Woman"), whose lyrics refer to a monetary exchange between a man and a prostitute. The director ironically pairs the soundtrack to the image, presenting what we could read metaphorically as a poorly paid Spain. Martín Patino's montage evokes a miserably "paid" population that had lost everything in a violent, three-year-long civil conflict. Martín Patino shows the harsh reality of the hunger and desolation that people suffered following the war, and at the same time reveals the implicit violence of the paternalistic and controlling character of the new regime. The triumphal

Figure 3.3   Poorly paid postwar Spain (*Canciones para después de una guerra*, 1971)

postwar discourse of the Civil War's victors was, as exposed by Martín Patino, in profound discord with the reality of the suffering population.

Director (Life and Works)

Basilio Martín Patino (b. Salamanca 1930)

Basilio Martín Patino was born in Salamanca in 1930, where he studied philosophy and literature at the Universidad Pontificia. There he collaborated on the creation of a university film club and the magazine *Cinema universitario*, which was eventually shut down by the Franco regime's censors. In 1954 Martín Patino moved to Madrid to enroll in the Escuela Oficial de Cinematografía (Official School of Cinematography), graduating as a director in 1960. In 1965 he wrote and directed *Nueve cartas a Berta*, a film that became one of the emblematic works of the so-called New Spanish Cinema. The film tells the story of Lorenzo, a law student in Salamanca, and his epistolary exchange with Berta, the daughter of an exiled Republican in London. Berta's impact on Lorenzo prompts a series of reflections on the suffocating nature of provincial life, the Francoist status quo, and the general feeling of discontent that pervaded the dictatorship. With this film the director won the Concha de Plata award at the San Sebastián Film Festival. During this period Martín Patino also worked in advertising, and it was his early experience making commercials that taught him the editing and screenwriting techniques that would later influence his film career.

In 1968 *Del amor y otras soledades* was released, starring the popular actress Lucía Bosé. Martín Patino then made the celebrated *Canciones para después de una guerra* (1971), a brilliant exercise in documentary montage that engages intensely with the Spanish postwar past, as well as the meaning and construction of collective and popular historical memory. The censorship and delay it encountered also occurred with his later films: *Queridísimos verdugos* (1973), a documentary that incorporates interviews with executioners during the Franco regime, and *Caudillo* (1974), a critical portrait of Franco; neither film premiered until 1977.

In 1985 he directed *Los paraísos perdidos*, in which he recreates life in Salamanca at the beginning of the socialist government, which came to power in 1982. Shortly thereafter, Martín Patino filmed *Madrid* (1987), a historical and political contemplation of the Spanish capital and its role in the Civil War and the postwar period, using similar collage and editing techniques to those employed in his renowned *Canciones para después de una guerra*. Despite their critical success, these films were not well received by the public. *Canciones para después de una guerra, Caudillo* (1974), and *Madrid* (1987) comprise his "trilogy of memory," with which he participates in the recuperation of Spain's collective memory.

In 1991 Martín Patino directed *La seducción del caos* for television, and in 1996 he filmed the series *Andalucía, un siglo de fascinación*, comprised of seven short films for television. In 2002 he presented his final film, *Octavia*, and appeared alongside directors like José Luis Borau and Miguel Picazo in the documentary *De Salamanca a ninguna parte*, directed by Chema de la Peña, about film censorship during the Franco dictatorship.

4

The Autarky: Papier-Mâché Cinema (1939–1950)

1 *Raza* (José Luis Sáenz de Heredia, 1941)
2 *Locura de amor* (Juan de Orduña, 1948)

Historical and Political Overview of the Period

The Nationalist victory and the end of the Spanish Civil War on April 1, 1939, prompted Spain's decades-long isolation from the rest of Europe and the world. The Spanish fascist regime faced political and economic ostracism from all but Germany and Italy, the Axis powers that had supported Franco's army during the war. Paradoxically, Franco embraced this rejection through the politics of autarky, a policy that attempts to create a self-sufficient national economy entirely insulated from international trade. In the case of Spain, it was both an economic measure and an element of Franco's Nationalist rhetoric in which the country's postwar ostracism was modified and affirmed. The consequences of autarky were disastrous because they accentuated the general crisis in the country, leading to problems such as the development of the black market (*el estraperlo*), hunger, unemployment, and increased prostitution. So dire was the situation that the postwar decade was and still is commonly referred to as "the years of hunger" (*los años de hambre*).[40]

In this isolated climate the legitimization of the new Nationalist dictatorship was tied to the validation of what was deemed to be the "authentic" Spain. Already apparent during the Civil War, the Nationalists' views of history and their defense of a supposed national culture, tradition, and religion were now articulated even more forcefully. During the postwar years the defeated side of the Civil War faced severe political repression in the form of executions, concentration camps, forced labor, and exile. It is important to emphasize that the Nationalists were not a homogeneous entity, and those factions that had supported Franco during the war – the Falange, the military, the Catholic church, large landowners, and conservative industrial bourgeoisie – now engaged in a power struggle. However, Franco, Spain's head of state and its *caudillo*,[41] was a skilled political maneuverer determined "to allow no single group to challenge his own firm grip on power" (Boyd, "History, Politics, and Culture 1936–1965," p. 92).

Francoist cinematographic politics reflected a more general climate of political repression. The Nationalists' wartime lack of interest in the medium was now replaced by an excessive attention to regulations and laws that mirrored the policing of other spheres of cultural production. The National Department of Cinematography (Departamento Nacional de Cinematografía) was created in May of 1938 as an offshoot of the Delegation of Press and Propaganda (la Delegación de Prensa y Propaganda). Thereafter, a complex mixture of state institutions became responsible for overseeing film production. Between 1939 and 1951 film production and regulation were under the control of four different state departments: Home Office (Gobernación), Commerce and Industry (Comercio e Industria), General Secretary of the Movement (Secretaria General del Movimiento), and National Education (Educación Nacional).

The politics of film production in 1940s Spain was controlled by two mechanisms: repressive measures and protectionist measures; the former consisted of censorship and obligatory dubbing while the latter offered state subsidies for film production. Censorship included supervision and approval of film scripts, prohibition of particular scenes, requests for modifications of particular scenes, issuing of filming permits, and issuing of permits allowing for the exhibition of Spanish and foreign films on national territory. Despite the strong political and moral motivation behind censorship, the censorial apparatus was surprisingly arbitrary and ambiguous. There was no explicit set of rules, criteria, or guidelines for censorship until as late as 1962.[42]

Even though Spanish films were occasionally dubbed before the Civil War, the practice become obligatory in April of 1941 when the Ministry of Industry and Commerce issued a decree ordering that Spanish be the sole language of films shown in the country.[43] This measure had several important repercussions. Spanish films could no longer compete with foreign films that were already more popular with the Spanish public. The practice was also part of a complex government regulation that tied dubbing licenses to the granting of lucrative import licenses. In this profitable business, Spanish films became only a secondary factor: "the dispensing of dubbing licenses was tied to the production of Spanish films; therefore, in reality, the films themselves were not the objective, but an inevitable means for importing foreign film" (Monterde, "El cine de la autarquía (1939–1950)," p. 196). Hence the governmental politics of protection and subvention was in reality a politics of speculation.

CIFESA (Compañía Industrial Film Española S.A.), already powerful before the war, became the most important production company in the 1940s. CIFESA's conservative and traditionalist tendencies matched the new regime's politics. Thanks to a favorable ideological climate and a solid industrial infrastructure, CIFESA produced 41 films between 1939 and 1950. While many of these films reflected the thematic and ideological preferences of the regime, typified by the production of Francoist historical epics, CIFESA also made several less explicitly political films, ranging from light comedies geared toward a mass audience to profitable escapist musicals. As in the pre-war era, CIFESA's success continued to be rooted in its imitation of the Hollywood film industry, in its efficient production mechanisms, and in its impressive national star system. CIFESA did not have a serious competitor among production companies until the middle of the decade. Cesáreo González's Suevia Films became the most serious competitor, making 38 films, followed by Barcelona-based Ignacio Iquino's Emisora Films, which made 25, and Aureliano Campa, who produced 19.

The postwar period saw both continuities with and breaks from previously preferred themes, genres, and styles. Benito Perojo and Florián Rey, veterans from the silent era, continued filming. Benito Perojo made several important films in Spain and Argentina, where he worked between 1942 and 1948. Florián Rey, however, never regained the pre-war success he had had with his films starring Imperio Argentina. His tried and tested formulas did not connect as well with the postwar public and his new star, Concha Piquer, was not as glamorous as Imperio Argentina, although she was extremely popular because her songs, essentially verses and couplets, played constantly on Spanish radio. In addition to these veteran directors, there were also a considerable number of filmmakers trained during the Republic and the war years, such as José Luis Sáenz de Heredia, Luis Marquina, Eduardo García Maroto, Ignacio F. Iquino, and Edgar Neville, among others. As with the production companies, some directors' political orientations were closer to Franco's regime than others. Rafael Gil and Juan de Orduña were the most talented and prolific of the directors involved in the new Francoist regime. José Luis Sáenz de Heredia was also seen as a regime proponent, while Edgar Neville was considered a more independent and avant-garde voice. The Spanish star system solidified as well, and both veteran actors and new stars flourished in the 1940s, as illustrated by the immense popularity of Aurora Bautista, Antoñita Colomé, Imperio Argentina, Sara

Montiel, Ana Mariscal, Conchita Montes, Antonio Casal, Rafael Durán, José Isbert, Miguel Ligero, Alfredo Mayo, and Jorge Mistral.

Despite the oppressive political climate, the film panorama of the post-war years was more diverse than is commonly thought. In "El cine de la autarquía (1939–1950)" José Enrique Monterde points out that between 1939 and 1950 Spain had produced "55 comedies, 66 dramatic comedies, 83 sentimental comedies, 19 contemporary comedies, 20 historical films, 18 war and spy films, 21 folkloric films, 3 sports films, 3 cartoons, 22 musicals, 58 dramas, 13 melodramas, 31 police flicks, 7 religious films, 15 adventures, 6 bullfighting films and 3 children's films" (p. 230).

However, within these diverse tendencies, we can still discern some common and recurrent thematic and ideological traits. This is especially noticeable in genres that were more involved in the formation of the new state, such as historical epics and war films. These works exalted the "Spanish race" and *castizo* values; the revindication of the notion of *hispanidad*, especially in reference to Spanish colonialism in the Americas; the opposition between victors and vanquished; patriotism, folklore and regional stereotypes; and the veneration of traditional and Catholic religious values.[44] In these films Spanish history was often reduced to the greatness of the imperial Spain and Castile of the expansionist Catholic Monarchs Isabel and Fernando. The historical periods and events that were left out were as significant as those that were overplayed. The seventeenth century was rarely depicted on screen because it was thought of as a century of Spanish decadence; the eighteenth century was seen as too enlightened; and contemporary, twentieth-century social movements were perceived as too dangerous. Paradoxically, the Franco regime's repressive national project that can be seen in these films also opened up the process of cultural negotiation and reappropriation. As Jo Labanyi showed in her readings of postwar films, "heavy censorship made Spanish audiences adept at the art of resignification" ("Race, Gender and Disavowal in Spanish Cinema of the Early Franco Period: The Missionary Film and the Folkloric Musical," p. 216).

Raza and *Locura de amor*, the two films chosen for this chapter, are representative of the more ideological cinema of the 1940s. In both films the official history depicted on the screen legitimized the establishment of the new Francoist state. Both films illustrate an attempt to establish national unity through an imaginary common patrimony and past. The films belong to the cinema of heroes and ideals, honor, virility, patriotic and military actions, noble queens, and ultimately, distorted historical views.

General Franco himself, under the pseudonym Jaime de Andrade, scripted *Raza*. Filmed by José Luis Sáenz de Heredia, one of the most prolific Spanish directors of the time, the film can be seen as a microcosm of the country's larger political issues. It can also be read as a "portrait" of the Spanish nation from 1898 to 1939. It is an allegorical tale of archetypal rival brothers, torn apart by opposing allegiances; one is a Republican, the other a Nationalist. The external conflict, the Spanish Civil War, is replayed within the borders of the family itself. The family's crises and ideological rifts highlight the crisis in the country's existing, broader social structure. *Raza* is also typical of fascism's melodramatic and conservative vision of history. This exalting Nationalist epic intertwines historical narratives with those of war, love, and romance. The link was made even more tangible through the dramatic performances of Alfredo Mayo and Ana Mariscal – both beloved film stars of the 1940s.

Locura de amor is an extravagant historical melodrama adapted from Manuel Tamayo y Baus's nineteenth-century drama of the same title. It tells the story of Juana de Castilla, daughter of the Catholic Monarchs Isabel and Fernando. Juana's love for Felipe *el Hermoso* ("the Handsome"), her emotionally and politically fickle and irresponsible husband, is not reciprocated. As in *Raza*, the personal story is mapped onto a larger socio-economic and political structure. In this case, the focus is on the plot to shift the center of power away from the Castilian crown and into the hands of foreign powers. Felipe el Hermoso represents the political and sexual corruption of the court of Flanders.

Locura de amor, filmed in 1948 by Juan de Orduña, precedes his other historical masterpieces *Agustina de Aragón* (1950), *La leona de Castilla* (1951), and *Alba de América* (1951). The film belongs to CIFESA's pseudo-historical, epic style. As José Enrique Monterde points out, "Orduña was not the originator of this tendency, but its culmination. He went beyond all sense of ridiculousness and contention to the point of constructing his papier-mâché[45] into an authentic stylistic motif" ("El cine de la autarquía (1939–1950)," p. 227). As in *Raza*, the film's stars were instrumental to its success. Juana de Castilla's madness and hysteria is captured in Aurora Bautista's outstanding performance. The stunningly beautiful Sara Montiel, a newcomer at this point, played the queen's rival, Aldara, a disguised Moorish princess. The charged emotions of this mad love story, the brilliant performances, opulent costumes, and Orduña's lavish style made *Locura de amor* an immense commercial success. These two talented actresses and their female characters dominated the screen, which highlights a curious paradox. Isolina Ballesteros notes: "Never before had woman been so omnipresent and visible on the movie screen, nor so absent and invisible in the political and social reconstruction of the country" ("Mujer y nación en el cine español de posguerra: los años 40," p. 54).

Significantly, both films, in their insistence on national destiny, a glorious past, and the greatness of imperial Spain, conceal all the pressing issues of the postwar years: hunger, poverty, political oppression, and social and class conflict. Only the following generation of filmmakers would start to question this ideological insistence on lavish superproductions. While the following decade would continue the generic thematic tendencies of the 1940s, it would also be significantly marked by the dismantling of this outlandish and excessive cinema, appropriately denoted the "cinema of gorgets and frock coats" (*cine de gola y levita*).

1   *Raza* (José Luis Sáenz de Heredia, 1941)

Context and Critical Commentary

Production credits

Director: José Luis Sáenz de Heredia
Production: Consejo de la Hispanidad (Hispanic Council)
Cinematography: Enrique Guerner
Screenplay: José Luis Sáenz de Heredia, based on the novel *Raza* by "Jaime de Andrade" (Francisco Franco)
Score: Manuel Parada
Genre: Drama, black and white
Country: Spain
Runtime: 113 minutes

Cast

Alfredo Mayo
Ana Mariscal
José Nieto
Blanca de Silos
Luis Arroyo

José Churruca
Marisol Mendoza
Pedro Churruca
Isabel Churruca
Jaime Curruca

Raul Cancio

Julio Rey de las Heras

Rosina Mendía

Vicente Soler

Pablo Hidalfo

Carmen Trejo

María Saco

José Luis Sáenz de Heredia

Luis Echevarría

Pedro Churruca, father

Isabel Acuña de Churruca, mother

Doctor Vera

Don Luis

"Nationalist" spy

Tía Lola

Bus driver

Synopsis

The action starts just before 1898, when Pedro Churruca, the captain of the Spanish ship *Marina*, returns to his home in Galicia (a region in the northeast of Spain) following a military mission. His wife Isabel and their four children – José, Pedro, Isabel, and Jaime – are waiting for him. After the homecoming, Churruca explains to his children the sense of pride that comes with being in the Spanish military, reminding them that among their ancestors is Admiral Damián Churruca, who died fighting five English ships in the battle of Trafalgar (1805). The father is then sent to fight in the war in Cuba (1898) and dies in combat defending the last Spanish colony.

Time passes and the following sequence is set in 1928. It is the wedding of Isabel Churruca to her brother José's best friend, Luis Echevarría, both of whom are in the military. Her other brother Jaime plans to follow his religious calling and join a convent, while Pedro has decided to study law and perhaps dedicate himself to politics. At the wedding, José and Pedro display their political antagonism in an argument. This ideological opposition between the two brothers will be a determining factor in the development of the plot.

Later the Civil War breaks out and José, united with the Nationalists, is captured and condemned to death by the Republican army. Miraculously, his girlfriend Marisol finds him seemingly resurrected from the dead when she comes to claim the body. Once he has recovered, he moves to the front in Bilbao, where he finds his brother-in-law, Luis Echevarría. Depressed by the long separation from his family, Luis has plans to desert. However, in reaction to his wife's opposition to the idea and José's advice, Luis changes his mind. Their other brother Jaime, now a priest in Catalonia, is executed by Republican troops who attack the convent where he lives. For his part, after collaborating with the Republic and feeling tormented by the thought that he didn't do enough to save his brother José, whom he believes to be dead, Pedro finally decides to collaborate with the Nationalists by turning in the Republican army's plans to a spy. Pedro is discovered, and before his execution he gives a speech in which he repudiates the Republic's ideals. The film ends with Franco's victory march into Madrid, in which José Churruca and Luis Echevarría participate. It is important to note that *Raza* incorporates documentary footage of the Nationalists' actual parade into the capital city.

Critical commentary

Raza could be classified as one of the so-called "patriotic war films" that were produced in Spain during the 1940s, such as *Harka* (Luis Peña, 1940) or *A mi la legión* by Juan de Orduña (1942). *Raza* exalts Spain's past glories and distorts its historical context in order to legitimize the implantation of the Franco regime. Moreover, General Francisco Franco, under the pseudonym Jaime de Andrade, wrote the screenplay. The dictator himself proposed the idea for the film, while his recently created Consejo de la Hispanidad (Hispanic Council), an institution that was dedicated to the diffusion of Spanish culture, supported its production. José Sáenz de Heredia, selected from among the best-known film directors at the time, was put in charge of the film. Sáenz de Heredia was the cousin of the executed José Antonio Primo de Rivera, the founder of the Falange and the so-called Principios del Movimiento (Principles of the Movement), the authentic ideological corpus that sustained Franco's regime.[46] In addition to selecting Sáenz de Heredia, Franco personally supervised the casting as well as the final version of the script and the definitive editing of the film, making it a truly propagandistic manifesto for his cause.

Marsha Kinder suggests that *Raza* is formally influenced by Russian expressionism (*Blood Cinema*, p. 457). For example, *Raza*'s final parade scene with its canon-lined streets recalls Eisenstein's *Battleship Potemkin*. However, this scene was not orchestrated by Sáenz de Heredia, but was documentary footage from *El gran desfile de la victoria en Madrid* (*The Great Victory Parade in Madrid*), produced by the National Department of Cinematography. The parade illustrates, as one of the characters asserts, the "spirit of the race," and thus underscores the deliberate homogenization of the newly consolidated nation. Hence the Republicans, who lost the war, are strategically erased and the differences that separate the "two Spains" are deliberately diluted. Moreover, the film does not outwardly show scenes of the cruelty of war or violent massacres, but focuses its attention on heroism and the epic qualities of war. The grandiose fascist aesthetics and strong propagandistic elements, reminiscent of Nationalist Socialist German films of the same era, can be read as an attempt to provoke empathy with the regime.

Franco's script also has strong autobiographical overtones. It is not difficult to recognize Franco's mother in the virginal, sacrificial Isabel Acuña de Churruca, and more obviously, the character also shares Franco's mother's last name. Additionally, just like Franco, José enrolled in the Military Academy of Toledo and his first destination was Morocco. Pedro, the Republican brother who finally recovers and identifies with the Nationalists, is very similar to the figure of Ramón Franco, the dictator's brother. The one exception is the paternal figure, Pedro Churruca, a military hero who died in the war. He has very little to do with Franco's actual father, a drinker and gambler who abandoned the family to live with his common-law wife and illegitimate son.

Raza's archetypal characters – the Nationalist, the priest, the military hero, the sacrificial mother, and the converted Republican – endorse Franco's new regime and its supposed "salvation of Spain." Pedro's final conversion to Nationalist causes is therefore didactic and central to the film's ideological underpinning. Family members are divided along the political lines where familial and national boundaries conflate. External conflict (war) is replaying itself within the borders of the family and in turn, the family crisis serves to point out the broader crisis in the existing social structure. *Raza*, characterized by its emphasis on national destiny, power, conquest, sacrifice, the exaltation of militarism, and distorted historical views, is dissociated from its real cultural and social milieu and conceals other pressing postwar issues such as hunger, poverty, domestic relations, and social and class conflicts.[47]

In 1950 a modified version of the film was re-released with the title *Espíritu de una raza* (*The Spirit of a Race*). The new version eliminated scenes that were considered inopportune for the regime, like images of the fascist salute (banned in Spain in 1947), gestures that implied a rejection of the United States due to their participation in the war of 1898, and the vilification of politicians who were blamed for "Spain's ruin." The changes in the 1950 version spoke to the regime's attempts to be internationally accepted by democratic governments. A film like *Raza*, a key tool of propaganda for the regime, could not reflect images that were reminiscent of fascism. Even the dialogue was revised; if in the first *Raza* someone says to Pedro, "you're a real anti-fascist!" in the 1950 version the line was changed to, "you're a communist!" clearly indicating who the regime was using as the common enemy at that moment. *Raza* and its later version, *Espíritu de una raza*, are genuine propagandistic tools that aided the Franco regime in its quest to consolidate power.

Film Scenes: Close Readings

Scene 1   History and myth

Pedro Churruca tells his children (José, Pedro, Jaime, and Isabel) the story of their heroic ancestors, particularly of Damián Churruca, who died in the battle of Trafalgar in 1805. In addition to the battle of Trafalgar, the film references key historical moments in Spain's tumultuous history, specifically the war with Cuba, in which Spain lost its last colony (1898), and the Spanish Civil War (1936–9) that was barely over when *Raza* was filmed in 1941.

The patriarch Pedro Churruca passes his didactic and patriotic lesson down to his children, Spain's next generation. The father's conception of Spanishness emphasizes attributes like the spirit of sacrifice for the fatherland, glorification of the military, and the exaltation of the figure of the hero. Saturated with references to Spain's allegedly glorious past and characterized by a solemn and exaggerated tone, *Raza* belongs to the cinema of heroes and ideals, patriotic and military actions, and distorted historical views. By foregrounding historical scenes, the film also establishes a link between Spain's supposed "legitimate" history and the newly established dictatorial regime. In other words the "official" history depicted on the screen legitimized the establishment of the new state, illustrating its propagandistic essence.

The final scene of the film, the victory parade of Franco's Nationalist troops, is tied to this first sequence of the film and reinforces the father's initial patriotic discourse. Now, however, it is his son that participates in the march of history, continuing in his father's and ancestors' footsteps. The succession of historical events is analogous to the progression of the Churruca family: from the battle of Trafalgar to the war in Cuba to the Spanish Civil War, from grandfather to father to sons, the men of the Churruca family patriotically sacrifice themselves for their country. The rest of the family is also present at the military parade, symbolizing Franco's unified Spain and conflating family unity with national accord. In this way, historical discourse is embodied in the experience of this "exemplary" family. Furthermore, the film ends with Isabel, Pedro Churruca's daughter, explaining to her young child that the triumphal march of Franco's troops represents "the spirit of our race."

Scene 2   *Family division and the two Spains*

The country's tensions and political divisions are reflected allegorically in the Churruca family dynamics, specifically those of the two sons, Pedro and José. They symbolize the two opposing Spains: Nationalist and Republican. In José's case, his heroism, his spirit of sacrifice for the fatherland, and the glorification of his military career stand out. Pedro, on the other hand, reflects the Republican values that are characterized negatively in the film. In contrast to José and within the film's ideological aim, Pedro is selfish, weak, and cowardly. This scene, framed by the initial dispute over the father's inheritance, is symbolical of a wider conflict: the ideological difference between the two brothers.

Throughout the film, the brothers' ideological rift is highlighted by a detailed description of their drastically different lives. Sáenz de Heredia shoots many parallel scenes of their lives in which we see the juxtaposition of military and bourgeois lifestyles. The mundane, frivolous material luxury that Pedro acquires is contrasted with José's spiritual possessions, such as military glory and self-sacrifice for the nation. Pedro is enslaved by material goods, while José's spirituality is timeless and everlasting.

Toward the end of the film Pedro, disenchanted with the Republicans, strongly and publicly repudiates their cause. The film's final scene – Franco's triumphal entrance into the capital city and the seat of power – reinforces Pedro's conversion to the Nationalist side. In his repentance, Pedro adopts the discourse of the "glorious race," the race that has received the divine gift of heroism, sacrifice, and above all, an "opportunity" to redeem its past, as he has redeemed his own.

Scene 3   *The massacre of the priests*

In this scene, the Catholic priests, whom the film portrays as caring souls dedicated to providing for the most needy – in this case the orphans of war – are brutally taken from their monastery, which they had converted into an orphanage. This sequence consists of a series of extreme long shots of priests walking to their death. The Republicans, who are portrayed as indifferent murderers, line up the priests along the seashore and riddle them with bullets. It is significant and symbolic that Jaime, the youngest son of the Churruca family, now a priest in Catalonia, is also executed in this scene. Religious conflict, one of the key issues of the Spanish Civil War, is also at the heart of the film and this scene, in which the conflict between the Nationalists' Catholic values and the Republican laic, atheist ethos results in brutal violence.

The defense of religion portrayed in this scene is tied to the misuses of history, perceptible in other key scenes of *Raza*. There is a conscious attempt to root the formation of Franco's new nation not only in a glorious and imaginary past, but in Spain's supposedly authentic religious beliefs as well. Furthermore, as there was no possibility of territorial greatness and expansion (Spain faced economic misery at home and ostracism abroad), Franco's political mission was spiritual rather then territorial. Franco was focused on the exaltation of spiritual greatness and superiority, trying to achieve hegemony and national unity through a patrimony that supposedly belonged to everybody. He sought to convert the war-torn and hetero-geneous group into a homogeneous modern nation where Catholicism was the only religious and moral option.

In sum, the scene is symbolic of the confrontation between the old and the new, tradition and progress, conservative and liberal, Spain and the so-called "anti-Spain." It illustrates the Republicans' brutality as well as their rejection of religion, an aspect that is exaggerated by the film's pro-pagandistic message. In presenting such a negative model of Republicans, the film establishes a discourse that legitimizes the Franco regime and its usurpation of the legitimate political power that Republicans had before the outbreak of Spanish Civil War.

Director (Life and Works)

José Luis Sáenz de Heredia (b. Madrid 1911, d. Madrid 1992)

José Luis Sáenz de Heredia is one of the most important directors of the 1930s and the Spanish postwar period. He was born in Madrid in 1911, where he lived his entire life. He studied architecture, which he eventually abandoned to begin his film career in 1934. The same year, he wrote the screenplay for *Patricio miró una estrella*, which was directed by his best friend Serafín Ballesteros. The script impressed Luis Buñuel, who at that time had just become the executive producer of the company Filmófono, which then produced *Patricio miró una estrella*. Buñuel decided to contract Sáenz de Heredia to direct two films: *La hija de Juan Simón* and *Quién me quiere a mí?*, released in 1935 and 1936, respectively.

Following the end of the Civil War the Consejo de la Hispanidad, under the supervision of General Franco, selected Sáenz de Heredia (cousin of Franco regime icon José Antonio Primo de Rivera) to direct *Raza* in 1940. Based on the script that Franco wrote under the pseudonym Jaime de Andrade, the film finally premiered in 1942. *Raza*'s success and its political significance brought Sáenz de Heredia recognition and fame. From the 1940s on, he was considered one of the most prestigious directors of the period.

Because of his work on *Raza*, many critics consider Sáenz de Heredia the "official" director of the Franco regime. Nevertheless, his later thematically and aesthetically complex films should be seen as an exploration of Spanish popular culture rather than political propaganda. These works include the comedy *El destino se disculpa* (1944) and the popular melodramas *El escándalo* (1943) and *Mariona Rebull* (1947). In 1948 he directed *Las aguas bajas negras*, which was influenced by neorealism – an Italian movement that was just beginning to be explored in Spanish cinema at that time. Sáenz de Heredia's most commercial and, according to many critics, best work is *Historias de la radio*. Released in 1955, this comedy's plot revolves around characters that take part in a radio game-show contest, and reflects the complexity of Spanish society in the 1950s. Undoubtedly, in this film, the well-known Spanish actor José Isbert gave one of the best comedic interpretations of his entire career.

Although Sáenz de Heredia had progressively distanced himself from the regime's propaganda, in 1964 he was required to direct a documentary film commemorating the anniversary of Franco's triumph, which the regime baptized as "25 years of peace." The film *Franco, ese hombre* serves as a reminder of the relationship between Sáenz de Heredia and the Franco regime's propaganda apparatus.

During the 1960s and 1970s, Sáenz de Heredia continued to direct films influenced by popular culture, such as *La verbena de la Paloma* (1963), *Historias de la televisión* (1965), and *Don Erre que erre* (1970). During this last stage of his career the quality of the director's work diminished, along with his popular success. His final film, *Solo ante el streaking*, premiered in 1975, the year of Franco's death. In 1984 he published his memoirs, *En clave de mí*, and in 1992 he died in Madrid after a long battle with lung disease.

2   *Locura de amor* (Juan de Orduña, 1948)

Context and Critical Commentary

Production credits

Director: Juan de Orduña
Production: CIFESA
Cinematography: José F. Aguayo
Screenplay: Manuel Tamayo; Alredo Echegaray; based on the 1855 book
Locura de amor by Manuel Tamayo y Baus (the screenwriter's grandfather)
Score: Juan Quintero
Genre: Melodrama, black and white
Country: Spain
Runtime: 110 minutes

Cast

Aurora Bautista	Juana
Fernando Rey	Philip the Handsome
Sara Montiel	Aldara
Jorge Mistral	Captain don Alvar
Jesús Tordesillas	Don Filiberto de Were
Manuel Luna	Don Juan Manuel
Juan Espantaleón	Admiral of Castile
Ricardo Acero	Don Carlos
Eduardo Fajardo	Marquis of Villena
Manuel Arbó	Mariano, the queen's doctor
Carmen Lucio	The archduke's lover
Conrado San Martín	Hernán
Encarna Paso	Queen's maid

Synopsis

The future emperor Carlos V goes to visit his mother, Queen Juana, in
the castle of Mota, situated on the outskirts of Valladolid (Castile), the
capital of the kingdom at that time. His mother, suffering from an attack

of dementia, does not recognize him. At Carlos's request, Don Alvar, a nobleman who has been loyal to the queen throughout her rule, recounts her story. The action flashes back to November of 1504, when Queen Isabel the Catholic dies. At that moment Juana, Queen Isabel's only daughter, lives in the court of Flanders and is married to Philip, the archduke of Austria, also known as Philip the Handsome (Felipe *el Hermoso*). Don Alvar goes to the court of Flanders to tell Juana that her mother has died and to oversee her return to Spain in the company of her husband.

Once back in Spain, in the region of Tudela de Duero, the queen's subjects praise her leadership, while her frequently absent husband occupies himself with adulterous affairs. Juana discovers one of these exploits when she finds her husband at an inn with Aldara, a young Moorish princess. Despite the fact that she actually is in love with Don Alvar, Aldara has an affair with the king to avenge her father's assassination. At first the queen chooses to ignore the affair, but her jealousy and suspicion intensify.

Because of her jealousy and persistent obsession with the king, rumors about the queen's possible madness begin circulating. The Council of Castile examines the situation and is divided into those who favor Juana and those who side with her husband; the latter want to proclaim the queen incompetent and call for Philip to reign over the kingdom. Eventually the nobles of the Council confirm Juana's supposed madness. However, after assuming the reign of Castile, Philip dies suddenly. On his deathbed he repents of all of the pain he caused Juana and the kingdom. Juana, overcome by a profound sadness, lingers around her husband's coffin. Ultimately, she is confined in the castle of Mota, where her son Carlos visits her at the beginning of the film.

Critical commentary

Locura de amor fits into the genre of "papier-mâché cinema" characteristic of the 1940s. Although postwar production was diverse (comedy, folkloric musical, melodrama) in both style and theme, so-called papier-mâché cinema is the most representative of the Franco regime's ideological pretenses. In this genre, the mostly historical films exalt Spanish history and mythical national values, like the imperial past *Locura de amor* portrays. These films also tend to be characterized by an exaggerated interpretive style and an artificial and grandiose aesthetic, with entire sets made out of papier-mâché – hence the genre's name.

In 1944 the production company CIFESA, which had an important role in the creation of Spanish postwar national cinema, acquired the rights to make a film of the novel *Locura de amor*, written in 1855 by Manuel Tamayo y Baus, the grandfather of one of the film's screenwriters. After delaying the filming on various occasions, CIFESA began making it in 1947. The film recreates the history of Queen Juana, called the Mad Queen, beginning with her young son Carlos (the future emperor Carlos V) visiting her at the castle where she is incarcerated. Through the use of a flashback, the film reconstructs Juana's past, starting with the death of her mother, Queen Isabel the Catholic.[48] Castile's dominance in the film is significant, as it fits well with Franco's own conception of Castile as the cradle of the "true" Spain and supports the claim of Nationalist historiography that Castile was central to the shaping of the Spanish nation.[49] Thus, the focus on Castile and Spain's past glories is symbolically utilized by the Franco regime to propagandistic ends in an attempt to present itself as the legitimate heir to Spanish historical lineage.

Issues of national identity, patriotism, political power, and gender are at the heart of the film. The female protagonists, Juana and Aldara – Christian queen and Moorish princess – are symbolically linked with the nation; thus the motherland is equated with the feminine. Although from different perspectives, both Juana and Aldara are ultimately characterized, above all else, by their patriotism. It is precisely in the contraposition of these two characters, embodying their respective nations, that the ideological underpinning of the film resides. Therefore, the film demonstrates the mythification of the symbols and patriotic stereotypes symbolically assigned to women, who were idealized and understood as the safeguard of patriotic values and the transmitters of national consciousness (Ballesteros, "Mujer y nación en el cine español de posguerra: los años 40," pp. 51–7).

The centrality and importance of feminine roles in *Locura de amor* creates the possibility for complex layers of interpretation. On the one hand, Juana and Aldara are indispensable to the plot, and thus are a dynamic presence in strong contrast to the passive role imposed on Spanish women in the postwar years of Franco's dictatorship. On the other hand, both Juana and Aldara are women who struggle to obtain love that they are both denied, and are represented as having crazy and hysterical tendencies, implying that they are unqualified to exercise power. Nevertheless, or rather despite these representations, the spectator feels empathy with Juana and Aldara and questions the perpetuation of the submission of women that was characteristic of the social order that operated under the Franco regime, and that this film symbolically exalts and justifies under the guise of historical epic. Thus paradoxically, through this elaboration of the female characters, the film ironically denounces the patriarchal system and the oppression and injustice that it imposes on women (Ballesteros, "Mujer y nación en el cine español de posguerra: los años 40," pp. 51–7).

In the context of historical papier-mâché epics, the fact that the action begins and ends in the castle of Mota is significant. It was there that not only Juana, but also Isabel the Catholic and Saint Teresa,[50] were confined and eventually died. The Franco regime considered these women to be feminine national icons while banalizing and reducing their real historical and political significance. Furthermore, the regime utilized the castle of Mota as the headquarters of La Sección Femenina (The Feminine Section),[51] the most formative as well as oppressive women's institution during Franco's reign. Papier-mâché cinema undoubtedly served the Franco regime's propagandistic ends by using a very particular aesthetic to transmit a stereotypical reproduction of the nation's mythical valor.

Film Scenes: Close Readings

Scene 1   Juana and Aldara

The film reflects the political and religious conflicts that characterize Spain's history through the two central female characters: Juana, the Christian queen of Castile, and Aldara, a Moorish princess who intends to take revenge on Juana for the assassination of Aldara's father (Zagal the Caliph), which put an end to her family's reign. Both Juana and Aldara seek to exercise their function as prominent political voices of their kingdoms, but because of their secondary position as women, they have neither the space nor the circumstances to directly act in the positions of power that they have inherited. The relationship between the two protagonists is always mediated and manipulated by the male characters and by the social function that the protagonists serve as women. In this scene Aldara writes a love letter in an attempt to destroy the queen, but her actions are suggested and then manipulated by the king's adviser. In this case Aldara thinks that she is influencing the state of the Spanish crown, but in reality she is playing the simple role of the mistress. The conflict between Aldara and Juana, while political, is therefore imbued with female competition and jealousy, characteristics coded and depreciated as feminine. In a similar manner, Juana lives locked in the castle, overcome with the anguish caused by her husband's exploits, which impedes her from making any political decisions or exercising her power. Through these female characters the film para-doxically denounces the patriarchal system and the oppression and injustice it exercises over women. This scene also registers the complex interplay of power determined by gender, religion, and national identity.

Scene 2   Love's madness

Juana, a chaste, sober, and just queen, gradually loses the political leadership she once exercised. Her steady slip into madness stems from her husband's infidelity, and that insanity in turn delegitimizes her political power, which is already compromised by her being a woman. Submission, hysteria, and madness, coded and depreciated as feminine traits, gradually exclude Juana from participating in political life. These aspects intensify with the fact that she slowly assumes the discourse of insanity, which is articulated when she states that she would rather be "crazy than betrayed." Thus Juana relinquishes her political power because of her emotional turmoil.

The theme of political power sacrificed to the "madness of love" is emphasized in the film through the repetition of Juana's oscillation between reason and insanity. After her first lapse into madness, provoked by jeal-ousy, she goes to the inn where she discovers Philip with his lover, Aldara. In response, she decides to retake her political power and assume the role of queen that the people of Castile are asking her to fulfill. But once again she falls victim to further scheming, and has another episode of anxiety and madness, which culminates at the end of the film, after her husband's death. It is also important to note the skill with which the actress Aurora Bautista plays Juana, interpreting the character's madness with hyperbolic gestures and a crazed affect, thus underlining the film's theme through the form and stylistic exaggerations characteristic of papier-mâché cinema.

Scene 3   The infidelities of the archduke of Flanders

One of the central political conflicts the film focuses on is the tension and difference between the kingdom of Castile and the court of Flanders (present-day Belgium). At the heart of the conflict is a geopolitical realignment of power in sixteenth-century Europe. The marriage between Juana and Philip illustrates the alliances between various European kingdoms as well as their internal struggle for primacy in ruling. In the film, Juana's honorable Christian state of Castile contrasts with the corrupt court of Flanders, exemplified in the figure of the archduke, who became King Philip I through his marriage to Juana, but was perceived by Castilian nobles as a foreigner who might usurp their power and political dominance.

This theme is metaphorically developed in the film through Philip's infidelities. Beneath a deceptive façade, the king repeatedly commits adultery and openly serves foreign interests. Furthermore, his constant infidelity progressively feeds the queen's madness. His various exploits, including adulterous relationships with other women, lead him into a relationship with the Moorish princess, Aldara, whose attractiveness and exoticism are contrasted with the Christian queen. The king thus transgresses against not only the queen's fidelity, but also the Christian people he is supposed to govern. As Isolina Ballesteros points out, "the king's nationality [Flemish] and his lover's religion [Islam] aggravate the offense of adultery" ("Mujer y nación en el cine español de posguerra: los años 40," p. 64). The queen's honor is thus tied to that of her kingdom of Castile, and its Christian faith is seen as desecrated by Islamic betrayal, represented here by adultery.

Papier-mâché cinema frequently served the Franco regime's propagandistic ends and its stereotypical reproduction of the national myths. The defense of Juana's and Castile's honor is tied to the exaltation of Spain's past imperial glories and the ideological, Castilian-centered view of Spanish history. Thus the sequence can be read as a pseudo-historical justification of Franco's own insistence on the political and economic primacy of Castile during his dictatorship and the repression of Spain's other national minorities, especially Basques and Catalans. The political manipulation and repression of Francoism were therefore defended under the guise of historical "truth."

Director (Life and Works)

Juan de Orduña (b. Madrid 1907, d. Madrid 1974)

Born in Madrid in 1907, Juan de Orduña began acting in theater at a young age. In 1924 he made his filmic debut in the movie *La casa de Troya*, directed by Florián Rey. However, it is in the film *Boy*, directed by Benito Perojo, that he had his first great success as the lead actor. Later he participated in Florián Rey's well-known folkloric film *Nobleza baturra* (1935), but after the Civil War he began directing short films. Eventually CIFESA contracted him to direct a variety of movies, beginning with *Porque te vi llorar* (1941), followed by the war film *A mí la legión* (1942), a big success with a marked patriotic, propagandistic tone that corresponded to the spirit of the times.

He added, to what would become a prolific list of works, films like *Tuvo la culpa Adán* and *Deliciosamente tontos*, two comedies released in 1943, and *Ella, él y sus millones* (1944), which launched the actress Amparo Rivelles toward stardom. In 1945 he released *Misión blanca*, which could be interpreted as a Catholic propaganda film, and in 1948 directed *Locura de amor*. This papier-mâché, historic melodrama was a resounding success with audiences and made Orduñez's protagonist, Aurora Bautista, famous. One year later she would return to act in another one of his films, *Pequeñeces*.

In 1955 two more historical melodramas were released: *Alba de América* and *La leona de Castilla*, which added to the stock of grandiose and artificial films representative of the papier-mâché cinema that came to characterize Orduñez's repertoire. Later he directed two films based on literary works, *Cañas y barro* and *Zalacaín el aventurero* (1956), and in 1957 he released one of his biggest successes, *El último cuplé*, the film that consecrated Sara Montiel as an actress and one of Spain's leading film stars of the 1950s.

Following *El último cuplé* Orduña's acclaim as a filmmaker began to decline with movies like *Teresa de Jesús* (1961) and *Bochorno* (1964), which had little resonance with critics and mainstream audiences. Between 1967 and 1969 he adapted for television traditional *zarzuela*s like *La revoltosa* and *Gigantes y cabezudos*, among other titles. His last films were the comedies *La Tonta del Bote* (1971) and *Me has hecho perder el juicio* (1973), which were rejected by critics and audiences alike. Following the release of his final film, Juan de Orduña died in Madrid on February 3, 1974.

5

Neorealism: Status Quo and Dissent (1951–1961)

1   *El cochecito* (Marco Ferreri, 1960)
2   *Viridiana* (Luis Buñuel, 1961)

Historical and Political Overview of the Period

The second decade of the Franco dictatorship was a time of various political, economic, and cultural changes. The 1950s brought international
legitimization of the dictatorial regime: Spain was admitted to UNESCO
on November 17, 1952, signed a concordat with the Vatican on August 27,
1953, and was finally admitted to the United Nations in December of 1955.
Autarchic Spain was becoming technocratic. Franco's restructured cabinet
of February 1957 included Laureano López Rodó as *secretario general técnico
de la presidencia de gobierno* (general technical secretary of the presidency
of the government), the new minister of finance, Mariano Navarro Rubio,
and the new minister of commerce, Alberto Ullastres Calvo. Advocates of
a technological society and progress, technocrats valued efficiency, com-
petence, and professionalism. They also supported the state-led modernization drive and economic liberalization. The new technocratic ministers
endorsed the unrestrained embrace of modern capitalism, foreign investment, massive industrialization, population migration, urbanization, and
educational expansion.[52]

The beginning of this decade was symbolic. In March of 1952 the
government stopped issuing the ration card (*cartilla de racionamiento*) that
they had provided since the end of the war. Economists aptly named this
period the Hinge Decade (*decenio bisagra*), a metaphor that illustrates the
shift from the postwar insistence on moderation, restriction, and rationing
to the beginning of a new consumer society.[53] The first car for mass consumption, the Fiat 600, appeared in June of 1957. The first TV program
was aired on October 28, 1956. However, this incipient consumer paradise

revealed its darker sides. Modernization and political liberalization provoked crises in all realms of culture, politics, and economics. Among the most worrying developments (for the regime) were labor strikes and student unrest, fertile ground for a new generation of political activists.

In September of 1951 José María García Escudero was appointed general director of cinematography and theater (*director general de cinematografía y teatro*). García Escudero was a proponent of renovation. His reforms articulated more clearly the politics of state subsidies, censorship, import/export licenses, and the politics of the film industry in general. Nevertheless, he was a victim of the inner contradictions of the Franco regime, which paradoxically required both political control and liberalization. García Escudero was appointed general director of cinematography and theater to help project a more liberal image of Spain abroad, but was subsequently seen as too liberal and forced to resign in February of 1952. His resignation, prompted by the so-called *Surcos* scandal, illustrates well the complex politics of 1950s Spain. García Escudero nominated for a lucrative *interés nacional* ("national interest") category[54] the film *Surcos* (1951) instead of the more ideologically appropriate *Alba de América* (1951), Juan de Orduña's historical epic about Columbus's discovery of America. Despite its Falangist values, *Surcos* centered on social and contemporary issues such as immigration, the black market, corruption, unemployment, and prostitution. The nomination of *Surcos* faced bitter opposition from the traditional sectors of the regime, which then forced García Escudero's resignation. His brief appearance and impact on the Spanish film scene was nevertheless very important. Furthermore, he was returned to the post in 1962, becoming one of the leading champions and a crucial figure of the New Spanish Cinema.

Some of the other important changes of the period were reflected in the structure of Spain's cinematographic apparatus. The Board of Classification and Censorship (La Junta de Clasificación y Censura) split into two branches: "one dedicated to censorship or evaluation of the film's 'ethical, political and social aspects' while the other classification related to its 'technical and artistic qualities and its economic circumstances'" (Monterde, "Continuismo y disidencia (1951–1962)," p. 249). There was also an attempt to separate production subsidies from import and dubbing licenses and to redefine and modernize governmental policies of protection and subvention.

The changing panorama of institutional film practices and censorship politics had a direct impact on production companies. After years of dominance CIFESA lost its unquestioned sovereignty on the Spanish film scene. CIFESA's decline was tied to the demise of the historical cinema genre that had embodied Spain's dissipating autarkic principles. In 1951 CIFESA produced the last three historical films: *Alba de América*, *La leona de Castilla*, and *Lola la Piconera*. Despite being in the prestigious national interest category, *Alba de América* is a film that marks the closure of the postwar cycle of historical epics, the end of Juan de Orduña's prolific career, and the end of CIFESA's production dominance. Thereafter CIFESA would only stay competitive with a few commercially successful films such as Luis García Berlanga's *Calabuch* from 1956 and one of the biggest hits of the 1950s, Orduña's *El último cuplé* (1957) starring the spectacular Sara Montiel.

In contrast, Cesáreo González's Suevia Films became one of the most powerful production companies of this period. Ignacio F. Iquino's Barcelona-based Ifisa, founded subsequent to his company Emisora Films and geared more toward low-budget films, began growing in importance as well, producing 46 films between 1951 and 1962. The 1950s also saw activity from some smaller production companies such as Aspa Films (geared toward religious themes), as well as Agata Films (José Luis Dibildos and Pedro Lazaga) and Asturias Films (Pedro Masó and R. J. Salvia), two companies that were oriented toward comedy, especially comedies of tourism and development (*desarrollo*), a sub-genre that would become extremely popular in the following decade.

The institutional and production politics of the 1950s influenced experienced and emerging film directors alike. With a few exceptions, old-timers continued to make conventional, unpoliticized works that fared well with the regime and the public. The film culture of the fifties also saw the rise of a new generation, tied to the Instituto de Investigaciones y Experiencias Cinematográficas (Institute for Cinematic Investigation and Experimentation, or IIEC), the film school created on February 18, 1947. The two most important young voices were Juan Antonio Bardem and Luis García Berlanga, graduates of IIEC. In 1951 they co-directed *Esa pareja feliz*, a film that reflects the social reality of the times while parodying and reworking the historical cinema of the previous decade. In *Esa pareja feliz*, Lola Gaos, an actress playing the role of a medieval queen, literally collapses through the stage in a parody of Aurora Bautista in the historical epic *Locura de amor*. Berlanga also made one of the most celebrated films of the 1950s, *¡Bienvenido Mister Marshall!* The film explored the myths and realities of Francoist Spain, Spanish bureaucracy, and the Marshall Plan, an American policy that provided financial aid to underdeveloped Spain. In addition to making pointed comments on economic dependency, Berlanga also centers on the film form itself. The film was originally commissioned as an *española*, a genre that was, as we have seen in the previous decade, particularly (ab)used to depict clichés of "archetypal" Spanishness.[55] *¡Bienvenido Mister Marshall!* simultaneously uses and departs from the genre, thus exploring its subversive potential. Berlanga's force lies in his multiple critique of (inter)national politics, Hollywood, Francoist *folklorismo*, and even neorealist aesthetics.[56]

In the 1950s, the IIEC opened up a space for an oppositional cinema. This cinema of dissent was partially inspired by the Italian Institute of Culture's "Week of Italian Cinema" that took place in Madrid in 1951 and 1953. The first event in November 1951 screened *Cronaca di un amore* (Antonioni, 1950) and *Miracolo a Milano* (De Sica, 1951). The second festival in March 1953 presented *Umberto D* (De Sica), *Bellísima* (Visconti), *Due soldi di speranza* (Castellani), *Proceso a la ciudad* (Zampa), and *Il camino della speranza* (Germi), all filmed in 1951. There were additional private screenings that gave Spanish filmmakers access to other films such as *Paisá* (Rossellini, 1946) and *Ossessione* (Visconti, 1942). Several Italian directors came to Madrid to accompany the screenings: Vittorio de Sica, Alberto Lattuada, Luciano Emmer, Luigi Zampa, and Cesare Zavattini.[57]

The "Week of Italian Cinema" introduced Spanish film directors to Italian neorealism, a genre developed partially in reaction to fascist cinematographic aesthetics. Italian neorealism, engaged with social reality and problems, gave the IIEC directors an aesthetic and political framework for an exploration of their own social reality. Their demand for a different cinema closely resembled an Italian insistence on dismantling the grandiose fascist spectacles that dominated their film screens in the 1940s. In addition to a preoccupation with poverty and social problems, neorealism was also prompted by a need for cinematographic and formal renovation. Low budgets, exterior setting, non-professional actors, an emphasis on the "documentary" aspect of film art, natural lighting, extremely lengthy takes, and deep focus photography were some of the defining characteristics of the new genre.

The Italian influence, newly formed *cine clubs* showing alternative films, and a proliferation of more radical film journals such as *Objetivo* and *Cinema universitario* shaped the film culture of the 1950s and helped to articulate a dissident cinema that contrasted with films of the previous period. The zeitgeist was captured in a congress held in May of 1955 entitled Conversaciones de Salamanca. The Salamanca congress was the first national film conference organized by the younger generation of filmmakers and critics who were not direct participants in the Spanish Civil War. They were nevertheless marked by war's consequences, the Francoist dictatorship, and the drab ideological rhetoric of the postwar era. They came from all political persuasions and were also supported by progressive filmmakers from the preceding generation. From the left, Juan Antonio Bardem offered his diagnosis of Spanish cinema as "politically ineffectual, socially false, intellectually base, aesthetically void, [and] industrially weak," an opinion that was seconded by the Falangist Marcelo Arroita-Jáuregui, who called for "a cinema that is revolutionary, religiously correct, politically valid, socially educational, and aesthetically valuable."[58] The Salamanca congress's motto, "Spanish cinema is dead. Long live Spanish cinema!" articulated theoretically what was already discernible in the innovative film practices of the 1950s.

Neorealism was established as the primary aesthetic model for Spanish dissident cinema in the 1950s. Nevertheless within Spain's oppressive political and social context, the reception and appropriation of neorealism were also problematic and ambiguous. Several film critics have spoken of "*españolization* of neorealism," since Spanish circumstances, in contrast to Italy's, did not permit the movement's more radical political posture to develop. Spanish neorealism has been criticized for absorbing only empty formalist traits of the movement, void of the social criticism that characterized its Italian counterparts. Furthermore, neorealism, which was originally associated with a leftist worldview, became ideologically reinscribed in the Spanish context. The most notorious example of this reinscription was José Antonio Nieves Conde's *Surcos* (1951), a film that can paradoxically be categorized as Falangist neorealism.[59]

However, Spanish dissident cinema did turn its gaze toward reality, as put forward by the Salamanca postulates. Spain's idiosyncratic neorealist aesthetic was characterized by the vicious and corrosive black humor that was partially inspired by *esperpento*, a literary technique developed by Spanish playwright Valle-Inclán, which portrays grotesque and absurdist "deformations" of reality. Valle-Inclán's assertion that "The tragic sense of life can be rendered only through an aesthetic that is systematically deformed" (*Luces de Bohemia*, 1920) is transported to the big screen by Marco Ferreri, Rafael Azcona, and Luis García Berlanga. The team of Marco Fererri, an Italian director who transplanted himself to Spain, and screenwriter Rafael Azcona became almost synonymous with this dark, biting form of Spanish neorealism. Berlanga, especially when working with Azcona, displayed a similar sensibility. Some of the best films of the period and the most indicative of this tendency were *El pisito* (1958), *El cochecito* (1960), *Plácido* (1961), and *El verdugo* (1963).

One characteristic that distinguishes Spanish neorealism from its Italian counterpart is its use of *esperpento*. As the renowned director Pedro Almodóvar said, "In the 1950s and 60s Spain experienced a kind of neorealism which was far less sentimental than the Italian brand and far more ferocious and amusing" (Vidal, *El cine de Pedro Almodóvar*, p. 116). In Marco Ferreri's *El pisito*, for example, a young couple schemes to get housing by marrying off the boyfriend to an old widow whose apartment they hope to inherit once she has died. The plan fails miserably as the widow is rejuvenated by her new, young husband. Berlanga's *Plácido* is a dark Christmas comedy of errors, originated by a government campaign: "Seat a poor man at your table." Acidic and unsentimental, the film uncovers the hypocritical dominant discourses surrounding traditional family values and Christian charity at the very heart of the Francoist state. *El verdugo* is a dark comedy that examines the moral ambiguities of Spain's death-penalty system. The panorama of this oppositional wave would not be complete without mentioning actor and film director Fernando Fernán Gómez, who filmed *La vida por delante* (1958) and *La vida alrededor* (1959), followed by his two masterpieces *El mundo sigue* (1963) and *El extraño viaje* (1964). Finally, in 1959 Carlos Saura, one of the most important directors of the following period, debuted with *Los golfos* (1959), whose forgotten and marginalized "hooligans" of the title are depicted by a non-professional cast of actors in authentic street locales in Madrid.

This cinema of dissent was partly enabled by the rise of alternative, more politicized production companies and models. In addition to directing, IIEC students also became involved in film production. Bardem and Berlanga's debut *Esa pareja feliz* was produced by Altamira S.L., created in 1949. Manuel Goyanes, one of the most successful and commercial producers of the 1960s (linked to the child star phenomenon), appeared on the scene at this time producing several important, politicized films by Juan Antonio Bardem such as *Muerte de un ciclista* (1955), *Calle Mayor* (1956), and *Venganza* (1957). Pere Portabella and his more oppositional Films 59 made Carlos Saura's first feature *Los golfos* and Marco Ferreri's *El cochecito*, and collaborated in the production of *Viridiana*, Buñuel's sacrilegious 1961 masterpiece.

Besides the oppositional current of the 1950s, there was also a continuation of the folkloric cinema prominent in earlier decades, a strong religious cinema presence, the appearance of urban comedy geared to the rising middle class, and the establishment of a children's cinema. As emphasized by Carlos Heredero, cinematic practices of the period were characterized by "generic promiscuity" ("promiscuidad genérica"). As Heredero emphasized, "it is not at all strange that pious themes are dressed in historic clothes, that children star in musicals, comedies, melodramas, or religious movies, that nuns sing, that folkloric singers turn up in historic films or that religion and politics walk hand in hand through the takes of more than one film" (*Las huellas del tiempo*, p. 163).

The popularity of folkloric films was tied to prominent female stars such as Lola Flores, Carmen Sevilla, Marujita Díaz, and Paquita Rico. Antonio Molina, a leading male star, debuted in *El pescador de coplas* (1953). Folkloric cinema very rarely departed from a set of stereotypical formulas. One of the rare examples is *Duende y misterio del flamenco* by Edgar Neville from 1952. *Cuplé* cinema was as popular, partially due to the nostalgic revival of this pre-war musical genre and partially because of Sara Montiel, the star of *El último cuplé*, who reached the height of her popularity in the mid 1950s.[60] Urban romantic comedy, *comedia rosa*, both portrayed and catered to the emerging middle class. The commercial success of *Las chicas de la Cruz Roja* (Rafael J. Salvia, 1958), *Muchachas de azul* (Pedro Lazaga, 1957), *Las aeroguapas* (Eduardo Manzanos, 1957), and *Ya tenemos coche* (Julio Salvador, 1959) can be seen as precursors of the immensely popular comedies about tourism, sex, and development (*desarrollo*) that reached their height in the following decade.

There is a consensus among critics that the 1954 film *Marcelino, pan y vino* marks the onset of child-star films in Spain. *Marcelino, pan y vino*, the melodrama of an orphan, Marcelino (played by Pablito Calvo), adopted by friars, captivated audiences and created a formula for success that was exploited in subsequent child films. Pablito Calvo's fame was followed by the emergence of the two biggest child stars of the time, Joselito and Marisol. The undisputable hits of this genre were Joselito's *El pequeño ruiseñor* (1956), *Saeta del ruiseñor* (1957), and *El ruiseñor de las cumbres* (1958) and Marisol's *Un rayo de luz* (1960), *Ha llegado un ángel* (1961), and *Tómbola* (1962). Religious cinema coexisted with these more frivolous films and subjects. Its heyday in the 1950s can be partially explained by the space that was opened up by the decline of the patriotic war-films genre. This move from the Falangist 1940s to the National-Catholic 1950s is exemplified in *Balarrasa* where "a soldier of Franco's becomes a soldier of Christ" (Heredero, *Las huellas del tiempo*, p. 194). Other significant titles were Rafael Gil's *La señora de Fátima* (1951), *Sor Intrépida* (1952), *La guerra de Dios* (1953), and *Cerca de la ciudad* (Luis Lucia, 1952) as well as missionary films such as *Molokay* (Luis Lucia, 1959) and *La mies es mucha* (José Luis Sáenz de Heredia, 1948).[61]

The two films featured in this chapter are *El cochecito* (1960) and *Viridiana* (1961). *El cochecito* exemplifies Marco Fererri and Rafael Azcona's collaboration, characterized by their dark, critical, and biting humor. It centers on the misery and solitude of the protagonist Don Anselmo (played by José Isbert) and his obsessive efforts to obtain *el cochecito*, his own motorized wheelchair, to be able to spend time with his disabled, albeit motorized, friends. The film is reflective of Spain's moment of industrialization in the late 1950s and its entrance into modern capitalism and a consumer economy. The film's ending, a darkly comedic scene in which Don Anselmo poisons his family in "exchange" for a motorized wheelchair, can be read as a critique of capitalism and its false promises of mobility and autonomy. The film is also a striking visual testimony of its times, capturing Madrid's renewal and ongoing process of industrialization in the late 1950s. The film has a documentary quality that is prompted by formal concerns as well as a neorealist preoccupation with poverty and social issues.

Viridiana, the second film examined in this chapter, is Luis Buñuel's tour de force and one of the most radical critiques of Francoism and Spanish tradition, particularly religion. *Viridiana* unsettled both the Francoist establishment and the dissident artistic and cultural milieu. The film was instrumental in (re)connecting Spanish filmmakers with Luis Buñuel, who was living in Mexico and whose films were largely unknown in his own country. The Francoist government attempted to co-opt the film to project and foment a more liberal image abroad. While *Viridiana*'s prestigious Golden Palm at the 1961 Cannes Film Festival worked to that end, the Vatican newspaper *L'osservatore romano*'s accusation of the film's anti-Christian blasphemy had harsh consequences. Instead of illustrating Francoist government liberalization, *Viridiana* testified to its limits. The scandal cost José Muñoz Fontán his post as director general of cinematography. *Viridiana* was prohibited from exhibition, the official documentation of its production disappeared, and the film premiered in Spain only after Franco's death.

The Vatican's accusation of the film's anti-Christian blasphemy was not unfounded. Profoundly unsettling, the film links sexuality, perversion, and religion, themes characteristic of Buñuel's opus in general. Buñuel's questioning of the "true" premises of Christianity was particularly evident in *Viridiana*'s notorious Last Supper scene, which is re-enacted by a group of beggars and prostitutes to the sound of Handel's *Messiah*. Buñuel's film also links Christianity to modernization and capitalism. Through radical juxtapositions of the capitalist sphere (exemplified by the protagonist Jorge, who attempts to modernize the countryside) and the Christian sphere (exemplified by Viridiana, her "devoted" beggars, and the daily regime of prayer), Buñuel's film reveals the contradictions at the very core of 1950s Francoist technocratic reform. Christian spirit and capital, individuality and family, tradition and modernization – themes already explored in *El cochecito* – are pushed to the extreme in *Viridiana*. This film significantly impacted the cinematographic panorama of the time, and although it doesn't exactly fit the parameters of neorealism, it does share some of its aesthetic characteristics. The cruel, demystifying portrait of the world's miseries that we find in Buñuel's films is reminiscent of both neorealism and the picaresque tradition, reflected in the director's corrosive humor and his focus on social outcasts. Both films in this chapter reveal the limits and contradictions at the very heart of Franco's regime, and the necessity for change inscribed in the paradoxes of a rapidly developing dictatorial Spain.

The neorealist aesthetic, characterized by black-and-white photography, communicates the nameless characters' gray reality. Some of the formal characteristics that define the genre are the use of non-professional actors and a focus on daily life. Many of the films were made with modest budgets and on location, as opposed to in the studio, thereby using natural light and avoiding prefabricated sets. For Spanish film, the neorealist style heralded a renovation, both formally and in terms of subject matter. Using a documentary style, it attempted to provide testimony of a certain time, and sought the complicity of the audience by featuring characters whose lives resonated with the drama of the spectator's own existence. Neorealism employed these techniques despite the fact that filmgoers frequently preferred the entertaining commercial films associated with official cinema, which avoided representing a rather colorless daily reality.

1   *El cochecito* (Marco Ferreri, 1960)

Context and Critical Commentary

Production credits

Director: Marco Ferreri
Production: Pere Portabella; Films 59
Cinematography: Juan Julio Baena

Screenplay: Rafael Azcona; Marco Ferreri
Score: Miguel Asins Arbó
Genre: Comedy, black and white
Country: Spain
Runtime: 88 minutes

Cast

José Isbert	Don Anselmo
Pedro Porcel	Carlos Proharán
José Luis López Vázquez	Alvarito
María Luisa Ponte	Matilde
José Alvarez "Lepe"	Don Lucas
Antonio Riquelme	Médico
Antonio Gavilán	Don Hilario
Angel Alvarez	Alvarez
Chus Lampreave	Yolandita
Carmen Santonja	Julita
Rafael Azcona, Carlos Saura	Frailes

Synopsis

Don Anselmo Proharán, a retired civil servant and a widower, lives with his children in Madrid. Almost every Sunday he meets up with his best friend Don Lucas and their disabled friends, who all have motorized wheelchairs (*cochecitos*), and Don Anselmo becomes obsessed with owning one himself. In order to convince his family to buy him one he pretends he is losing the ability to walk. He goes to Don Hilario's orthopedic shop to order a *cochecito*, and while there he meets Alvarez, the caretaker of the physically and mentally disabled son of a marquis. The wheelchair that Don Anselmo had ordered finally arrives at Don Hilario's shop. Don Anselmo takes the wheelchair on a test drive with his friends through the park, El Retiro, and is absolutely enamored of the new apparatus. However, he must convince his family to help him pay for it. He pretends to have an accident on the stairs, in front of his son Carlos, but the stunt is unconvincing and Don Anselmo decides to pawn his deceased wife's jewels. When Carlos finds out, he becomes furious with his father and he forces Don Anselmo to go with him to retrieve the jewels and return the wheelchair. Once at the shop, Don Hilario refuses to return the money Don Anselmo has already paid. But, out of Carlos's earshot, Don Hilario promises Don Anselmo that he will hold on to the *cochecito* for three more days if he can come up with the remainder of the money he owes. Three days later one of the employees shows up at the Proharán house to collect on the debt. As a result, Don Anselmo's son threatens to send him to a nursing home and the rest of the family agrees. Don Anselmo bursts into tears and goes into the kitchen, where he empties a bottle of poison into a pot of food cooking on the stove. Then he takes a roll of money from a box in his son's desk to pay for the motorized wheelchair. Now the owner of his own *cochecito*, Don Anselmo returns to the house, where he learns his whole family has died. As he tries to escape down the highway on his wheelchair, two Civil Guards detain him and take him to jail.

Critical commentary

The script is based on a novella, published in the 1950s, as *El paralítico* (*The Paralytic*) by Rafael Azcona. The story grew out of an anecdote that Azcona previously published in *La Codorniz*, a weekly cultural magazine that was critical of the Franco regime. The story recounts how a group of disabled men criticizes the players of a soccer game as they leave the stadium in their motorized wheelchairs. The story piqued the interest of the Italian director, Marco Ferreri, who had already successfully adapted Azcona's critically and publicly acclaimed *El pisito* for the screen. He immediately envisioned José Isbert in the role of the protagonist. This was an ideal choice, given Isbert's outstanding performance and his ability to communicate the black humor that is so characteristic of neorealism.

Don Anselmo, the film's central character, can be seen as an *esperpento*-influenced rendition of one of the most famous characters in Italian neo-realism, Umberto D., from the film of the same name, directed by Vittorio de Sica in 1952. Nevertheless, in contrast with Umberto D., Don Anselmo's character provokes empathy in the spectator, even though he kills his entire family in order to pay for the motorized wheelchair he wants so badly. For exactly this reason, the censors suppressed the scene in which Don Anselmo poisons his family. The director had to film the scene over again in a shorter, simpler version in order to make the end of the story morally acceptable.

The film's visual quality and strength are products of the outstanding work of photographer Juan Julio Baena. He captured equally well the exterior shots of Madrid and the claustrophobic interior of the apartment where the Proharán family lives, reflecting the conflict within this limited space and the family's inability to live together. The use of sound is also noteworthy. The diverse synthetic sounds, like those of the street, traffic, the exaggerated ambulance siren, along with human sounds, like Don Anselmo's agonized breathing and the family's arguments, are superimposed on each other to emphasize the characters' existential anguish.

Don Anselmo's outings around Madrid give the audience an insight into the social fabric of 1950s Spain: the city and its anonymous characters' struggles for daily subsistence. Baena's camera captures the day-to-day context of Madrid's urban space in the 1950s, and is key in reflecting the world of social marginalization. The backdrop of this black comedy is the conflict between the dizzying industrial modernization taking place at that moment (the so-called "economic miracle" that carried Spain into a new period) and the persistently outdated structure of the Franco dictatorship. The crisis occurring within certain social structures – family, neighborhood, and friends – critiques the scarcity of solidarity and the cruelty of the group toward the individual. In essence, the crisis that society faced at that moment is one of being trapped between the old social models and new dictates of modernity. In this way *El cochecito* evokes the neorealism that Ferreri had initiated in his Spanish stage, first with *El pisito* and later with *Los chicos* (1959).

Film Scenes: Close Readings

Scene 1   *The disabled go for a ride*

In this scene, Don Anselmo travels with his friends to the outskirts of Madrid, the very countryside idealized in the Francoist imaginary, liberating himself from the oppression that his family represents. Don Anselmo's dissatisfaction at home with his family is juxtaposed with the almost child-like joy he experiences after an idyllic day with his crippled friends, where they sing, drink, and frolic on their motorized wheelchairs. By contrasting the healthy body of the protagonist, Don Anselmo, with the crippled bodies of his friends in their *cochecitos*, Ferreri emphasizes Don

Figure 5.1   The disabled go for a ride (*El cochecito*, 1960)

Anselmo's need to own a wheelchair in order to belong to a group that, although crippled, is still motorized, liberated, and modernized. The ability to socialize with his friends is juxtaposed with the exclusion and lack of communication that Don Anselmo suffers within his own family. The same problematic is reflected in earlier scenes. Both Don Anselmo and Don Lucas are treated disparagingly and perceived as useless, mentally senile, and irritating, although they are still integrated into the family dynamic.

As Don Anselmo's day in the country comes to an end, his friends abruptly abandon him to find his own way home, reinforcing the fact that in order to belong to this mobilized group he must acquire the unifying element: the wheelchair. The solitary figure of Don Anselmo in the countryside is contrasted with his friends' joy as they proceed without him on their outing. We hear the sound of the motors as they drive away, contrasted with the still sound of the leaves rustling in the trees. Therefore, the irony of the scene, steeped in black humor, resides in the paradox of mobility, where what marks the group's difference is their possession of the fetishized *cochecito*.

Scene 2   The poisoned family

When Don Anselmo sees his desire to obtain the expensive wheelchair that would integrate him into the group of motorized friends unfulfilled, he takes drastic measures. In order to convince his family, and his son in particular, that he needs the wheelchair, Don Anselmo pretends to fall down the stairs. He then stays in bed complaining that he can't move his legs, until the doctor visits. Once his farce is uncovered, he decides to sell his dead wife's jewels and convinces the wheelchair vendor to sell him the precious object in installments. When Don Anselmo's son finds out, he returns the wheelchair and denounces his father as senile. Don Anselmo, with the conviction that losing the wheelchair means he will be excluded from his only group of friends, poisons his family's food. His obsession overcomes his moral judgment and, therefore, black humor and *esperpento* achieve their maximum intensity in this scene. This intensity reaches its height in the take where we see Don Anselmo in a tight close-up, as he returns to his house after taking his new wheelchair – the envy of all his friends for its multiple speeds – for a ride, and sees the bodies of his dead family as they are being taken from his house. The exaggerated ambulance sirens mix with various street sounds to punctuate the film's climax. This scene manifests the particular form of corrosive, acidic humor that Spanish neorealism developed, and that distinguishes it from Italian neorealism.

Scene 3   Don Anselmo and the Civil Guard

In a final scene charged with irony and black humor, two Civil Guards on bicycles detain Don Anselmo as he tries to escape Madrid on his motorized wheelchair. The protagonist is seen driving down a long highway that promises to distance him from the reality that oppresses him. In an absolute lack of understanding, the family failed to realize the extent of Don Anselmo's desire (and insanity). The final scene reiterates Don Anselmo's amorality and his persistent fetishization of the *cochecito*. After the guards ask him for his papers and realize who he is, they ask Don Anselmo to follow them to prison. In this way, the object of his liberation becomes the motive for his incarceration. However, the lack of physical freedom is not exactly what Don Anselmo is worried about. He asks: "Will they let me keep my little wheelchair in jail?" At that moment we hear a very loud braying sound, possibly in mockery of certain aspects of society: the patriarchal system, the law, consumer society, modernization, and individual freedom.

Director (Life and Works)

Marco Ferreri (b. Milan 1928, d. Rome 1997)

Marco Ferreri was born in Milan (Italy), but his career began in Spain. The three films he directed there are widely recognized as key contributions to the development of Spanish film of the 1960s. Ferreri originally studied to be a veterinarian, but later abandoned that field for a degree in journalism. He published the magazine *Documento mensile*, which quickly became popular, with articles by well-known directors of Italian cinema such as Visconti, De Sica, and Antonioni. Ferreri then began working as an assistant director for renowned filmmakers Antonioni, Fellini, and Lattuada. In 1955 he traveled to Madrid where he met Rafael Azcona, who would later become one of his closest collaborators.

In 1958 he co-directed *El pisito* with Isidoro Ferry in Spain. The screenplay, written by Azcona and based on the novella *Pobre, paralítico y muerto* (*Poor, Paralyzed, and Dead*), became a great critical and popular success. The film reflects the lack of housing available at the time and the subventions that the state granted for the construction of a number of moderately priced apartments. With its black humor the film levels the same type of social critique of corruption and urban land speculation that is characteristic of later works by both Ferreri and Azcona.

Ferreri's next film was *Los chicos* (1959), which shows the daily life of a group of adolescents in Madrid's suburbs. The film clearly shows the influence of the Italian neorealism that definitively marked Ferreri's Spanish period and is best exemplified by *El cochecito*, the last film he made there. A common thread throughout his films is the conflict between society and the individual, the friction between old social models and the new consumer society.

It is important to note that Ferreri's films were influenced not only by Italian neorealism but by Spanish *esperpento*, as evidenced by his use of ironic black humor. Ferreri was a model for filmmakers like Berlanga (*El verdugo*, 1962) and Fernando Fernán Gómez (*El extraño viaje*, 1963). Following his Spanish period, Ferreri continued to work with Rafael Azcona on the majority of his films, the best-known being *La grande abbuffata* in 1973. Marco Ferreri died in Rome in 1997.

2   *Viridiana* (Luis Buñuel, 1961)

Context and Critical Commentary

Production credits

Director: Luis Buñuel
Production: UNINCI (Madrid); Films 59 (Madrid); Gustavo Alatriste (México D.F.)
Cinematography: José Fernández Aguayo
Screenplay: Luis Buñuel; Julio Alejandro
Score: *Requiem* by Mozart, Händel's *Messiah*, and Beethoven's Ninth Symphony, selected by Gustavo Pittaluga
Genre: Drama, black and white
Country: Mexico/Spain
Runtime: 86 minutes

Cast

Silvia Pinal	Viridiana
Francisco Rabal	Jorge
Fernando Rey	Don Jaime
Margarita Lozano	Ramona
Victoria Zinny	Lucía
Teresa Rabal	Rita
José Calvo	Don Amalio
Luis Heredia	El Poca
Joaquín Roa	Don Zequiel
José Manuel Martín	El Cojo
Lola Gaos	Enedina
Juan García Tienda	José El Leproso
Sergio Mendizábal	El Pelón

Synopsis

The young novice Viridiana is at the point of donning the habit when she leaves the convent to visit her uncle Don Jaime, her only living relative and benefactor. During her visit, Don Jaime tries to keep her, as he is profoundly fascinated by her likeness to his dead wife. He tries to seduce her but Viridiana refuses his advances. In spite of her resistance to her uncle's advances, Viridiana does agree to put on the wedding dress that her aunt was wearing when she died in Don Jaime's arms on their wedding night. With the help of his servant, Ramona, Don Jaime drugs Viridiana and carries her to the bed in which his bride died. The next morning, in his last attempt to prevent Viridiana from leaving, Don Jaime lies to his niece, telling her that he had raped her the night before, even though in actuality he could not bring himself to the act. Horrified, Viridiana decides to leave. Seeing that he has lost her, Don Jaime confesses that he had actually lied to her and asks for her forgiveness. Viridiana leaves anyway, and Don Jaime commits suicide by hanging himself from a tree. Viridiana assumes responsibility for the suicide, and as a form of penitence renounces the habit and stays at the newly inherited mansion. However, it turns out that she shares this inheritance with her cousin Jorge, Don Jaime's son. Viridiana's attempts to practice Christian charity by sheltering beggars conflict with Jorge's plans for modernizing the property, but at the same time she is attracted to him.

Critical commentary

After nearly 20 years of not filming in Spain, Buñuel decided to face the challenge of returning to his homeland to film *Viridiana*, which, according to Víctor Fuentes, became "the greatest and most divine erotic orgy on film" (*Buñuel: cine y literatura*, p. 139). Buñuel's decision to film *Viridiana* in Spain evoked strong criticism from Spanish Republicans in exile. In the eyes of many exiles, the filmmaker had relented in his criticism of the Franco regime and returned to Spain forsaking his radical political postures. Nevertheless, it is precisely with this film that Luis Buñuel produced his strongest critique of the most emblematic elements promoted during Francoism. His irreverence for Catholic symbolism earned him the condemnation of the Vatican when *Viridiana* premiered.

Buñuel's directorial return to Spain is the result of complicated circumstances. Two important production companies converged during *Viridiana*'s germination: UNINCI (Madrid) and Pere Portabella's Films 59 (Madrid), together with Mexican producer Gustavo Alatriste. UNINCI, the first production company to even attempt to go beyond the parameters dictated by the regime, produced *Sonatas*, a film that Juan Antonio Bardem made in Mexico in 1959. UNINCI wanted to attract politically involved and outspoken directors, and in Mexico they offered Buñuel the chance to return to Spain to film a movie. It is also important to note that Pere Portabella, who produced Carlos Saura's *Los golfos*, met Buñuel at the Cannes festival in 1960 and proposed that they do a project together. Finally, Gustavo Alatriste decided to get involved in the project as well, partly because his wife, Silvia Pinal, wanted to work with a director of international prestige like Luis Buñuel.

Upon reading the preliminary screenplay the censors had various objections of a moral and religious character. For example, they took issue with the inclusion of the pious symbols that Viridiana carries with her, the attempts of her uncle and cousin at seduction, the presumably fake rape, and the morbid suggestions of necrophilia and masochism. The censors especially insisted on changes to the final scene of the film, in which Viridiana's cousin Jorge seduces her. Buñuel ignored all of their suggestions, with the exception of the one related to the final scene. This change, paradoxically, makes the ending even more provocative by adding a shot – suggestive of a ménage à trois – that shows Viridiana, Jorge, and the servant Ramona playing cards together.

Viridiana was filmed in Madrid at filmmaker Juan Antonio Bardem's studios and on location. Buñuel did not encounter any problems during the filming, thanks to an adequate budget and high-quality technical and artistic crews. The relative ease with which he was able to film *Viridiana* in Spain contrasted with the scandal that followed its release. *Viridiana*, with its transgressive topics, was reminiscent of Buñuel's most radical surrealist productions like *L'Âge d'or* (1930). *Viridiana*, filmed during Buñuel's long period of residence in Mexico, shows the fusion of elements that stand out in both Spain and Mexico: the obsession with morality, the figure of the patriarch, Christian ritual, and the eroticism underlined by religion and death. This is clearly seen in *Los olvidados* (1950), *Él* (1952), and of course, *Viridiana*.

The director general of cinematography, José Muñoz Fontán, chose *Viridiana* to represent Spain at the Cannes Film Festival with the intention of gaining international recognition by reclaiming Spanish cinema's great exile, Luis Buñuel. This gesture represents one of the many paradoxes of the period of opening up (*apertura*) in Franco's Spain. The film won the Palme d'Or, the festival's highest honor, and received a unanimous standing ovation from the public and the jury. Nevertheless, the film brought with it a wave of questioning because it presented images that were extremely provocative to the Spanish Catholic mores of the time. The film immediately became the subject of a resounding international debate. *L'osservatore romano* attacked it for being sacrilegious and blasphemous, the Spanish censor prohibited it (the film was not authorized for screening until 1977), but the film achieved worldwide success beyond Spain's borders. The furious denouncements from the ecclesiastical powers forced the resignation of José Muñoz Fontán, who had personally accepted the award at Cannes on the advice of Pere Portabella and Juan Antonio Bardem. As a result of the scandal, Luis Buñuel would not film again in Spain until 1970, when he made *Tristana*.

Film Scenes: Close Readings

Scene 1   The impossibility of desire

Throughout the film, Viridiana appears in various scenes that evoke her as an erotic object. For example, in the scene prior to this one, she sleepwalks through the house in her nightgown, with bare feet and her hair undone. As the script itself indicates: "When Viridiana sits down, her skirt is maladjusted and shows her leg and the beginning of her thigh" (*Viridiana*, 52). It is important to note that in her sleepwalking trance, Viridiana surprises Don Jaime in the act of trying on his deceased wife's wedding attire: the white shoes, her wedding veil, flowers, and finally, her corset. The next night when Viridiana agrees to put on her aunt's wedding gown she is complying with Don Jaime's desire to reincarnate the figure of his dead wife.

We see Buñuel's characteristic iconography played out in this scene. After drugging Viridiana, Don Jaime carries her to the bed in which his wife died, in hopes of satisfying a desire that is seemingly impossible: to resurrect his dead wife through the body of his young niece. To the uncle, to have Viridiana is to materialize the lost object, as she is the living image of her dead aunt. Viridiana lies still, as if dead, in the matrimonial bed. Her uncle's gaze travels the length of Viridiana's body, fragmented by a series of close-up shots: feet, hands, crossed arms, lips, and chest. The uncle's desire, as it searches for satisfaction in Viridiana's "substitute" body, literally becomes a protagonist in this scene, as the script itself indicates: "Don Jaime's eyes are fixed on this white, pure flesh, without looking at any other body part. He is obviously disturbed" (*Viridiana*, 52).

Figure 5.2   The impossibility of desire (*Viridiana*, 1961)

The eroticism of the scene is emphasized by the use of Catholic symbolism. The attempted rape is tied to elements of a Catholic mass: the white dress and candelabra suggest the desecration of a novice. In this scene Buñuel subverts the meaning of one of the most sacred institutions in the Catholic religion: marriage. Viridiana's wearing the wedding dress, in addition to constituting a symbolic marriage, results in the "resurrection" of the dead object of desire. Furthermore, Mozart's *Requiem* provides the ambience for the scene, evoking the coexistence of life and death, which the visual elements of the night scene also reinforce. It is also important to point out that the sequence, shot from a high camera angle, is seen from the perspective of Rita, the servant's young daughter. This juxtaposition, in addition to evoking infantile innocence and profanation through the attempted rape of Viridiana, is also a questioning of the function of the gaze in film. In this way, various gazes converge on Viridiana's immobile body: the uncle's, the young girl's, the spectator's, and the camera's.

Scene 2   Viridiana's utopia

In this scene the recitation of the angelus, a devotional prayer that commemorates the Annunciation, symbolically reflects the way in which Viridiana attempts to achieve her own utopia. Don Jaime's suicide leaves Viridiana with no referents: she is no longer part of the convent, nor does she have the patriarchal protection that family provides. Upon finding herself alone, Viridiana initiates an act of Christian charity, but within her own parameters. She decides to bring all of the beggars in town to live in the huge, old house in an effort to create a Christian utopia. However, Viridiana's modern, innovative, and seductive cousin has his own new ideas for his father's land, which had stopped being productive.

Both cousins reclaim the inherited property with the same intensity: for Viridiana it is an idyllic place to establish her Christian utopia, and for Jorge it holds the possibility of progress and modernity. This scene juxtaposes Viridiana and her beggars, the reciters of the angelus, with the incessant construction being carried out by workers whom Jorge has contracted. The images of the reciters frame various symbolic pairs in both close-up and medium shots; for example, Viridiana and Refugio (a pregnant beggar) and Viridiana with the crippled beggar who will later attempt to rape her. Through three long shots of the group, Buñuel evokes the famous painting by J. F. Millet, *The Angelus*, so revered by the surrealists.

In the fragments of the angelus, words underline images: "The angel of God illuminated Maria," prays Viridiana, "and she conceived through the work of the Spirit," answers her future rapist; "He made the flesh," prays Viridiana, "from your womb," Refugio answers. It is important to note that Buñuel also resorts to using two literary genres of the Spanish tradition: mysticism, through Viridiana's utopian Christianity, and the picaresque, through the harsh reality of the beggars whom society marginalizes. The use of sound, a recognizably Buñuelian element, is important in this scene. The "Pray for us Maria, conceived without sin" is indistinguishable from the sound of the construction taking place on the property: a saw cutting wood, hammering, and the sound of material being unloaded. The two auditory registers, the praying and the reconstruction, become indistinguishable background noise. This visual and auditory struggle is symbolically reminiscent of the conflict and coexistence of progress and religion in Spain during the 1960s – the contradiction underlying the fact that the modernizing Planes de Desarrollo, or Development Plans, were being pushed by the ministers of Opus Dei.[62]

Viridiana's proposal to establish a different order, a utopian "republic of beggars," fails because, in the end, these new citizens don't seem to actually share in the project. Just like her cousin, Jorge, the beggars are more interested in enjoying the property. The film's opening and closing music reinforce this leitmotif of the two conflicting economic-symbolic orders:

the spirituality of Handel's *Messiah* against the modernity symbolized by the jazz playing in the final scene.

Scene 3   The decadent dinner

As Viridiana's and Jorge's plans conflict with each other, the beggars take advantage of their patrons' absence to live out their fantasy of belonging to the order that even in their utopia they are denied: the huge house. They break into the prohibited space and organize a decadent dinner. In this scene the beggars invade the space that is socially prohibited: the opulent and bourgeois dinner table. Here we see a familiar trope in Buñuel's films: ceremonies linked to the dinner table. In this specific scene he questions the bourgeois formalities of dining by putting silverware into the hands of beggars. Buñuel levels a strong social critique while also signaling the beggars' desire to appropriate their masters' objects instead of forming part of Viridiana's religious utopia. As one of the beggars affirms, "I don't want to die without having eaten on such handsome table cloths." Here Buñuel very effectively applies theatrical techniques to the film medium. Everything occurs in enclosed space, the semi-darkness of which allows the temporary rupturing of the social stratum.

Because of its parody of the Last Supper, this is one of the most lauded and criticized scenes of the film. Buñuel visually references Leonardo da Vinci's *The Last Supper*, the emblematic image of the Christian imaginary.

Figure 5.3   The decadent dinner (*Viridiana*, 1961)

This scene is tied to the film's "blasphemy" and is precisely what makes Viridiana "the greatest and most divine erotic orgy on film" (Fuentes, *Buñuel: cine y literatura*, p. 139). The desecration of *The Last Supper* is symbolically tied to Viridiana's own desecration. The 12 beggars personify the 12 apostles, who through their orgy become characters that incarnate the lowest of human passions. The sex scene between two of the beggars focuses on their feet; their thick socks and wasted skin are a foil to the elegant fetishism of the white wedding shoes and the delicate skin on Viridiana's legs. Handel's *Messiah* provides background music again, as the Leper puts on the dead aunt's wedding dress and performs a grotesque dance, throwing around the feathers of the pigeon he has just killed. This bird's death symbolizes the loss of purity that foreshadows the transformation from Pious Viridiana to Carnal Viridiana. The orgy culminates with a photo of the huge table of beggar-apostles that Enedina pretends to take with her vagina. At this moment we also hear a rooster crow, symbolizing the way the beggars have betrayed Viridiana. The scene ends, as does the disorder imposed by the beggars, with the return of the masters, Viridiana and Jorge, to the house. They restore order by definitively expelling the beggars from and inviting modernity into the old house.

Director (Life and Works)

See pp. 36–8.

6

The "Liberal" Dictatorship and its Agony (1962–1975)

1 *El verdugo* (Luis García Berlanga, 1963)
2 *El jardín de las delicias* (Carlos Saura, 1970)

Historical and Political Overview of the Period

The implementation of the First Economic Development Plan (Primer Plan de Desarrollo Económico) in 1963, elaborated by the technocratic government in collaboration with the World Bank, ushered Spain into a new era. Above all, the plan encouraged the development of tourism and the augmentation of foreign investment. The tourist industry increased from hosting a few million visitors in the beginning of 1958 to 14 million in 1964. A vertiginous economic takeoff and modernization at home were accompanied by Spanish migration to Western Europe. These changes indicated the beginning of economic prosperity in Spain. However, the rapid introduction of consumer capitalism and the influx of foreigners brought with them new cultural values that conflicted with traditional Spanish mores.

There were major changes in both domestic and foreign politics. Manuel Fraga Iribarne, a liberal voice that fit well with the increasingly modernizing political climate, replaced Gabriel Arias Salgado as minister of information and tourism in 1962. Fraga Iribarne worked toward political reform (such as a program for the right to political association) and drafted a more liberal press law.[63] However, along with Spain's rapid political and cultural changes came growing social tension and unrest caused by striking students and workers, who were calling for political and unionizing rights. The student unrest culminated in the closing of Madrid and Barcelona universities in February of 1967, while working-class organizations became more organized, powerful, and threatening to the dictatorial system. Worker activism provoked the suspension of constitutional rights in 1968 in Guipúzcoa and then in the rest of Spain in 1969. The liberal opening halted in 1969, coinciding with the naming of Prince Juan Carlos as Franco's successor and the forced resignation of Manuel Fraga Iribarne, who in 1966 passed the freedom of the press law, albeit within the limits of the Franco dictatorship.

The early 1970s saw even more turmoil, and opposition to the regime became more violent at the very end of Franco's dictatorship. Even sectors of the two most typical Francoist institutions, the church and the military, were starting to abandon the regime, as exemplified by the creation of the Unión Militar Democrática (Democratic Military Union, or UMD), and certain Catholic priests' ties to leftist parties. The tension culminated on December 20, 1973, in the assassination of Franco's hard-line ideological successor, Admiral Carrero Blanco, who had recently been appointed president. The radical Basque separatist group Euskadi Ta Askatasuna (ETA), which had a degree of popular support in the final years of the dictatorship given the severity of the Franco regime, carried out the operation. The years between the deaths of Carrero Blanco and Franco were characterized by violence, political tension, and social uncertainty. The regime's return to harsh authoritarianism was illustrated by a series of governmental executions that preceded Franco's death. A Catalan anarchist, Salvador Puig Antich, was executed on March 2, 1974, by strangulation (*garrote vil*) along with Heinz Chez, a common criminal not connected with politics. These two death sentences were followed by another 11 executions approved by Franco, who seemed unmoved by the diplomatic outcry in the rest of Europe.

The cultural and political backlash, as well as the return to several repressive measures, can be seen as a result of a contradiction at the heart of dictatorship: a desire to reach a point of modernization, but without the tools of modernity and democratization. As Helen Graham and Jo Labanyi pointed out, and as we will see in the following period, "Francoism set itself the (ultimately unachievable) goal of securing the permanent separation of cultural and political modernity from the modernization process" ("Culture and Modernity: The Case of Spain," p. 10). Thus the move toward modernity and modernization was inexorable, but never smooth; it entailed a continuous process of struggle and negotiation. Spain's complex and ambiguous changes entered a new phase after Franco's long-awaited death. After 36 years in power, Franco was officially pronounced dead at 5:25 a.m. on November 20, 1975, when he was taken off of life-support.

Spain's political and economic changes from 1962 until Franco's death in 1975 were reflected in film politics and practices. Manuel Fraga Iribarne, the aforementioned minister of information and tourism, appointed José María García Escudero, who had held the same post briefly from 1951 to 1952, as general director of cinematography. García Escudero's term (1962–7) saw significant liberalization and innovation in the Spanish film industry. These years corresponded to the vitality of the Escuela Oficial de Cinematografía (Official School of Cinematography, or EOC), formerly the IIEC (Instituto de Investigaciones y Experiencias Cinematográficas, or Institute for Cinematic Investigation and Experimentation), and the rise of the New Spanish Cinema movement. García Escudero's promotion of New Spanish Cinema sought to revitalize the film industry as well as to project a more liberal image abroad, especially at film festivals. Overall, García Escudero's pioneering measures were fitting for the general Europeanizing tendencies of the First Development Plan.

In contrast to the flourishing period between 1962 and 1967, film culture and industry suffered repression in the final years of the dictatorship under the influence of Alfredo Sánchez Bella, then minister of information and tourism. His 1969–73 term was marked by a series of political and cultural setbacks. Sánchez Bella appointed the conservative Enrique Thomas de Carranza as a director of cinematography. Unfortunately, the film politics implemented by the latter mirrored the state of Spanish politics and its return to oppressive, authoritarian measures.

New Spanish Cinema (1962–1967) and commercial trends

García Escudero's assertive revitalization of the film industry led to the flourishing of New Spanish Cinema. However, the movement was also criticized for being directed from above and for its deliberate, conscious, self-serving endorsement by the state. As García Escudero himself wrote: "A film is a flag. We must have that flag unfurled" (Hopewell, *Out of the Past*, p. 65).[64] Nevertheless, García Escudero's appointment and his pioneering vision opened up the space for a cinema less dependent on commercial interests. The film sector, from directors to producers, encountered favorable circumstances for producing more personal as well as more political pictures, despite the implementation of new protectionist measures supported by the state.

García Escudero introduced the "special interest" category (*interés especial*), granted to works that emphasized the formal and thematic qualities of film, which distinguished them from the cheap, mass-produced films that were flooding the market. Therefore, the creation of the "special interest" category was geared toward promising young students and filmmakers from the EOC, as it replaced outdated categories that had been in use since 1952. The special protection policies and financing mechanisms were designed to promote the incorporation of EOC graduates into the industry, facilitating their transition from students to feature-film directors. García Escudero had an ally in José Luis Sáenz de Heredia, the EOC's director, who also supported new talent and promoted student films, as well as screened them for the public in Madrid's famed theater, the Palacio de la Música.

However, García Escudero's measures were also criticized for their ties to the state, especially because the politics of subvention also served as a mechanism of state control. For example, one of his ministerial decrees stipulated that for every three days of foreign films shown in a theater, one Spanish film from the special interest category had to be projected. The problem with state-subsidized cinema, as in previous periods, was its lack of connection with the larger public, as it did not depend on its audience for financing. Consequently, New Spanish Cinema has been criticized for being an intellectual ghetto with elitist tendencies. The creation of Experimental Art Cinemas (Salas de Arte y Ensayo y Especiales) in January of 1967 additionally testified to the intellectualizing tendencies within film circles and of cinematographic politics of the time. The creation of specialty venues like the Experimental Art Cinemas was a contradictory gesture, as John Hopewell points out, since it "encourage[d] a 'social cinema' but discourage[d] its social impact by consigning it to the cultural ghettoes of 'art' cinemas" (*Out of the Past*, p. 65).

Parallel to these changes in protection mechanisms there was also a significant change in censorship politics. In 1963, for the first time in Franco's Spain, the censorship code was officially articulated. However, the inconsistency of censorship persisted because, as many critics have noted, the norms were too broad, vague, and open to interpretation. General Norm #4 is an excellent illustration of the above-mentioned ambiguities: "The film should logically proceed toward a condemnation of evil, . . . but it is not necessary to show this condemnation explicitly on the screen if the film gives enough elements to produce the desired effect in the viewer's conscience" (Santos Fontenla, "1962–1967," pp. 245, 246). Due to this intentional interpretive ambiguity, García Escudero's successor, Carlos Robles Piquer, was able to be intransigent while using the very same censorship codes. The intentional vagueness of the norms is in keeping with the "paradoxical opening" that was taking place in Spain during this period.

In terms of the New Spanish Cinema itself, the EOC students who formed the movement are difficult to classify as a group. Their interests ranged from the introspective tendencies and highly personalized works of Basilio Martín Patino to Carlos Saura's use of allegory. Nevertheless, this generation was troubled by the status quo of the political dictatorship and was frustrated by the limits placed on political and creative freedom of expression. This context prompted the use of a complex film language: elliptical editing, opaque allusions, dense symbolism, and multiple meanings. This group was also familiar with foreign film tendencies, and the theoretical and practical innovations of the New Spanish Cinema were in the spirit of other European film movements such as French New Wave or Nouvelle Vague, Free Cinema, and Junger Deutscher Film.

Carlos Saura's first feature *Los golfos* (1959), produced by Pere Portabella's Films 59, is often seen as a precursor to the movement. Saura's film was made in the midst of the neorealist period but can nevertheless be seen, aesthetically and politically, as a starting point for New Spanish Cinema. While Saura's filmmaking is both too prolific and too diverse to be solely tied to New Spanish Cinema, his first three films – *Los golfos* (1959), *Llanto por un bandido* (1963), and *La caza* (1965) – fit some of the movement's more general tendencies. *La caza*'s production team was tied to other New Spanish Cinema projects as well; its producer, Elías Querejeta, was also instrumental in promoting films and talented new directors who were EOC graduates. The visual style of Saura's cinematographer, Luis Cuadrado, became a signature of several other films of the New Spanish Cinema.

Other talented filmmakers from this era include Miguel Picazo, who made *Habitación de alquiler* (1960), and Julio Diamante, who in 1962 made *Los que no fuimos a la guerra* (*Those who Didn't Go to War*) – whose original title, *Cuando estalló la paz* (*When Peace Broke Out*), was changed by the censors – followed by *Tiempo de amor* (1964). Jorge Grau's first feature was *Noche de verano* (1962), Francisco Regueiro's was *El buen amor* (1963), and Manuel Summers made *Del rosa al amarillo* (1963), followed by *La niña de luto* (1964). Mario Camus made *Los farsantes* (1963) and *Young Sánchez* (1963), an adaptation of Ignacio Aldecoa's story about amateur boxing, followed by *Muere una mujer* (1964). That same year Picazo directed *La tía Tula* (1964) starring Aurora Bautista, and in 1965 Jaime Camino made *Los felices 60*.

Basilio Martín Patino's *Nueve cartas a Berta* sums up many of the issues postulated by the EOC and New Spanish Cinema. It was shot in 1965 and premiered at the 1966 San Sebastián Film Festival, where it won the Concha de Plata for the best first film. *Nueve cartas a Berta* introduces what would become Martín Patino's distinguishing traits: masterful montage, experimentation with sound, use of offscreen space, and use of the voice-over as a dislocating element. Lorenzo, the protagonist of the film (played by Emilio Gutiérrez Caba), meets Berta, the daughter of an exiled Republican intellectual, in London. Upon his return to Salamanca, the encounter prompts a series of reflections on the suffocating nature of provincial life, the Francoist status quo, and the general feeling of discontent that pervaded these years of the dictatorship. The film is a depiction of socio-cultural malaise and the physical and intellectual claustrophobia of 1960s conservative Salamanca (Spain), in contrast to the freedom and creativity that Lorenzo projects onto Berta and her London milieu.

Another important figure, Angelino Fons, made *La busca* (1966). These filmmakers were some of the most promising voices of the EOC and they loosely adhered to the tendencies of New Spanish Cinema. Several of the new directors were not as successful with their subsequent features, or were hindered by a lack of continuity; many directors were dependent on García Escudero's subventions, which were helpful, but unfortunately not linked to the realities of the film industry and the market. At the end of García Escudero's term as general director of cinematography in 1967 the movement also faded, sending each of the filmmakers on to separate career paths and artistic choices.

Luis García Berlanga and Juan Antonio Bardem, the most prolific film-makers from the previous generation, continued filming, though the 1960s were not as fruitful for them as the previous decade, with the exception of Berlanga's two masterpieces *Plácido* (1961) and *El verdugo* (1963). Fernando Fernán Gómez, whose 1950s films *La vida por delante* (1958) and *La vida alrededor* (1959) showed great promise, made two of his most important films in the 1960s: *El mundo sigue* (1963) and *El extraño viaje* (1964). Unlike the heavily promoted EOC students, Berlanga, Bardem, and Fernán Gómez did not have the support of García Escudero, mainly due to political disagreements.

The Madrid-based New Spanish Cinema was not the only space for arti-culating innovative film tendencies. The Escuela de Barcelona (Barcelona School) also put forth a radical cultural and aesthetic program. While realism and intimate portraits were traits of the New Spanish Cinema, the Barcelona School articulated their artistic preoccupations through experimentation, avant-garde tendencies, fantasy, and the exploration of marginalized film genres such as science fiction. They were known for delving into the world of fashion, photography, the 1960s cultural industry, advertising, and the modernity of Barcelona itself, a city that inspired and reflected the tendencies of the movement. The actresses and muses of these films came from the world of fashion (such as Teresa Gimpera and Italy's Serena Vergano). Vicente Aranda's *Fata Morgana* (1966) marks the birth of the Barcelona School, launching its muse Teresa Gimpera toward stardom. *Dante no es únicamente severo*, made in 1967 by Joaquín Jorda and Jacinto Esteva, is considered the most prominent film of the movement.[65]

In addition to New Spanish Cinema and the Barcelona School there was also a flourishing of commercial film, typified by "child-prodigy" cinema (*niños-prodigio*). Joselito and Marisol, two leading child stars of the times, emerged in the late 1950s and early 1960s. Joselito's hits *El pequeño ruiseñor* (1956), *Saeta del ruiseñor* (1957), and *El ruiseñor de las cumbres* (1958) brought him unprecedented success. Marisol's *Un rayo de luz* (1960), *Ha llegado un ángel* (1961), and *Tómbola* (1962) established her as an indisputable child star of the 1960s.

Along with the child-stardom phenomenon, this period saw the mass production of cheap comedies by directors like Mariano Ozores, Ramón Fernández, Pedro Lazaga, and Fernando Palacios, who benefited from the easing of censorship. These films featured some of the most popular comic stars of 1960s Spain: Paco Martínez Soria, José Luis López Vázquez, and Alfredo Landa. The critical disdain for these films was inverse to their popularity with the Spanish public.

A significant number of spaghetti westerns were also produced during this period. The *spaghettis*, a bastardized Italian offspring of the western film genre, dominated European and US screens in the early 1960s. Spain was the onsite location for most of the Italian westerns. The elaborate film sets of the Wild West, with its saloons, mining towns, train tracks, and cowboys and Indians, were recreated first near Madrid, in Hoyo de Manzanares, and later in Almería, in southern Spain. Some foreign impresarios took advantage of Spain's lower production costs to build their film empires there instead of in their native countries. For example, Samuel Bronston, an adventurer and US film producer, made a series of lavish superproductions including *King of Kings* (1961) and *55 Days in Pekin* (1962), directed by Nicholas Ray, and *El Cid* (1961) and *The Fall of the Roman Empire* (1963), directed by Anthony Mann.[66]

The last years of Francoism

Besides the political and cultural factors already outlined in the beginning of this section, certain economic aspects are crucial for understanding late Francoism and its film politics. For example, one of the biggest financial fraud scandals of the late Francoist period, the "Matesa scandal,"[67] had a direct impact on cinema and film subsidies. Under García Escudero's previous policy the Banco de Crédito Industrial granted 15 percent of the government's subsidies, which were then blocked in the Matesa aftermath. Therefore, the state froze all credit granted for film production. The world economic crisis of the 1970s further impacted Spanish film production negatively. As a result of these problems, the Spanish film industry entered a period of severe crisis that was especially noticeable between 1969 and 1977. As in the rest of the industrialized world, television and video became unrivalled competitors for film industry markets. The introduction of video prompted a radical change in consumer habits that contributed to the decline of cinema and cinema-going. These economic and structural weaknesses were further exacerbated by the return of fierce censorship, especially applied to filmmakers critical of the regime, such as Carlos Saura, whose *La prima Angélica* (1973) suffered 64 cuts, and Basilio Martín Patino, whose *Canciones para después de una guerra* (1971) was only screened in 1976, just one year after Franco's death.

During this complex period of late Francoism, Carlos Saura, Basilio Martín Patino, Víctor Erice, and José Luis Borau were considered the strongest oppositional voices to the regime. Their films explored the ideological impact of Francoism and portrayed oppressive familial worlds that were seen as symbolic of dictatorial structures. They explored the implications of the long Francoist dictatorship and its relation to Spanish society. Their cinema connected well with the intellectual public, university spectators, and the middle class of the transition period. During the last five years of the dictatorship Saura directed some of his most powerfully anti-Francoist films: *El jardín de las delicias* (1970), *Ana y los lobos* (1972), *La prima Angélica*, and *Cría cuervos* (1975). Víctor Erice's celebrated film *El espíritu de la colmena* (1973) is a layered and powerful critique of dictatorship woven through dense textual allusions and the creative use of the horror genre. José Luis Borau's *Furtivos* (1975) is a compelling exploration of violence, authoritarianism, and power. *Canciones para después de una guerra* is the first film in Basilio Martín Patino's celebrated trilogy of remembrance, followed by *Caudillo* (1974) and *Madrid* (1987). The film questions historical memory through the innovative use of archival footage and popular cultural forms of the period.

It is also important to mention the Tercera Vía (Third Way), a movement that emerged as a compromise between the "oppositional" cinema (intellectually elliptical and dense films) and "commercial" cinema (cheap popular comedies) of the 1970s. The Third Way was formed by progressive filmmakers who geared their films to the urban middle class. They appropriated the formulas of sophisticated Hollywood comedies that rested on clever dialogues and solid teams of actors and producers. Among some of their favorite themes were sexuality, abortion, and other contemporary issues facing Spanish society. Two important producers involved with the emergence of the Third Way were José Luis Dibildos with Ágata Films and Antonio Cuevas with Kalender Films. Some of the most interesting productions were Manuel Summers's *Adiós, cigüeña, adiós* (1970), *El niño es nuestro* (1972), *Ya soy mujer* (1974), and *Mi primer pecado* (1976), and Roberto Bodegas's *Españolas en París* (1969), *Vida conyugal sana* (1973), and *Los nuevos españoles* (1974). Antonio Drove filmed *Toca y fuga de Lolita* (1974) and *Mi mujer es muy decente dentro de lo que cabe* (1974).

This period of late Francoism also saw a strong presence of women directors for the first time in Spanish film history. In a similar way, Catalan and Basque cinemas started to flourish, exploring long-suppressed national identities, linguistic particularities, and their political singularity. These tendencies will be explored in the next chapter.

The two films featured in this chapter are *El verdugo* (Luis García Berlanga, 1963) and *El jardín de las delicias* (Carlos Saura, 1970). *El verdugo (The Executioner)* tells the story of a man who, upon marrying the daughter of the state executioner, is condemned to inherit his father-in-law's practice. The script, a cruel black comedy that muses on the death penalty, was written in collaboration with Rafael Azcona. Significantly, the young *verdugo*'s debut – his first execution – takes place in Palma de Mallorca, a seaside resort whose popularity is typical of the country's 1960s tourist boom. The film is an ethical probing and criticism of tourism's coexistence with the practice of the death penalty, highlighting the contradictions between Spain's opening up to the rest of the world and the persistence of its dictatorial structures. *El verdugo* was timely, filmed just before the regime attracted international attention and outrage by executing three of its political opponents.

El jardín de las delicias is one of Saura's masterpieces and it garnered the prolific director international recognition. *El jardín de las delicias* dissects Franco's historical and political legacy. The film depicts the downfall of Antonio, a powerful patriarchal figure and former successful businessman who is confined to a wheelchair after a serious car accident. Having lost his memory, Antonio is at the mercy of his greedy family, which is interested solely in obtaining his Swiss bank account. The backdrop of this black tragicomedy of greed is the conflict between Spain's rapid industrial modernization – the *milagro económico* (economic miracle) that ushered Spain into a new era – and the residual dictatorial structures of the time. In *El jardín de las delicias*, the protagonist's amnesia symbolizes the willful obliteration of historical memory during the Francoist dictatorship. Personal amnesia is equated with a collective forgetting, and Saura seems to suggest that the recuperation of personal identity can only be grasped through collective history.

1   *El verdugo* (Luis García Berlanga, 1963)

Context and Critical Commentary

Production credits

Director: Luis García Berlanga
Production: Naga Films (Madrid); Zebra Films (Rome)
Cinematography: Tonino Delli Colli
Screenplay: Luis García Berlanga; Rafael Azcona; Ennio Flaiano
Score: Miguel Asins Arbó
Genre: Melodramatic comedy, black and white
Country: Spain/Italy
Runtime: 87 minutes

Cast

Nino Manfredi	José Luis
Emma Penella	Carmen
José Isbert	Amadeo
José Luis López Vázquez	Antonio
Ángel Álvarez	Álvarez
María Luisa Ponte	Estefanía
Mulia Caba Alba	Working woman 1
Lola Gaos	Working woman 2
Chus Lampreave	Working woman 3
Guido Alberti	Prison director
María Isbert	Ignacia
José Sazatornil	Administrator
Antonio Ferrandis	Chief of services
Alfredo Landa	Sacristan
José Luis Coll	Organist

Synopsis

A young undertaker named José Luis meets Amadeo, an old executioner (*verdugo*) who is about to retire. The executioner leaves his briefcase at José Luis's funeral home, so the undertaker goes to Amadeo's house to return it. There he meets Carmen, the executioner's daughter. Though she is no longer a young woman, Carmen is still single because all of her suitors abandon her once they discover what her father does for a living. When Amadeo returns home one day to find José Luis and Carmen in a compromising position, he tries to force them to get married. Although José Luis had dreamed of migrating to Germany to find work, he finally agrees to marry Carmen when he finds out that she is pregnant.

José Luis finds himself in the position of having to support the family, but the only way they can afford to live is by qualifying for a state-subsidized apartment – which would require him to be a state employee. As Amadeo will no longer be eligible once he retires, he convinces José Luis to take over his job as executioner, thereby insuring that the family keeps the apartment. José Luis very reluctantly accepts on condition that he will resign if he is ever actually called to perform the macabre work. The family lives in the apartment for a year or two before José Luis is finally called upon to perform an execution in Mallorca, a Spanish island that had at that time recently become a popular tourist destination. Amadeo convinces him that the whole family should go, arguing that the victim will end up being pardoned anyway, and, he adds, the newlyweds never did take a honeymoon. The whole family travels to the island as if on vacation. However, the happy couple's excursion to the touristy Drach Caves is interrupted when Civil Guard officers come looking for José Luis to perform the execution. Eventually, despite his stalling, José Luis fulfills his job as executioner and the family returns to Madrid.

Critical commentary

In 1963 when *El verdugo* (*The Executioner*) premiered at the Venice Film Festival, the Spanish ambassador to Rome, Alfredo Sánchez Bella, publicly condemned the film as anti-Francoist propaganda. Although it won the International Critic's Prize, the official reproach condemned Berlanga and temporarily paralyzed his career. Berlanga's executioner was timely: shortly before the film's release three people were executed in Spain under the death penalty: Julián Grimau, a communist, and the anarchists Francisco Granados Mata and Joaquín Delgado Martínez. These incidents provoked a wave of international criticism condemning the backwardness of the Franco regime and sparked a debate over the death penalty in Spain. In this socio-political context, Berlanga's film was understood as tendentious and complicit with the international rejection of Francoism.

El verdugo not only condemns the practice of the death penalty in Spain, but also denounces the social paralysis that resulted from the still-oppressive dictatorial regime that was only apparently beginning to liberalize. The repressive political climate was at odds with the cultural transformations of the 1960s and the social changes that were affecting Spain, such as rapid economic development and the arrival of mass tourism. Berlanga illustrates Spain's ambivalent reality by contrasting the persistence of archaic practices, like administering the death penalty with the gruesome *garrote vil* – a crude asphyxiating machine – with images of modernity represented by tourism in Mallorca. One could argue that Berlanga also critiques the repressive, patriarchal nature of the Franco regime through the character of José Luis and his submission to his father-in-law's mandates. Finally, Berlanga casts an ironic and critical gaze at Francoist urban policies and the difficulty in finding affordable housing in the expanding urban areas.

The extraordinary command of humor operating throughout the tragic story makes this film a classic black comedy and reflects the outstanding work of co-writer Rafael Azcona, whose earlier experience with neorealism clearly influenced *El verdugo*'s form and content. The extraordinary performance of José Isbert, an icon of black comedies from the 1950s and 1960s, and his ability to convey the subtlety of *El verdugo*'s tragicomic tone are another outstanding feature of the film. In sum, *El verdugo* is critically acclaimed as one of the best Spanish films of all time.

Film Scenes: Close Readings

Scene 1   Deceptive modernity

In the first part of the film we see the executioner Don Amadeo and his daughter living in a dilapidated house, in a working-class neighborhood. Similarly, José Luis, who works as an undertaker in a funeral home, shares a small apartment with his brother's large family. In both cases, the lack

Figure 6.1 Deceptive modernity (*El verdugo*, 1963)

of housing reflects the urban crisis of the 1960s. Once José Luis marries the executioner's daughter, they need a larger, more modern living space for the child they are expecting. Luckily, thanks to his job with the government, Amadeo is granted a new apartment that promises to be more modern and comfortable. However, in order to keep the apartment once Amadeo retires, José Luis must follow in his father-in-law's footsteps and keep the work of the executioner in the family. After an intense internal struggle, José Luis accepts the position of executioner in order to resolve his housing problem.

The key moment of this scene is when the family arrives at the construction site of the future apartment. Because of a bureaucratic error, the flat has also been promised to another group of people. After a ridiculous conflict, Amadeo's family eventually wins the apartment, albeit in a less-than-dignified manner. Even at the construction stage, the potential of having a large apartment actually gestures toward modernity's failed promises; ironically, the new apartment turns out to be even smaller than the old one, and what they predicted would be the best space in the flat ends up actually belonging to the neighbors. The new space is even more suffocating than the old one. The situation with the apartment ends up confirming the family's immobility; for them, change and progress are out of reach.[68]

Scene 2 *Mallorca: vacation and the death penalty*

Life seems to calmly transpire for everyone except José Luis, the new executioner. He spends his new life following the news for possible death-penalty cases and attempting to quell any violence around him that, in his paranoid state, he thinks might lead to murder and a subsequent death sentence. When he least expects it, the government sends an order requiring José Luis to travel to Mallorca to perform an execution. Once again the family is divided: Amadeo tries to persuade his son-in-law that there's always the possibility of a pardon, as his wife mediates the argument by suggesting they combine the morbid obligation with a pleasure trip. This tragicomic scene touches on a significant contradiction of the late-Francoist era. While the island of Mallorca represents the most attractive destination on the international tourism market, the executioner's presence and duty there allude to one of the regime's tensest moments: the execution of the communist Julián Grimau and the anarchists Francisco Granados Mata and Joaquín Delgado Martínez, who were killed the same year Berlanga filmed *El verdugo*.

The family enjoys Mallorca while waiting either for the charged man to be pardoned or for José Luis to be summoned for work. While José Luis and Carmen are on a sightseeing trip to the famous Drach Caves, a typical boat full of musicians playing *La Barcarola* floats toward the seated spectators. Suddenly, a different boat full of Civil Guards interrupts the show to summon José Luis. The film ingeniously ties together the contradiction between the Spanish state's attempt to open itself up to the international community through tourism after years of isolationism, and the persistence of the anachronistic structures that characterized the Franco regime.

Scene 3   The price of modernity

The officers of the Civil Guard lead José Luis to the jail to perform his work as executioner. José Luis is "pale, trembling, disconnected, and panic-stricken," according to the screenplay. In an ironic and cruel inversion, he is in a state as bad as (or worse than) the man who is actually condemned to die. Both are carried in the guard's arms to the gallows. Several critics have recognized this scene as the most aesthetically successful in the film because it breaks with the tone of *costumbrismo*, or the representation of local customs and manners, of the rest of the film through the creation of complex and stylized shots (Tonino Delli Colli was behind the impressive camera work).

After the execution the family reunites on the boat that will take them back to the peninsula. José Luis, looking extremely disturbed and defeated as he pulls the money he has just made out of an envelope, declares: "I

Figure 6.2   The price of modernity (*El verdugo*, 1963)

won't do it again. Do you understand me? I won't do it again." Don Amadeo, in contrast, fixates on the cash José Luis received for his first job, and says, "that's what I said the first time I did it." José Luis incarnates the role of both the executioner and the victim. Being inserted into this profession "against his will" is emblematic of a larger failure in his life: instead of moving to Germany he stayed in Spain, got married out of obligation, and accepted the job as executioner in order to keep the new apartment, despite the psychological cost. Following the blunt dialogue that implies that José Luis is destined to continue working as an executioner, the scene closes with women dancing on a yacht and young men racing cars alongside the beach. In this way, the film concludes by emphasizing the paradox of the Franco regime's blatant but contradictory turn toward modernity.

Director (Life and Works)

Luis García Berlanga (b. Valencia 1921)

Luis García Berlanga was born into a bourgeois Republican family in Valencia in 1921. At the start of World War II Berlanga enlisted in the Spanish Blue Division that fought in the Soviet Union on the side of the German army. Once Berlanga returned from the war he finished his studies in philosophy and began working as a film critic for radio and newspapers in Valencia. In 1947 he enrolled in the recently opened IIEC, where he directed his first short films and was exposed to the Italian neorealism that would influence his subsequent works. There he met Juan Antonio Bardem and together they started the production company Altamira.

Berlanga's first full-length film, *Esa pareja feliz* (1951), co-directed with Bardem, depicts the daily existential and economic struggles of a recently married couple who get to live one fantasy day after they win a "happy couple" radio contest. He followed that film with the acclaimed *¡Bienvenido Mister Marshall!* (1952), which tells how a small Castilian Spanish town prepares for a visiting North American economic delegation by disguising itself as a stereotypical "Andalusian" town. The film is a strong critique of Spain's economic backwardness and the stereotypical and folkloric image that the Franco regime attempted to project to the outside world, as well as of American economic imperialism. In 1953 Berlanga directed *Novio a la vista*, and later in 1956 *Calabuch*, which along with his later film *Los jueves, milagro* (1958) conclude what some critics have termed his early neorealist phase, even though Berlanga's complex opus cannot be reduced to one single film movement or influence.

The film *Plácido* (1961), which blends social criticism with black humor, initiated a second period in Berlanga's cinematic work, marked above all by the beginning of his collaboration with one of the most successful Spanish screenwriters, Rafael Azcona. This and other films, such as *El verdugo*, were highly critical of the dictatorship and thus condemned by official sectors of the Franco regime, forcing Berlanga to put his career on hold until the late 1960s.

In 1969 he directed *Vivan los novios*, about a controlling and oppressive mother figure. This film begins a third phase that satirizes Spain's transition from dictatorship to democracy. We then find titles like *La escopeta nacional* (1977), whose critical and public success enabled Berlanga to make his two subsequent films: *Patrimonio nacional* (1980) and *Nacional III* (1982). Berlanga went on to make *La vaquilla* (1984), a well-received film that deals openly with the Spanish Civil War. He then made two comedies about the social reality of his birthplace, Valencia: *Moros y cristianos* (1987) and *Todos a la cárcel* (1994). In 1999 Berlanga directed *París Tombuctú*, which can be seen as his return to the characteristic black humor of his early films.

In addition to his work as director, Berlanga taught cinematography courses at both the IIEC and the EOC. He was named in the early 1980s as director of the Filmoteca Nacional (National Film Archives), but he resigned shortly thereafter, claiming that he did not have the spirit for bureaucratic and institutional matters. He was also president of the committee that awards the Premio Sonrisa Vertical (Vertical Smile Prize), a prestigious literary award for erotic novels.

2　*El jardín de las delicias* (Carlos Saura, 1970)

Context and Critical Commentary

Production credits

Director: Carlos Saura
Production: Elías Querejeta
Cinematography: Luis Cuadrado
Screenplay: Carlos Saura; Rafael Azcona
Score: Luis de Pablo
Genre: Drama
Country: Spain
Runtime: 95 minutes

Cast

José Luis López	Antonio
Luchy Soto	Luchy
Francisco Pierra	Don Pedro
Charo Serrano	Mother
Lina Canalejas	Aunt
Julia Peña	Julia
Mayrata O'Wisedo	Ana
Esperanza Roy	Nicole

Synopsis

Antonio Cano, a wealthy industrialist in the cement and construction business, has a car accident and subsequently loses his memory, is paralyzed, and is rendered almost mute. Unfortunately for the family he supports financially, he is the only person who knows the secret number to the Swiss bank account that holds his millions. Therefore, his family attempts to help him regain his memory through various tactics, one of which is to re-enact scenes from his life. In an interesting plot twist, the protagonist begins to regain his memory, but hides it from his family. The film ends ambiguously, suspended between actual vengeance and its symbolic representation.

Critical commentary

Carlos Saura directed *El jardin de las delicias* in 1970, just five years before the long-awaited death of Francisco Franco. These final years of the Franco regime were marked by a profound crisis that was reflected by the dictator's own physical decline. Like the protagonist Antonio, Francoism was incommunicado, frozen in time, and its political structure was outdated. In the same way that Antonio's family members continued to depend on him, members of the Franco regime continued to support the dictator during his physical and mental decline in order to take advantage of his prerogatives and insure their own future. The uncertainty of Spain's future permeated Spanish society, a feeling that Saura successfully instills in the viewer throughout *El jardin de las delicias*.

Though the dictatorship was nearing an end, the censors continued exercising strict control over cultural production, forcing opposition filmmakers to develop metaphorical narratives to articulate their discontent with the regime; had their criticism been more explicit, the films wouldn't have survived the censors' cuts. It was in this context that Saura, already well versed in dense intertextual filmmaking, delivered an allegorical critique of the late Franco dictatorship with a storyline that enables multiple readings of the film.

El jardin de las delicias explores the relationship between Antonio, who is immersed in the personal isolation of his memory loss, paralysis, and muteness, and his family members, who only seem to be interested in his money. Antonio is subjected to violent dramatizations of his own life (traumas from his childhood and his adult years) by his rapacious and merciless family. *El jardín de las delicias* is an extraordinarily complex film because of the interpenetrating narrative planes through which it unfolds: staged past, evoked past, present-day frames, oneiric world, and future.[69] Antonio's amnesia links all five continua, each one structured around memory recuperation, either deliberately by the family members trying to gain access to Antonio's Swiss bank account number, or through Antonio's own efforts as he struggles to remember, reinterpret, or recover his identity.

It is important to point out that the backdrop of this black tragicomedy of greed is the conflict between Spain's rapid industrial modernization, the *milagro económico* that ushered Spain into a new era, and the residual dictatorial structures of the time. Antonio's life is thus inseparable from the national dimension. The re-enacted performances of his personal traumas also overlap with Spain's other central historical events: the beginning of the Spanish Civil War in 1936, the Nationalist victory, and the First Development Plan elaborated by Spanish technocrats in the early 1960s. These national "traumas" give rise to personal ones, showing how the individual is an intricate product of the nation. The re-enactments of Antonio's past function as a critique of the dictatorship and its legacy. Saura takes Antonio, a prototypical product of the dictatorial structure, an embodiment of the Francoist zeitgeist, and turns him into the victim of the very system that he himself helped to forge.

Luis Cuadrado's outstanding camera work and Pablo G. del Amo's highly original editing manipulate formal techniques to serve the film's thematic elements. Like Antonio, the spectator is forced to constantly interpret a multiple, fractured meaning. As Marvin D'Lugo points out, in *El jardín de las delicias*, "the function of the spectator's sharing Antonio's way of seeing the world appears to be to simulate for the real audience their own cultural position as subjects of the ideological message of Francoism" (*The Films of Carlos Saura: The Practice of Seeing*, p. 102). In *El jardín de las delicias*, the protagonist's amnesia symbolizes the willful obliteration of historical memory during the Franco dictatorship. Personal amnesia is equated with the collective; therefore, the recuperation of personal meaning, Saura seems to suggest, can only be grasped through collective history.

Film Scenes: Close Readings

Scene 1   Pig punishment

By acting out a series of critical moments in the protagonist Antonio Cano's life, his family hopes to help him recuperate the memory he lost following an automobile accident. At the beginning of the film his father and an actress hired to play his mother re-create the moment in which Antonio, at five years old, was punished and locked in the barn with a pig. The re-enactment of the first childhood event opens with the staging of what appears to be a mid-1920s bourgeois bedroom set. An elderly man, Antonio's father, orchestrates workers as they bring in props (ranging from the authentic period-pieces such as paintings and lamps to more bizarre elements, such as a live pig whose meaning will only be understood later). Antonio's father also directs the actress who plays Antonio's mother and sets the mood with the music, Imperio Argentina's "Recordar" ("Remember"), an aural reiteration of the film's main theme of recollection. The extravagant and deliberately artificial setting, with its minuscule details ranging from furniture and music to hairstyle and make-up, suggests a theatrical montage. Before knowing the purpose of this scene, therefore, the spectators are well aware of its staged nature.

Saura then foregrounds an extreme close-up of a mute, stunned face, which contrasts with the rapid movements and agitation on the "set." A few moments later a middle-aged man in a wheelchair is slowly rolled into the staged bedroom. The audience discovers only later that the mute figure is Antonio Cano, a wealthy industrialist who has lost his memory in a car crash. Antonio's father explains that he is about to re-enact a childhood episode in which a five-year-old Antonio made his mother cry and was then locked up in a room with a pig that "would eat his hands off." The traumatic childhood punishment is repeated as Antonio is once again locked in with the pig. Antonio, forced into violent dramatizations of his own life, is at first an unwilling spectator of a performance that he does not comprehend, and then an unwilling participant in a life he neither grasps nor remembers. Antonio's family, nevertheless, believes that they are doing the right thing in returning the "signs" that will make him remember who he is, where he comes from, and, most importantly, the numbers of his Swiss bank account. The film gradually reveals that the family's interest in helping Antonio recover his memory is purely economic.

Scene 2   The professional past

This scene is set in the family warehouse, which has been converted into an exhibition room whose walls are covered with a collection of oversized photographs from Antonio's professional past, tracing the development of his business from its modest beginnings to the factory's most recent modernization. Antonio Cano's monstrous building projects, a testament to Spain's boom of the 1960s (dams, ports, roads, tourist amenities), were made possible through large postwar government contracts that built his

Figure 6.3   The professional past (*El jardín de las delicias*, 1970)

empire. Antonio's life is therefore inseparable from the national dimension, as seen in this re-enactment of his professional career. Spain's rapid industrial modernization – the *milagro económico* that ushered Spain into a new era – empowered Antonio's trajectory as a businessman and enabled him to create a financial empire.

Over the loudspeaker we hear Antonio's speech about productivity and the role of the workers in his business. Antonio enthusiastically shouts "yo, yo, yo, yo" ("me, me, me, me") and then recites the speech, his voice in sync with the recording heard over the loudspeakers. The paternalistic economic discourse – a lingering legacy of fascism – heard over the speakers provides a moment of self-recognition and encapsulates Spain's path toward progress and mobility. This scene strikingly juxtaposes the mobile nation with an immobile, wheelchair-bound Antonio. Antonio's figure, now abject and useless, is contrasted with Spain's booming productivity. However, the representation of his professional life is ultimately successful in recuperating Antonio to the hostile and despotic character as which he was remembered.

Scene 3   Multiple wheelchairs in the garden, or Antonio's revenge

In this final scene of the film Antonio recalls his accident. Mesmerized and possibly hallucinating, Antonio imagines the scene of the crash: wreckage, battered cars on the lawn that seem to have collided head-on; his own bloody body crushed amidst metal and twisted wires next to his injured female lover. In the same space of the garden the family members then appear in wheelchairs. The family don't speak or look at him, but stoically circle him in their wheelchairs. Antonio now orchestrates whole scenarios for his family. Crippled and bound to wheelchairs, they circle endlessly through the lush gardens surrounding the Cano estate, endlessly mirroring Antonio's crippled body. The motion of the wheelchairs is carefully choreographed. The camera follows them, accentuating the rhythm of the movement. Sutured so that it flows effortlessly, this sequence of tracking shots is matched by a state of emotional vacancy. The participants seem artificial and puppet-like, each one in his or her own world, as still shots capture their solipsism. Alternate long shots of the characters, framed by a proscenium screen,[70] produce an onstage effect. As Marvin D'Lugo observes, "the film ends with this image, frozen to produce a tableau-effect approximating a contemporary version of Bosch's panel in his 'Garden of Earthly Delights'" (*The Films of Carlos Saura: The Practice of Seeing*, p. 106). Saura's garden of delights, as seen in this final scene of *El jardín de las delicias*, is thus a dystopic, false paradise. All of the characters are wounded by the legacy of the dictatorial regime, and Antonio's twisted revenge points to the endless proliferation of cruelty in a system where both victims and victimizers are irreparably crippled.

Director (Life and Works)

Carlos Saura (b. Huesca 1932)

From a very young age Carlos Saura had an affinity for photography, and he was a professional photographer before he started his film career. In 1950 Saura moved to Madrid to study industrial engineering, which he abandoned in 1955 to enroll in the IIEC. There he specialized first in photography and documentary film, but then gradually became interested in making feature-length films. In 1959 he directed his first film, *Los golfos* (*Hooligans*), which depicts the lives of a group of hooligans in the marginal suburbs of Madrid. The work, which is clearly influenced by Italian neorealism, was a great critical success, despite the fact that it was censored and didn't come out until 1962. Nevertheless, this film introduced Saura to the critics, who quickly recognized his talent as a director. His following film, *Llanto por un bandido* (1963), was followed by *La caza* (1965), an emblematic work of his early career. *La caza* is a brutal portrait of male camaraderie and violence, and can be read as an allegory of the implicit violence of postwar Spanish society. It was the first of Saura's films to be produced by Elías Querejeta, and it won the Silver Bear at the Berlin International Film Festival in 1966. Saura's successful collaboration with Querejeta lasted for 16 years, during which they produced 13 films that all employ symbolism and allegory to critically denounce Francoist culture and the dictatorial regime.

In 1967 Saura directed *Peppermint Frappé*, starring Geraldine Chaplin, his companion, artistic muse, and a vital actress in the films he made during the late Francoist period. The film was an absolute critical success, and is somewhat reminiscent of Buñuel's work with respect to the character's double obsession with religion and sex. In 1969 he made *La madriguera*, and then in 1970 he directed *El jardín de las delicias*, which along with *Ana y los lobos* (1972) and *La prima Angélica* (1973) forms a trilogy that harshly critiques the ideological impact of Francoism. Saura deliberately employed elliptical editing and a dense allegorical style in order to elude the censors, a recourse that became one of his distinguishing "saurian" techniques. He then directed the highly successful commercial hit *Cría cuervos* (1975), one of the emblematic films of the Spanish transition to democracy. Through the eyes of Ana, a young girl played by Ana Torrent, the film depicts her oppressive family life in the later Franco years.

Following the death of Franco and the dismantling of the system of censorship, Saura turned to more intimate cinema, such as the outstanding *Elisa, vida mía* (1977) and *Mamá cumple cien años* (1979), which was nominated for an Oscar for Best Foreign Film. His following film, *Deprisa, deprisa* (1980), won the Golden Bear at the Berlin International Film Festival and can be seen as Saura's re-examination of the theme of urban marginalization that he explored in his first film, *Los golfos*. In the early 1980s Saura began collaborating with producer Emiliano Piedra and the flamenco choreographer Antonio Gades, making films that feature dance and adaptations of dramatic or musical pieces, such as *Bodas de sangre* (1981), *Carmen* (1983), and *El amor brujo* (1985). In 1990 he turned again to the theme of the Spanish Civil War with the comedy *¡Ay, Carmela!*, which won eight Goyas[71] and signaled Saura's strong comeback. He then continued with a series of films centered once again on music and dance, including *Sevillanas* (1992), *Flamenco* (1994), and *Tango* (1998). In 1999 he directed *Goya en Burdeos*, which won him yet another Goya award. In 2001 Saura made an homage to Buñuel entitled *Buñuel y la mesa del rey Salomón*, and in 2002 he directed *Salomé*. His most recent films to date are *El séptimo día* (2004), *Iberia* (2005), and *Fados* (2007).

7

Cinema of the Transition: The Period of Disenchantment (1975–1979)

1 *El desencanto* (Jaime Chávarri, 1976)
2 *El crimen de Cuenca* (Pilar Miró, 1979)

Historical and Political Overview of the Period

General Francisco Franco's long-awaited death on November 20, 1975, symbolically marked the already unfolding transition from dictatorship to democracy. Nevertheless, the dictator's death did not signify a radical rupture with the past. From as early as the beginning of the 1960s, Spain had experienced profound changes in the economic and political culture that were tied to a number of factors: a more aggressive implementation of the capitalist market economy; the makeover of the middle class (influenced greatly by a rise in managerial positions); transformations in the working class (related to changes in labor union politics, among other factors); urbanization (changes in social and cultural habits); and increased access to higher education (which tended to promote values of tolerance and pluralism). Significantly, the same political class that was once a pillar of the dictatorial regime was instrumental in shaping the new democratic system. Democracy was implemented without breaking the existing legal framework. Ironically, a referendum on the Ley para Reforma Política ("Law of Political Reform," 1976), which actually enabled democratic change to take place, was held by the very Francoist institutions that were abolished as a result of it. Strategically but paradoxically, the "dismantling" of Francoism was built upon a silent consensus, the so-called *pacto de olvido*. This "pact of forgetting" was perceived as necessary for the "national reconciliation" that might have been impossible without a deliberate erasure of memory (specifically of the traumas of the Spanish Civil War and the repression of the years that followed).

On November 22, 1975, two days after the death of the dictator, King Juan Carlos I, an instrumental figure in the peaceful transition to democracy, was designated the king of Spain according to the law of succession promulgated by Franco in 1969. Once in power, the king faced pressure from the influential remnants of the Francoist political elite, who were insisting on maintaining the dictatorship without Franco. Pressure also came from the oppositional reformists, who were supporting political reform based on the creation of a modernized post-dictatorial political arena and the legitimization of clandestine political parties. The opposition that formed around the Communist Party (PCE), the Spanish Socialist Workers' Party (PSOE), and the Democratic Junta called for the formation of a provisional government that would require general elections within a year of its constitution.

Chosen to guarantee the continuity of the dictatorial regime, Juan Carlos instead successfully oversaw Spain's transition to a democratic constitutional monarchy that opened up to more moderate sectors of the political spectrum. After the brief transitional term of Carlos Arias Navarro, the last president of the dictatorial era, Juan Carlos appointed Adolfo Suárez as the new president of the government on July 3, 1976. Suárez worked toward political transition by approving the Law of Political Reform, which led to Spain's first free general elections in 41 years, held on June 15, 1977. Among some of the most important political landmarks were the legalization of the Communist Party under the leadership of Santiago Carrillo, the restoration of the rights of meeting and association, release and amnesty for political prisoners, and the return of political exiles. In the spirit of the conciliatory *pacto de olvido*, Adolfo Suárez and his centrist coalition, the Central Democratic Union (UCD or Unión de Centro Democrático), an alliance of liberals, Christian democrats, and social democrats, won the first democratic elections. Suárez's UCD was closely followed by the PSOE, which became the main opposition party. The two parties claimed 70 percent of the seats between them, and their leaders Adolfo Suárez and Felipe González became major political figures during the transition period. They supported steady movement toward a capitalist market economy and, with their moderate political agenda, attempted to overcome the religious and ideological differences of their constituencies.

The democratic transition was, however, not altogether smooth and indeed was seriously endangered by an attempted military coup, known as "23-F," on February 23, 1981. One of its leaders, Antonio Tejero Molina, a Spanish lieutenant-colonel, stormed into the Spanish Congress of Deputies together with a group of 200 armed Civil Guards, the national military police force. When they entered, the Congress was in the process of electing the new president, Leopoldo Calvo Sotelo, to replace Adolfo Suárez. The startling image of Antonio Tejero with a gun in his hand, breaking into the Congress of Deputies, became emblematic of the transition. It pointed to the vulnerability and fragility of the country's democratic institutions during this period. King Juan Carlos acted decisively to maintain political stability, giving a televised speech in which he condemned the coup and called for support for Spain's democratic process. This speech, along with the arrest the following day of Colonel Tejero and the other coup participants, indicated the consolidation of the democratic system.

Thus, Spain's period of transition, which had already started in the 1960s, lasted through the beginning of the 1980s, when in 1982 the socialist PSOE won the second democratic elections. Their coming to power signaled the end of the transition period and the solidification of democracy. Spain's exemplary transition had its darker undertones, however. The social legacy of dictatorship, erasure of collective memory, and embracing of a politics of forgetting (the *pacto de olvido*) produced a strong feeling of disenchantment in several sectors of Spanish society, followed by an extremely low level of active political involvement.

The politics of the transition had a significant impact on Spain's film industry and its infrastructure. The film censorship that was instituted when Franco came to power was coming to an end at the time of his death in 1975, coinciding with the abolition of censorship in other political and cultural realms, like journalism and literary production. The final censorship norms were issued in 1975. While they were much more lenient than the earlier, authoritarian and repressive censoring measures of Sánchez Bella and Enrique Thomas de Carranza (1969 and 1973, respectively), they were nevertheless incongruous with the new air of democratic change. Censorship was finally abolished in the Royal Decree of November 11, 1977, the year that the UCD came to power. The UCD's politics contributed to many progressive changes in the realm of culture. Nevertheless, though it rejected previous repressive and authoritarian measures, the UCD did not envision alternative post-Franco cultural politics. Film culture and industries mirrored the ruling party's lack of a coherent cultural strategy. During the transition years, on average there was one general director of cinematography per year, a number that clearly suggests disarray and a lack of continuity in the realm of cinematographic institutional politics.

As in the previous periods, one of the most problematic areas continued to be the state's involvement in film production. While 15 percent of the government subsidies for Spanish films were reinstated, this measure was largely counteracted by the 1979 Supreme Court decision that revoked the obligatory screen quota (*la cuota de pantalla*), a protectionist measure that guaranteed the screening of Spanish films. When it was first introduced, the measure required one week of Spanish film for every six weeks that foreign films were shown. As expected, the decision resulted in an overwhelming predominance of foreign (mostly US) films. A reshaping of various other rigid measures followed, and at times film practices even challenged the Spanish legal system. Emblematic of testing the limits of the new democratic structure and freedom of expression, Pilar Miró's 1979 film *El crimen de Cuenca* challenged the legality of military tribunals regarding civilian cases (the military justice code). The film is set in the rural province of Cuenca during the early twentieth century. It tells the story of two men who suffer torture at the hands of the Civil Guard, and as a result confess to a murder that they did not commit. The military tried to suppress the film, bringing charges against Pilar Miró and her producer Alfredo Matas, who were prosecuted for maligning the reputation of the Civil Guard. The film was finally authorized in 1981. While the Miró affair showed the difficulties of doing away with the political censorship still operative during the transition, it did eventually invalidate the Civil Guard's claim to historical jurisdiction that pre-dated the 1978 constitution. Thereafter, and partially as a result of the Miró incident, civilians accused of military crimes had to be tried in a civilian court.

It is important to note that the Spanish film scene was particularly diverse during the transition period. Among the most important directors and trends were the continued presence of Luis García Berlanga and Juan Antonio Bardem, veteran directors from the 1950s; the active engagement of the New Spanish Cinema generation, formed at the Escuela Oficial de Cinematografía (EOC, or Official School of Cinematography) in the 1960s (Carlos Saura, Mario Camus, Basilio Martín Patino, Manuel Gutiérrez Aragón, and José Luis Borau); the emergence of New Madrid Comedy (Nueva Comedia Madrileña), led by a trio of directors who attempted to break with the heavy and oblique style of "political" films critical of the dictatorial regime (Fernando Colomo, Fernando Trueba, and José Luis Garci); the mass production of low-quality exploitation films focused on nudity and soft-core pornography; the strong presence of Elías Querejeta, a producer who financed some of the most polemical and visually noteworthy films of the 1960s and who continued to support new talent (Ricardo Franco and Jaime Chávarri); the presence of women directors, who finally had a substantial role in the national Spanish film scene (Cecilia Bartolomé, Josefina Molina, and Pilar Miró); and the institutionalization of the "cinema of the autonomous communities" (*el cine de autonomías*), especially Basque and Catalan cinema.

Luis García Berlanga continued his collaboration with scriptwriter Rafael Azcona. Berlanga achieved considerable commercial success with his post-Franco trilogy *La escopeta nacional* (1977), *Patrimonio nacional* (1980), and *Nacional III* (1982). Despite box-office success and the films' clever mixture of corrosive humor with a scrutiny of contemporary Spanish mores, Berlanga had lost the critical edge that characterized his earlier masterpieces. Juan Antonio Bardem, on the other hand, remained loyal to his political and ethical engagement, even though his films were less appealing to the public than Berlanga's. Bardem continued directing ambitious political dramas such as *El puente* (1977) and *Siete días de enero* (1979). *El puente* illustrates a complex panorama of Spain in 1976, one year after the death of Franco. The film won first prize at the Moscow Film Festival. In addition to communicating the social consciousness that Bardem was always known for, *El puente* was also an interesting attempt to "rehabilitate" icons of popular culture, such as Alfredo Landa, a popular star of the lowbrow comedy genre named after him (*landismo*). Despite his unique look at contemporary Spain, Bardem was overshadowed by the younger, more stylish generation of filmmakers engaged with similar issues and themes.

Luis Buñuel, the most revered Spanish filmmaker (though he was a Mexican citizen from 1949 on), returned to Spain in 1977 to make his last film *Cet obscur objet du désir* (*That Obscure Object of Desire*). A Spanish/ French co-production, the film featured Buñuel's beloved actor Fernando Rey. The film's female protagonist Conchita is portrayed by two actresses playing the same role, Carole Bouquet and Angela Molina. Adapted from *La femme et le pantin*, Pierre Louÿs's nineteenth-century novel, the film centers on quintessential Buñuelian themes: social mores and prohibitions, nature and the elusiveness of desire, the enigma of femininity, and illusions of freedom. The film also reiterates the extraordinary and peculiar formal traits of Buñuel's extensive opus. *Cet obscur objet du désir* is one of the most provocative films of its time, as well as a symbolic moment for Spanish cinema; it was made during Buñuel's last sojourn in Spain before his death in 1983 in Mexico. The film thus brings closure to Buñuel's extraordinary cinematographic career, which started in 1929 with *Un chien andalou*.

Carlos Saura's post-Franco opus lost some of its critical edge, but he nevertheless continued to be a prominent voice on the film scene. *Cría cuervos* (1975), depicting an oppressive family milieu in the last years of the dictatorship, was actually made before the death of Franco and thematically fits in with Saura's earlier period. Even though a political dimension is never completely absent from his films, from 1975 on Saura turned his gaze toward more personal subjects. *Elisa, vida mía* (1977), the first film Saura made after the death of the dictator, is an intricate narrative puzzle of the protagonist's life that focuses on the relationship with her aging father and failed marriage. Through Elisa, Saura explores social constraints and repressive conventions (namely those of gender) and their relation to Elisa's emotional and creative turmoil. *Mamá cumple cien años* (1979) was a comic sequel to *Ana y los lobos* (1972) that reiterated Saura's departure from his earlier somber looks at the Franco dictatorship. In the early 1980s, Saura started his flamenco trilogy; the first film, *Bodas de sangre* (1981), is an unusual and original adaptation of Federico García Lorca's well-known play. The film's exceptional nature is partially due to Saura's collaboration with Antonio Gades, a ballet dancer, flamenco choreographer, cultural icon, and communist activist. Gades's dramatic and powerful dance performance formed the core of their future collaborations: *Carmen* (1983), which was nominated for an Oscar in the Best Foreign Language Film category, and *El amor brujo* (1985).

Mario Camus had a fairly irregular career during this period. His work ranged from serious dramas and literary adaptations to lighter commercial works. At this time he also gradually moved toward television projects, the most famous one being an adaptation of Benito Pérez Galdós's nineteenth-century masterpiece *Fortunata and Jacinta* (1979). One of his more engaging films, *Los días del pasado*, filmed in 1977, centered on the pressing theme of the time: the recuperation of historical memory, in this case, of the militants from radical leftist groups (like the *maquis*, resistance fighters who continued to be a threat to the Franco regime until 1947).[72] His authorial voice once again emerged with more coherence and strength in the 1980s.

José Luis Borau's *Furtivos* (1975) explores the protracted Franco dictatorship's impact on Spanish society. However, Borau's engagement with Spanish cinema goes beyond filmmaking. He taught screenwriting at the

EOC from 1962 until 1970, participated in the making of several prominent Spanish films, and actively supported critical cinematic projects through his production company El Imán. He had a strong influence on several filmmakers from the next generation: Pilar Miró, Manuel Gutiérrez Aragón, and Iván Zulueta, among others. Borau produced Iván Zulueta's opera prima *Un, dos, tres . . . , al escondite inglés* (1969), a musical influenced by beat culture (reminiscent of the Beatles' film *Help!*). Zulueta's second film *Arrebato* (1979), an underground cult classic, is an exploration of the nature of the (film) image and fantasy, and its relation to heroin dependency and vampirism. In the film's compelling ending, the fictional filmmaker is progressively swallowed by the image and finally annihilated by his camera. Borau was instrumental in Zulueta's brief but stellar appearance on the Spanish film scene.

Many critics consider Manuel Gutiérrez Aragón to be a filmmaker of the transition years, especially with regard to his trilogy, which explores the nature of fascism, its persistence in post-Franco Spain, and its neo-fascist manifestations. *Camada negra* (1977), set in Madrid just after Franco's death, won the Silver Bear at the Berlin Film Festival. The film explores the tumultuous years of the immediate post-dictatorial society by looking at the culture of violence, the persistence of a fascist ethos, and the role of the oppressive family legacy. *Sonámbulos* (1978) continues with the same themes, but the action moves from the limited family space of *Camada negra* to the larger public space of the Spanish National Library, the hideout for a group of political terrorists. Gutiérrez Aragón's somnambulist explorations, suspended between dreams and reality, are reinforced by Strindberg's *Ghost Sonata* performed in the background. The last film of the trilogy, *El corazón del bosque* (1979) is a story of *maquis*. Set in the lush Cantabrian landscape, the political struggle is endowed with a poetic lyricism. While he never completely abandoned his focus on the legacy of the Francoist period and its manifestations in post-Franco Spain, Gutiérrez Aragón nevertheless turned toward more personal themes in his later films, which also explored the limits and boundaries between reality and fantasy, and truth and poetry. Even so, his final films, made in the 1990s, revisit some of the social themes that characterize his earlier work.

With the encouragement and financial support of Elías Querejeta's production team, Ricardo Franco made *Pascual Duarte* (1975) and Jaime Chávarri made *El desencanto* (1976); both are powerful films that are considered milestones of that period. Querejeta also co-wrote the script for

Pascual Duarte, an adaptation of Camilo José Cela's disturbing postwar novel of the same title. The film is representative of the cinematic trend that both depicts violence and explores it as subject matter that profoundly marked Spanish society during the transition. Ricardo Franco's film became a profound reflection on contemporary Spain. From his next film, *Los restos del naufragio* (1978), onward he focused on more personal themes.

Chávarri's *El desencanto* is a moving story of disenchantment, both national and personal, told through a portrait of and interviews with the troubled family of a deceased Francoist poet, Leopoldo Panero. Chávarri's first directorial feature was *Los viajes escolares* (1974), a partially autobiographical film that centered on complex and troublesome family relations – themes that anticipated *El desencanto*. Among Chávarri's other notable films is *A un dios desconocido* (1977), a subtle homage to Federico García Lorca. In an interesting turn of events that further ties these two filmmakers together, in 1994 Ricardo Franco filmed a sequel to Chávarri's *El desencanto*, entitled *Después de tantos años*. The film revisits members of the Panero family, providing even more insight into the personal and national complexities of the transition era.

Fernando Colomo and Fernando Trueba were the most prominent representatives of the New Madrid Comedy movement. Attempting to break with the elliptical style of their predecessors and films critical of the dictatorial regime, they instead focused on the progressive but somewhat apolitical middle class and their personal – sexual and professional – frustrations. References to politics were relegated to the background, with a focus instead on a quotidian chronicle of contemporary Madrid. Fernando Colomo's first feature-length film, *Tigres de papel* (1977), set the tone for these contemporary comedies of manners. These films were refreshing and welcomed by an audience that had been saturated with political and historical revisions. Throughout his career Colomo continued to master the genre that brought him considerable commercial success. Like Colomo, Fernando Trueba had a good rapport with the contemporary audience, producing several box-office hits, beginning with his very first feature-length film, *Opera prima* (1980). This sophisticated, comical love story is considered one of the key works of New Madrid Comedy. Despite his talent, Trueba's career continued on an uneven path, though he did receive a prestigious Oscar for Best Foreign Language Film in 1994 with *Belle Epoque*, discussed in the next chapter. José Luis Garci is another figure with certain thematic and formal ties to Colomo and Trueba. The beginning of Garci's career in cinema is tied to the Tercera Vía (Third Way), discussed in chapter 6. He scripted several of the most successful films of the Third Way trend between 1972 and 1977. His first directorial debut was *Asignatura pendiente*, filmed in 1977. It was a fairly successful first film that draws on the encounter of ex-lovers as a pretext for a bittersweet look at contemporary Spain and the frustrations of a generation disillusioned with the politics of the transition. Like Colomo's and Trueba's, Garci's films range from the predictable and sentimental – *Las verdes praderas* (1979) – to more experimental explorations of genre, such as film noir in *El crack* (1980). Garci's biggest international success, *Volver a empezar* (1982), is a sentimental story of a renowned Spanish poet who returns from exile in the United States, where he had fled from the Spanish Civil War. *Volver a empezar* was the first Spanish film to win an Oscar in the Best Foreign Language Film category (1983).

As could be expected, post-dictatorial Spain, with its de-centralizing project and more autonomous economic structure, was favorable to the recuperation of the cinema of the autonomous communities. With the 1978 constitution, Spain was organized as a federation of 17 autonomous regions. Basque and Catalan cinemas became the most prominent among the "regional" cinemas. Basque cinema flourished despite its relative lack of tradition and industrial infrastructure. However, Catalan cinema did not emerge as strongly in the post-Franco years as one would have expected, considering the region's renowned film history, culture, and tradition.

Filmmaking in Catalonia, the Basque country, and other autonomous regions suffered a lengthy suppression under the Castile-centered model of the Franco dictatorship. Therefore, once the repression was lifted, there was additional incentive to recover or reinvent these national cinemas. Additionally, film partially became a vehicle for the reassertion of regional and national identity and the recuperation of linguistic and cultural heritage. Some films were made in the long-suppressed languages of Eusquera (the language of the Basque country), Catalan, or Galician, while others continued to be made in Castilian in order to reach a bigger number of spectators and to be more competitive in the Spanish market. This paradoxical situation shows the difficulty in negotiating between national aspirations and the demands of the market.

Among the most successful Catalan films made during this period were Antoni Ribas's *La ciutat cremada* (1976), an exploration of Catalonia's past, and Josep María Forn's *Companys, procés a Catalunya* (1979), depicting the tumultuous history of Lluís Companys, executed in the 1940s by Franco's government after his extradition by French collaborators. Jaime

Camino started his career with *Los felices sesenta* (1963), which explores the ties between rapidly developing tourism in Catalonia's Costa Brava and European modernity. During the transition period Camino made films that reflect on nature and the recuperation of historical memory. *Las largas vacaciones del '36* (1976) is a chronicle of the fascist uprising as seen through a group of friends and family members stranded on vacation at the beginning of the Spanish Civil War in July 1936. Camino's exploration is timely; his revisionist account of this traumatic moment in Spanish history was made in 1976, just one year after Franco's death. The film received the critics' award at the Berlin film festival. *La vieja memoria*, filmed in 1977, follows Camino's earlier inquiry. It is a documentary that questions the nature and veracity of historical memory by interviewing Spaniards who fought on both sides of the Spanish Civil War.

José Juan Bigas Luna, a filmmaker who would go on to make several box-office hits in the 1980s, appeared on the film scene at this time with *Tatuaje* (1976), *Bilbao* (1978), and *Caniche* (1979). Marginal characters, prostitution, obsessive passion, pathological attachments, cannibalism, and consumerist culture became trademark themes in Bigas Luna's later career. Vicente Aranda, director of *Fata Morgana* (1965), *Las crueles* (1969), and *Clara es el precio* (1973), had a significant breakthrough at this time, emerging as a strong authorial voice with *Cambio de sexo* (1976) and casting a rising female star in the Spanish film scene, Victoria Abril. Ventura Pons, one of the most experimental contemporary Catalan voices, debuted with *Ocaña, retrat intermitent* (1977), a documentary about an Andalusian drag queen and artist, José Ocaña, who had moved to Barcelona. Captured on film by Pons, Ocaña's transvestism and his performances on Barcelona's famous Las Ramblas have significant testimonial and historical value. At the end of 1985 Ventura Pons created his own production company, Els Films de la Rambla, which made him a strong presence on the 1980s film scene.

In Basque cinema one of the most interesting new voices was Imanol Uribe. He filmed and lived in Madrid, but centered his films on Basque issues. His trilogy – *El proceso de Burgos* (1981), *La fuga de Segovia* (1981), and the critically acclaimed *La muerte de Mikel* (1983) – focuses on ETA and Basque militants. *La muerte de Mikel* also explores sexual marginalization (homosexuality) within the context of political struggle (Basque autonomy). Montxo Armendáriz, another vocal Basque filmmaker, made *Tasio* (1984), a depiction of several generations of Basque coal-workers, followed by *27 horas* (1986), which centers on drug addiction among Basque youths.

Eloy de la Iglesia started his filmmaking career in the late 1960s but achieved neither authorial nor commercial success until after Franco's death. The films that he made thereafter are noteworthy, especially for their complex exploration of gay themes. *Los placeres ocultos* (1976), *El diputado* (1978), and *El pico* (1983) examine the relationship between politics and (homo)-sexuality during the democratic transition. Furthermore, *El pico* specifically centers on Basque nationalism and separatism, tensions within the Basque political scene, and the region's alienated youth. In addition to homosexuality, most of de la Iglesia's films also center on drug culture, seedy milieus, working-class disenchantment, and economic marginalization.

Regional cinema that explored new directions and reflected post-dictatorial de-centralizing tendencies was offset by the return of the extreme right and their nostalgic political aspirations. Rafael Gil, a prominent filmmaker during Franco's dictatorship, concluded his career by adapting reactionary novelist Fernando Vizcaíno Casas's work in *Y al tercer año resucitó* (1981) and *De camisa vieja a chaqueta nueva* (1982). Exhibiting several residual issues of the unresolved *pacto de olvido*, the films reflect the right-wing political factions' disenchantment, stemming from their inability and unwillingness to accept Spain's new democratic political and social direction.

Prior to the 1970s there were only three women directing feature films in Spain: Rosario Pi made two films during the Second Republic in the 1930s; Ana Mariscal, a stage and screen star of the postwar era, directed 11 films from 1946 to 1968; and Margarita Alexandre acted in and co-directed three films in the 1950s with her husband. In the transition period three more vital female voices appeared on the film scene. Josefina Molina, Cecilia Bartolomé, and Pilar Miró all attended the renowned film school the EOC, in the second half of the 1960s, directing a total of seven feature films between 1973 and 1981. Centering on gender and identity, all three directors explore ties between feminist consciousness and issues confronting women in a country that was experiencing rapid social change.

Cecilia Bartolomé earned a degree from the EOC in 1970 with a practice film entitled *Margarita y el lobo*, a musical tragicomedy on marriage and its oppressive constraints. Bartolomé's first feature film, *Vámonos, Bárbara* (1977–8), is a feminist statement that powerfully explores the personal and political elements of gender. Its focus on divorce and female sexuality is a critical look at the inseparability of personal dimensions from larger legal structures and political issues. Together with her brother José J. Bartolomé, Cecilia Bartolomé coauthored *Después de . . .* (1979–81), an insightful testimonial and a reflection of political and social changes in post-Franco Spain.[73] The film is a collage of the dissonant ideological and political views of a broad sector of the Spanish population (rural, urban, liberal, and conservative), showing the persistent division, polarized pluralism, and extreme differences of the country in transition.

Josefina Molina completed her degree at the EOC in 1969 while simultaneously working for Spanish state television as a technical assistant to Pilar Miró. She was the first Spanish woman to receive a degree in film direction at the EOC. Molina already had experience directing television documentaries when she started to work on her first feature film, *Vera, un cuento cruel* (1973). The commissioned film (*película de encargo*) was a historical drama and a loose literary adaptation of a Gothic horror story by Villiers de L'Isle-Adam. Her second film, *Función de noche* (1981), was a remarkable documentary of Lola Herrera, a theater actress of the postwar generation. The film explores the relationships between gender, performance, professional struggle, and societal restrictions; its point of departure is Miguel Delibes's classic postwar masterpiece *Cinco horas con Mario* (1966), a work that Molina had earlier adapted for the stage in 1979 and whose female protagonist, Carmen, was played by Herrera. Through Delibes's text the actress Lola Herrera confronts her own demons: identity crisis, education, gender inequality, failed marriage, and her theater career during the long years of the dictatorship. Herrera's personal crisis is mapped onto the larger structure of family, stage, and state. The film points to the social construction of gender identity, exemplifying a feminist deconstruction of the deceptive dichotomy between public and private space. Formally innovative, the film combines cinéma vérité – Lola Herrera's monologues and interviews with Herrera's children and her ex-husband (actor Daniel Dicenta) – as well as flashbacks and documentary footage from Herrera's 1979 performance of Molina's adaptation of *Cinco horas con Mario*.

Pilar Miró directed her first feature film, *La petición* – a historical drama loosely adapted from the author Emile Zola – in 1976. The film was fairly controversial due to its explicit depictions of sexuality. Miró's next project, *El crimen de Cuenca* (1979), discussed in detail below, is one of the most controversial films of the transition period, responsible for Miró's notoriety and media exposure. Miró's third film, *Gary Cooper, que estás en los cielos* (1980), written prior to *El crimen de Cuenca*, is her most personal. It has an autobiographical resonance because of its focus on Andrea Soriano, an ambitious television director who discovers after a visit to the gynecologist that she must have potentially life-threatening surgery. Andrea's story, a narrative of a professional woman's emotional crisis, unfolds parallel to her reflection on larger issues confronting women such as feminist consciousness, abortion, reproductive rights, democratization, and modernization. The film had considerable appeal for a progressive, left-wing generation of women who belonged to an intellectual and privileged sector of Spanish society.

The scarcity of women directors in the Spanish film scene (until the very last decade of the twentieth century) is matched by the absence of critical texts on women filmmakers. The first challenging and in-depth study was Susan Martin-Márquez's *Feminist Discourse and Spanish Cinema: Sight Unseen*, published in 1999. Martin-Márquez's long-awaited study unearths unseen cinema by women, reconsidering the "lost" films of early female directors as well as giving an indispensable context for contemporary women's voices.[74]

The two films chosen for this chapter are Jaime Chávarri's *El desencanto* and Pilar Miró's *El crimen de Cuenca*. The point of departure of *El desencanto*, a story of personal and national disenchantment, is a tribute to Leopoldo Panero, an "official" poet of the Franco regime who died in 1962. The unveiling of Panero's statue at Astorga, his birthplace, on August 28, 1974, is the site of the first of Chávarri's interviews with the dead poet's family: Panero's widow Felicidad Blanc and their three sons Juan Luis, Leopoldo María, and Michi. An apparently simple reconstruction of Panero's family album becomes a story of lies, deception, concealment, and disenchantment. *El desencanto* became a cult movie and a tribute to a generation disillusioned with the political transition.

Filmed in 1979, Pilar Miró's *El crimen de Cuenca* is another powerful testament to the era of the transition. The film portrays explicit scenes of torture committed by the Civil Guard, including driving spikes through a prisoner's tongue and tying a prisoner's penis with a rope. *El crimen de Cuenca* is therefore representative of the violence that increasingly became a central element of the cinema of the transition, and a vehicle for critiquing the social legacy of the dictatorship. Miró's film shows that despite and because of the *pacto de olvido* there was a persistent desire for political and historical revision. In sum, *El crimen de Cuenca*, like other essential films of the transition, tests the limits of new post-dictatorial structures, negotiates the violence that erupted in response to Franco's dictatorial legacy, and reveals the persistence of historical memory despite the *pacto de olvido*.

1   *El desencanto* (Jaime Chávarri, 1976)

Context and Critical Commentary

Production credits

Director: Jaime Chávarri
Production: Elías Querejeta P.C.
Cinematography: Teodoro Escamilla
Screenplay: Jaime Chávarri
Genre: Documentary
Country: Spain
Runtime: 90 minutes

Cast

Felicidad Blanc
Juan Luis Panero
Leopoldo María Panero
Michi Panero

Synopsis

Leopoldo Panero, a well-known poet of the Franco regime, died in Astorga in 1962. Fourteen years later his widow Felicidad Blanc and their three sons Juan Luis, Leopoldo María, and Michi recount their experiences in the family of the great poet, evoking and then demythologizing the father figure. Each person's memories of Panero reveal how, even after his death, he continues to determine their lives. This conflicted and bankrupt family tells its story through oral testimony, documentary footage, and the memorabilia-filled house they used to live in. The reconstruction of Panero's life reveals a deceptive and dysfunctional familial environment, along with a deep sense of disenchantment. An attempt to maintain the façade of a happy, exemplary Francoist family is undermined by bitterness and antagonism between the family members. Chávarri's film, straight-forward on the surface, becomes a profound exploration of the deceptions of Francoist culture and society. The film can be read as an allegory for a Spain that was deeply disenchanted following the death of General Franco.

Critical commentary

Jaime Chávarri's *El desencanto*, an unsettling drama and reflection on the Panero family, became a cult film of the transition period, to the point that Vicente José Benet deemed the movie, "that generation's fetish" ("La nueva memoria: imágenes de la memoria en el cine español de la transición," p. 13). *El desencanto*'s point of departure is the unveiling of a statue in tribute to Leopoldo Panero. While this symbolic event honors Panero's importance during Franco's period, Chávarri's interviews with Panero's family offer a radically different image of the dead poet. An apparently simple reconstruction of Panero's family history through documentary footage, dialogue between family members, and their individual recollections, *El desencanto* gradually reveals the traumatic, bitter undercurrents of this "exemplary" Francoist family. Leopoldo Panero, symbolically unveiled in the very beginning of the film, is revealed as a castrating, patriarchal figure and an authoritarian father whose symbolic presence looms over his family like a shadow, despite his death. The death of the patriarch unleashes a visceral hatred between his family members, and the film captures the intense familial relations – ruptures and alliances – forged in the absence of the father/husband figure. Foregrounding the troubled relationship with their mother, Chávarri scrutinizes Juan Luis, Leopoldo María, and Michi, three brilliant, cynical, and Oedipal brothers. Moreover, the brothers – all writers – follow in their father's footsteps, their literary rivalry being as intense as their competition for their mother's attention.

El desencanto lays bare the disintegration of the Panero family. Chávarri made a film that is capable of showing the different facets not only of the Panero family's history, but of its and the nation's multiple fractures and contradictions. Hence the film symbolically interweaves personal trauma with that of the nation, and fills an important role in the recuperation and reconstruction of a traumatic historical memory. There is a painful discrepancy between the "ideal" Francoist family, so cherished in the dictatorship's National Catholic ideology, and the reality of its dark and grotesque reflection. The three brothers belong to the generation that came of age in the final moments of the dictatorship, and their complex tales of remembrance become an attempt to make sense of it. The film is an indispensable point of reference for the transition and its disenchantment, a tragic metaphor for the illusions, disillusions, and lies from which the country was emerging. Moreover, the title of Chávarri's film, *El desencanto* (disenchantment), became the catch-phrase for a generation of Spaniards disenchanted with the culture of dictatorship and the period directly following Franco's death.

Film Scenes: Close Readings

Scene 1   Juan Luis, incarnation of the father

In this scene Juan Luis, the oldest son of the Panero family, presents a series of objects that he has cherished and fetishized throughout his life, and which seem to function as symbolic protection against the inevitable disintegration of his family. As Chávarri's footage indicates, Juan Luis is most comfortable surrounded by pictures and memorabilia that depict the Panero family's supposedly blissful moments. He is the only one of the three sons who idolizes his father and cherishes his childhood. This attitude distinguishes him from his two brothers: the rebellious and troubled Leopoldo María, and the passive and resigned Michi. Juan Luis follows in his father's literary footsteps by becoming an intellectual and a writer. Identifying with his father, he incarnates the figure of the patriarchal male that Panero represented.

The objects that Juan Luis exhibits in this scene are remnants of the family's former splendor. They embody a spirit of nostalgia for the past that also pervades Juan Luis's narration of the family (hi)story. While *El desencanto* reveals the disintegration of the Panero family and reflects the crisis of patriarchal and dictatorial Spanish society, which for Juan Luis's generation was both obsolete and depressing, he still clings to the bygone times and to the mythic memory of his father. He is the only member of the family, besides their mother Felicidad Blanc, who attempts to maintain the façade of a harmonious family.

Scene 2   Leopoldo María, the black sheep

If there is any figure that incarnates the spirit of disenchantment in this film, it is Leopoldo María, the middle son. Appropriately, during the first part of *El desencanto* we only know of Leopoldo through his childhood photos and the various stories that the other family members tell about him, making his first actual appearance in the film even more dramatic. In this scene, Leopoldo takes on the role of the black sheep of the family. Rebellious and extremely creative since his childhood, Leopoldo's testimony is an attempt to unmask what he considers to be the hypocrisy of his family, his upbringing, and his sentimental education during the last years of

Francoism. Leopoldo articulately psychoanalyzes himself, and by extension his family, and goes as far as to say that one of the happiest moments of his life was, as he emphasizes several times in the film, the "happy death of our father." Thus, unlike Juan Luis, Leopoldo María rejects the willful forgetting (*pacto de olvido*) that characterized the transition period, opting instead for the recuperation and reconstruction of a traumatic memory of the past – personal, familial, and national.

Scene 3   Michi, the mediator

As he himself emphasizes in the film, because he is the youngest son of the family, Michi believes that both "the paths of identification [Juan Luis's] with and transgression [Leopoldo María's] against his elders had been closed off to him." After the death of his father, Michi, unlike Juan Luis, did not perpetuate his father's patriarchal ethos, nor did he assume Leopoldo María's rebellious attitude. His disenchantment seems to be inherent in the calm tone in which he speaks to his mother; of the three sons, he seems to be closest to her. Considering himself the last link of the Panero "race" (in an ironic reference to the racial ideals that characterized the Franco regime), Michi is conscious that he has taken on the role of mediator, in both the rivalry between his two brothers and the irresolvable conflict between Leopoldo and his mother. In trying to prevent his family from unraveling, he does not try to mirror his father, nor does he compete with his brothers; yet his identity is still determined by the strength of theirs.

Director (Life and Works)

Jaime Chávarri (b. Madrid 1943)

Jaime Chávarri was born in Madrid in 1943. After finishing his studies in law, he enrolled in the EOC in 1968. After the second year he dropped out of the EOC to dedicate himself to film criticism and to experiment with making Super 8 films. From 1969 to 1974 he contributed to various films as a technical assistant and screenwriter. In 1970 he collaborated on the script for *Vampiros lesbos*, directed by Jesús Franco, and in 1974 he made his directorial debut with the feature-length film *Los viajes escolares*, a complicated semi-autobiographical drama about a dysfunctional family. Two years later, in 1976, he explored the same theme in *El desencanto*, one of the most successful Spanish documentaries of the transition period. In 1977 Chávarri directed *A un dios desconocido*, about a professional magician in Madrid. The protagonist is a lonely gay man who ponders his homosexuality and existence, as well as the memory of his childhood in Granada and of the mythic writer Federico García Lorca. That year the film won the awards for Best Director and Best Actor at the San Sebastian Film Festival. Following a series of collaborations with cinematographer Teo Escamilla and producer Elias Querejeta, Chávarri directed *Dedicatoria* in 1980, which poses a series of ethical questions about political activism. From there he made a series of film adaptations of various literary works like *Bearn o la sala de muñecas*, which premiered in 1983, based on a Lorena Villalonga novel, and *Las bicicletas son para el verano* (1984), an adaptation of the play of the same name written by the actor Fernando Fernán Gómez, which takes place one summer during the Spanish Civil War. Continuing this tendency, in 1988 he adapted for television *Yo soy el que tú buscas*, based on a Gabriel García Márquez novel.

One year later, Chávarri filmed what would be his most successful commercial film, *Las cosas del querer*, a dramatic musical about traditional folkloric songs, or couplets, popular in postwar Madrid. In 1990 he continued making literary adaptations for television, most notably *La intrusa*, a series based on the short stories of Jorge Luis Borges. In 1993 he directed *Tierno verano de lujurias y azoteas*, a comedy of errors about a young man who goes to Russia one summer and ends up falling in love with his older cousin. In 1995 Chávarri made the second part of *Las cosas del querer*, though the sequel was not as successful as the first film, and one year later he released *Gran Slalom*, another comedy about love and intrigue. In 1997 in Argentina he filmed *Sus ojos se cerraron*, about a woman who dreams while listening to Carlos Gardel's tangos. In 2000 he directed *Besos para todos*, a melodrama situated in 1970s Spain about the amorous exploits of three medical students in Cadiz. In 2004 he released *El año del diluvio*, a film based on the Eduardo Mendoza novel of the same title. Set in the 1950s, it tells the story of the love between the mother superior of a charity hospital and a rich landowner who tries to raise enough money to open a nursing home. Chávarri's latest film, *Camarón*, is a biography of the legendary flamenco singer Camarón de la Isla. A critical and popular success, the film won three Goyas, including the award for best actor.[75]

2   *El crimen de Cuenca* (Pilar Miró, 1979)

Context and Critical Commentary

Production credits

Director: Pilar Miró
Production: Alfredo Matas
Cinematography: Hans Burman
Screenplay: Pilar Miró; Salvador Maldonado
Score: Antonio García Abril
Genre: Drama
Country: Spain
Runtime: 92 minutes

Cast

Hector Alterio	Judge Emilio Isasa
Daniel Dicenta	Gregorio Valero
José Manuel Cervino	León Sánchez Gascón
Amparo Soler Leal	Varona
Mary Carrillo	Juana
Guillermo Montesinos	José Grimaldos, "El Cepa"
Fernando Rey	Deputy Contreras
Mercedes Sampietro	Alejandra

Synopsis

Based on a true story, the film begins with a blind troubadour telling a popular tale in a village plaza. The film then re-enacts the events of the story, which takes place in 1910 in the village of Osa de La Vega, in the Cuenca province. A shepherd named José María Grimaldos, known as "El Cepa," disappears. Although El Cepa's mother, Juana, suspects he has been killed, the town's judge closes the case. Three years later a new judge, Emilio Isasa, is pressured by a politician and wealthy landowner, Deputy Contreras, to reopen the case and arrest two shepherds. Gregorio Valero and Leon Sanchez, friends and neighbors from the same village, are accused of killing El Cepa. The Civil Guard, with the judge's approval, torture the two suspects so brutally that each one accuses the other of committing the crime. Meanwhile, Varona, Gregorio's wife, denounces him in an attempt to get them to stop torturing her husband. Two years later the judge puts the men on trial and seeks the death penalty, though they are eventually sentenced to 18 years in prison instead.

The film then flashes forward to the blind troubadour telling the unfortunate story. A close-up shot focuses on the surprised face of a peasant as he realizes that he is listening to the tale of his own presumed murder and the gruesome consequences. The viewer then learns that El Cepa is very much alive, living in the village, and has just sent a letter to the priest of Osa de La Vega with regard to marrying the mother of his three children. The wives of the accused men find out about the letter, the priest admits he has received it, and the Civil Guard take El Cepa to the new judge, who then pardons the two accused men. During the walk to the courthouse, the entire town comes out into the street to insult El Cepa, who shouts in response that he was never dead. The film closes by informing the viewer that none of those responsible for the judicial error was punished; although legend has it they committed suicide.

Critical commentary

Through its sober setting and detailed reconstruction of historical events, particularly the scenes of torture, *El crimen de Cuenca* makes a strong argument against institutional violence and repression, in this case at the hands of the Civil Guard, and against judicial corruption and manipulation. The film also critiques Spain's historical submission to the abusive power of certain structures (landowners, bureaucrats, the corrupt military) that prevented the country from modernizing and achieving social justice.

Based on a screenplay written by Pilar Miró and author Salvador Maldonado, who would later publish a novel of the same title, this harsh portrait of Spanish reality was made in the first months of 1979, the period of transition to democracy. The film provoked significant social and political controversy around the cruelty depicted in the torture scenes, which were interpreted as a critique of the Civil Guard, the extremely influential and powerful military institution that policed the public during the Franco regime. The film's title, *El crimen de Cuenca*, or *The Crime in Cuenca*, is understood to reference the crime that the Civil Guards and the judge –

influenced by the powerful landowner – committed, not the one that the shepherds were accused of. The government in power at the time, the UCD under the presidency of Adolfo Suárez, was pressured by conservative opposition groups to take a position on the film.

In an effort to avoid conflict in his relationship with the army and the conservative sectors, the ministry of the interior in December of 1979 prohibited the film from being shown, and ordered that the director, Pilar Miró, face a military tribunal for slandering the Civil Guard and the judicial body. This extreme measure was an attempt to appease the army and the conservative groups, still loyal to Franco, during the new democratic regime's particularly unstable inception. Pilar Miró was the first civilian woman to face a military tribunal, and the film was the only one to be prohibited by the democratic government after the end of the Franco dictatorship and the abolition of censorship in 1977. Pilar Miró's trial in April of 1980 provoked an outpouring of national support for the director. Finally, in December of 1980, after abolishing the law of military trials for civilians, a civil court withdrew the charges against Pilar Miró. The highly anticipated film finally premiered in August of 1981, and just one year later, the new socialist government named Pilar Miró director general of cinematography.

Aside from the controversy surrounding its release, the film stands out for the excellent acting, its meticulous re-enactment of the mood of the turbulent era, and the brutal realism that the director achieved with the torture scenes. *El crimen de Cuenca* achieved great public and critical success, and is considered a fundamental film of the transition.

Film Scenes: Close Readings

Scene 1   Tyranny and corruption

Deputy Contreras, a wealthy landowner, pays a visit to Emilio Isasa, the new district judge. In the meeting, Contreras points out that the conservative party has taken over all of the communities in the province, with the exception of Osa de La Vega, which still remains under liberal control. He brings up the case of the disappearance of a local shepherd, El Cepa, and how the previous judge decided not to accuse the two suspected shepherds of murder because the judge was "a good man, though maybe a little too liberal." The deputy asks Judge Isasa to reopen the case because "we need a judge that can make people respect the law, and instill a little fear." A close-up of the silver lion's head on the judge's cane symbolically suggests that he will exercise power and control by force, not law, a characteristic that becomes instrumental in the story.

Toward the end of the scene the town's priest enters, completing the triumvirate of social powers: politics, justice, and religion – all accomplices and agents of tyranny as they use their positions of power to subjugate the citizens. With this scene of coercion and corruption, Miró critiques the abusive exercising of these forms of power, where justice is carried out through the pressure of the landowner, the deputy's political decisions are made to take revenge on a town controlled by liberals, and the priest enjoys the privilege of forming part of this powerful group.

Scene 2   The brutality of torture

In the shadows of the prison cell, the Civil Guards torture Gregorio and León. Their screams are heard while a close-up shot captures a nail being ripped from one of León's fingers. Gregorio witnesses the brutality, while the two guards taunt him by threatening, "don't worry, you're next." Unable to tolerate the pain, León screams, "it was him." The camera cuts between shots of León's contorted face and his mutilated hands. The other prisoner, Gregorio, desperately asks for the judge so he can submit a confession. The scene ends with a close-up of a Civil Guard's smiling face as he sews up Gregorio's ear with a needle, while background choral music provides a stark contrast to the brutal final image.

This scene is one of the most significant in the film for its meticulously realistic depiction of torture. Gregorio's and León's bloodcurdling screams pierce the darkness of the torture cell, accentuating the detainees' absolute fragility and the extreme pain inflicted by their torture. Miró's images are extremely raw and explicit, very effectively communicating the brutality of torture that drives these two innocent shepherds to implicate each other in a crime neither of them committed. These mutual accusations are not surprising given the horrific circumstances, which are heightened by the scene's closing score – disturbingly lyrical and smooth given the context. This is one of the most critical scenes of the film, not only for its impeccable construction, but also for the charge of slander Miró had to face for its depiction of the Civil Guard.

Scene 3   The blind troubadour in the village

In the town plaza, a blind man recounts how the shepherds, Gregorio and León, were tortured and condemned to prison for murdering El Cepa. He uses his cane as a pointer to draw the listeners' attention to drawings that recreate the story. The camera then closes in on the frightened face of a shepherd who has been listening intently to the troubadour. In addition to orally recounting the story, the blind man is also selling written versions of it. The shepherd buys one of the documents, and looks puzzled as he turns the paper over, revealing to the viewer that he does not know how to read. He quickly walks through the village's white streets back to his house, his image fading in the distance. The viewer later learns that this illiterate shepherd is El Cepa, whom León and Gregorio were convicted of killing.

In this scene Pilar Miró depicts the illiterate rural society of the early twentieth century, immersed in poverty, lacking primary education, and in the power of the landowner. At the same time, the troubadour's oral form of storytelling connects with Spain's historical, folkloric past, where oral legends and couplets, like the "couplet of the crime in Cuenca," were passed down through the generations, thereby avoiding institutional censorship. By utilizing the historically and culturally significant figure of the blind troubadour, Miró emphasizes how the story of *El crimen de Cuenca* belongs to Spain's own popular history, while also reinforcing the validity of the real-life events depicted in the film.

Director (Life and Works)

Pilar Miró (b. Madrid 1940, d. Madrid 1997)

In Spanish film history only a few female directors figure prominently prior to the 1980s. Some examples are Rosario Pi (1899–1968), Ana Mariscal (1921–95), and Margarita Alexandre (b. 1923). After the Franco regime's demise, women directors gained more visibility and important film-makers like Pilar Miró entered the Spanish film scene. Miró was born in Madrid in 1940. After abandoning a career in law, she studied both journalism and film, specializing in screenwriting. She was the first woman to graduate from the renowned EOC. Two other important, pioneering women filmmakers, Josefina Molina and Cecilia Bartolomé, also graduated from this film school in the late 1960s. All three filmmakers went on to focus on issues of gender, identity, and the changing roles of women in post-Franco Spain.

Before graduating from the EOC Miró had already ventured into directing through her work at Televisión Española (TVE), where she made numerous programs and literary adaptations. Not only did Miró gain hands-on experience in media at TVE, but she also learned to negotiate the male-dominated directorial profession. During the final years of the EOC's operation, Miró taught screenwriting and editing. In 1976 Miró made her film-directing debut with *La petición*, a film based on the novel by Emile Zola. The film was polemical, not just for its explicit sex scenes, but because of its controversial female protagonist. The main character seduces a member of the lower class in order to help her dispose of her ex-lover's cadaver, and then kills him to take on a different lover from a higher social class. Miró's second film, *El crimen de Cuenca*, depicts the true story of the wrongful conviction and torture of two men in 1910. Despite the fact that censorship had been abolished in Spain in 1977, two years before Miró filmed *El crimen de Cuenca*, the film was prohibited from being screened and Miró was charged with slandering the Civil Guard and faced a military tribunal. Given this politically charged context, *El crimen de Cuenca* remained stigmatized as scandalous and polemical for some time, although it was extremely successful once it was finally shown in 1981. The director was eventually absolved of the charges.

In 1980 Miró directed a semi-autobiographical film, *Gary Cooper, que estás en los cielos*. In this film, the protagonist, a director, reflects on the meaning of her existence after suffering from an illness that has required open-heart surgery. Miró herself had gone through this surgery and it would sadly be this same condition that caused her death in 1997. In 1982 Miró directed another controversial film, *Hablamos esta noche*, about the head of a newly constructed nuclear power plant. In late 1982, under the government of the PSOE, Miró was named the director general of cinematography during Felipe González's first administration. During her time in office Miró fought hard to establish laws that would protect Spanish film production and distribution, anticipating policies that the European Union would later impose. In 1983 she implemented the so-called Miró Law (Ley Miró), a controversial measure regarding state protection and subvention of Spanish film production. In 1986 she filmed *Werther*, a film that explores the female sensibility and reflects the director's personal, ideological, and emotional concerns. That same year she resigned from her post as director general of cinematography and accepted a new political position as director general of Servicio Público Centralizado RadioTelevisión Española (RTVE), which she would hold until 1989 when she resigned over a controversy regarding her administration. After leaving this position, Miró continued to direct films that garnered critical attention and awards: *Beltenebros* (1990), an adaptation of the literary work of Antonio Muñoz Molina, for which she won a Silver Bear for Outstanding Artistic Achievement at the Berlin Film Festival, along with various Goyas in Spain; *El pájaro de la felicidad* (1993), an intimate reflection on the director's own disenchantment with life's complexities; and *El perro del hortelano* (1996), adapted from the classic Lope de Vega work, which won several Goya awards the following year. In 1996 Miró directed the film *Tu nombre envenena mis sueños*, an adaptation of the novel by Joaquín Leguina, ex-president of the autonomous community of Madrid, which recounts a complex story of female revenge in the post-Franco period. Pilar Miró died of a heart attack in Madrid in 1997, at the pinnacle of her creative career.

8

Post-Franco Spain: The Pedro Almodóvar Phenomenon (1980–1991)

1   *Pepi, Luci, Bom y otras chicas del montón*
    (Pedro Almodóvar, 1980)
2   *¿Qué he hecho yo para merecer esto!*
    (Pedro Almodóvar, 1984)

Historical and Political Overview of the Period

Politically and culturally, this period is marked above all by the Spanish Socialist Workers' Party (Partido Socialista Obrero Español, PSOE) coming to power. The PSOE had already had a significant presence in the first free election in 1977 when they shared 70 percent of the seats with the UCD (Unión de Centro Democrático, or Central Democratic Union), but in the beginning of the 1980s their membership soared and the Socialist Party's stature increased. Their leader Felipe González gained more political power, and his popularity, as well as the newly proposed political reforms, won the PSOE an absolute majority in the polls in October of 1982, confirming the stability of Spain's new democracy.

Part of the PSOE's appeal could be traced to its abandoning of traditional leftist discourse and politics. The party's overwhelming victory at the polls stemmed from their ideology of moderate reformism. As Santos Juliá pointed out, "Socialists began to use new language in which the key words were no longer 'working class,' 'democratic socialism,' or 'Federal Republic,' but 'modernization,' 'Europeanization,' 'democratic consolidation,' and 'the strong internal unity of Spain'" ("History, Politics, and Culture, 1975–1996," p. 113). The political ambitions behind this "moderate" turn were based on the aspiration to join the European Community, into which Spain was accepted in 1986. The economic benefits, socially progressive politics, and innovative cultural initiatives firmly entrenched socialist government until the end of the decade.

In the early 1990s, however, the era of frustration began. Disenchantment with socialist politics was spurred by both financial scandals and the government's illegal antiterrorist operations. Involved in the embezzlement of public funds, the deputy prime minister of the Socialist Party, Alfonso Guerra, was forced to resign. Other members of the party were brought to trial for widespread corruption involving housing speculation and tax fraud. The government's clandestine war against ETA intensified, and the scandal exploded when the activities of the police-sponsored antiterrorist Grupo Antiterrorista de Liberación (GAL), or Antiterrorist Liberation Group, which had been active for about a decade, came to light in the mid-1990s. The economic recession and unemployment, which reached an unprecedented high of 24 percent, added to the increasing discontent with the Socialists. The last socialist victory achieved with an absolute majority (*mayoría absoluta*) was in 1989.

In 1992, at the end of the socialist administration, and despite the country's economic crisis, the government financed several elaborate international cultural events that coincided with the Socialists' decline in the political arena. Barcelona hosted the Olympics, Seville was the site of the World Exposition, and Madrid was proclaimed the European City of Culture. These opulent cultural exhibitions were an attempt to compensate for the loss of the government's political power and popularity. Furthermore, these events coincided with the five-hundredth anniversary of the "discovery" of America (el Quinto Centenario del Descubrimiento de América). Various celebrations of Spain's imperial past were critiqued for the revisionist history they celebrated and for their uncritical exaltation of the country's colonial legacy. In this context of political weakening, it was not surprising that the Socialists' last term in power – won only by a simple majority (*mayoría simple*) in 1993 – was followed by the loss of elections to the Partido Popular (PP), or Popular Party, in 1996.

The cultural politics of the Socialist Party had a significant impact on the film industry and its infrastructure. Cinema was seen as an effective vehicle for projecting a liberal, postmodern, and "post-Franco" image abroad – significant for a Spain that was still haunted by its dictatorial legacy. This strategy fit well with the Socialists' overall politics of Europeanization. Socialist reform advocated state involvement in film production and promotion, and this assertive support of Spanish cinema facilitated multiple subsidies to producers, films, and film directors. Already in 1978, four years before they won the elections, the PSOE had outlined their policies regarding cinema, to which they stayed remarkably faithful during their term in power. At the First Democratic Congress of Spanish Cinema (I Congreso Democrático del Cine Español), held in December of 1978, it was proclaimed that, "Film is a cultural good, a means of artistic expression, a fact of social communication, an industry, and an object of commerce, instruction, study, and investigation. Film is part of Spain's cultural patrimony, its nationalities, and its regions" (Llinás, *Cuatro años de cine español* (*1983–1986*), p. 16).

In 1982, Pilar Miró, the most prominent Spanish woman filmmaker (see chapter 7), was named director general of cinematography. A professional filmmaker trained in the very industry whose direction she was now able to shape, Miró held this powerful post from 1982 until 1986. She introduced several reforms, the most important being the measure named after her, the Miró Law (Ley Miró). The Miró Law was a controversial measure that reflected socialist politics by endorsing state intervention in cultural production. It was a protectionist measure geared above all to supporting "quality" cinema that, in the competitive market dominated by Hollywood, could never have been produced without a governmental subsidy. During Miró's term government subventions made up a sizeable portion of Spanish film budgets. Miró's elitist practice targeted the directors who could deliver "quality" cinema of highbrow aesthetic and formal experimentation, which often ended up being filmic adaptations of Spain's "great" literary works. The measure was criticized because it excluded small-budget, low-quality cinema and genres such as horror and soft-porn films.

Prompted by Miró's politics, Spanish films acquired a glossy, homogeneous look that guaranteed their directors a state subvention and were more attuned to the European film market. Miró's emphasis on "quality" cinema thus matched broader European film policies that were also geared toward producing "quality" films in an attempt to distinguish European cinema from American "commercial" cinema, its main rival in a particularly competitive market. The major drawback of this demand for so-called quality was that Spanish film production became increasingly formulaic, as Esteve Riambau outlines: "Contemporary films respond to the sum of these parameters (auteur film + genre + literary adaptation + star system + formal look) in different proportions but with an identical desire for polyvalence" ("El periodo 'socialista' (1982–1995)," p. 424).[76]

As the socialist period advanced, the party's internal ideological disagreements also affected film practices. In 1986 Fernando Méndez-Leite replaced Pilar Miró as director general of cinematography. His film politics were in line with Miró's, with the exception of changes that were introduced in 1986 with Spain's integration into Europe. The official incorporation into the European Community (EC) impacted cinematographic practices, especially with regard to the politics of film production and co-production. The year 1988, however, brought even more significant changes. Writer Jorge Semprún, then minister of culture, named Miguel Marías the new director general of cinematography. There was a significant push toward a free-market philosophy and a self-regulating industry, even though subventions continued to be linked to box-office returns. In August 1989, the so-called Semprún decree (el decreto Semprún) attempted to address and remedy film production's excessive reliance on the state, which Pilar Miró's politics encouraged. Almost 70 percent of films during Miró's term were financed by state subventions, prompting debates on the role of public financing in cinema production and distribution in Spain. In sum, while Miró's politics supported culture, public initiatives, state subventions, artistic quality, and film as artistic and cultural capital, Semprún's advocated industry, private financing, the free market, commercial success, and film as an economic commodity and technological product.

The end of the socialist period is seen as a moment of profound crisis for Spanish cinema: lavish state subsidies drained budgets; an industrially weak Spanish film industry was incapable of challenging the domination of American cinema; and the arrival of private-sector television in the 1990s only exacerbated the crisis. The result was a radical decline in Spanish film production accompanied by an alarming closure of theaters, whose numbers dropped from 3,109 in 1985 to 1,802 in 1990. Despite this dismal end result, Spanish directors welcomed most of the socialist protectionist measures because in reality only a handful of directors could compete on international commercial screens. However, they were more successful within a specialized art cinema context and at international film festivals. Starting in 1983 Spanish cinema – directors, producers, and actors – was becoming more visible and recognized abroad. José Luis Garci's *Volver a empezar* (1982) was the first Spanish film to win an Oscar in the Best Foreign Film category in 1983. *La colmena*, Mario Camus's 1982 film, won the Golden Bear at the Berlin Film Festival. Paco Rabal, a distinguished veteran actor, and Alfredo Landa, usually associated with lowbrow comedy, jointly won the prize for best actor at Cannes in 1985 for their performance in another Camus film, *Los santos inocentes* (1984). Carlos Saura's *Carmen* (1983) was nominated for an Oscar in the Best Foreign Language Film category, which it did not win, but it was nonetheless acknowledged for its artistic contribution (it featured a compelling dance performance by Antonio Gades and Cristina Hoyos, celebrated flamenco performers). Actor and director Fernando Fernán Gómez won a performance prize in Venice for his role in Saura's *Los zancos* (1984). The international recognition of Spanish cinema, it could be argued, culminated in 1988 with *Mujeres al borde de un ataque de nervios*, Pedro Almodóvar's worldwide artistic and commercial success.

Spanish cinema of the 1980s was rather diverse. Among the most important trends were those explicitly encouraged by socialist politics: the production of "high-quality" screen adaptations of literary masterworks and historical films, especially those centered on the historical inquiry into periods that had been suppressed during the Franco dictatorship. Comedy became even more commercially viable in the 1980s. Additionally, Spanish cinema continued to explore Basque and Catalan issues, and by this time, the cinema of the autonomous communities was gaining more visibility. In sum, as Marvin D'Lugo has suggested, "otherwise improbable clusters of films of this period may be understood as linked to the under-lying project of imagining a Spain which is able to confront and even thrive on the diversity and heterogeneity of its class and gender differences" ("Heterogeneity and Spanish Cinema of the Eighties," p. 56). The 1980s is also the decade of Pedro Almodóvar, a self-taught filmmaker who became an internationally recognized film auteur and the most prominent embodi-ment of Spanish cinema for the global audience to this day.

As emphasized earlier, films based on literary sources dominated this period. The screen adaptation of great works of literature served as a vehicle for the legitimization of the newly formed democratic nation. The literary works chosen for adaptation were also tied to the politics of the Socialists in power. The preferred authors mostly came from works canonized as *antifranquistas*, or anti-Francoist, such as novels and plays by Juan Marsé, Jesús Fernández Santos, Federico García Lorca, Ramón Sender, and Miguel Delibes. Camilo José Cela is another author whose work was prominently adapted, even though his political position was much more ambiguous. The two best-known directors of screen adaptations of literary works were Mario Camus and Vicente Aranda. Mario Camus's films are emblematic of Pilar Miró's politics. Until the 1980s, when his authorial voice fully emerged, Camus had a somewhat erratic career. *La colmena* was adapted from Camilo José Cela's popular postwar novel, and *Los santos inocentes* was a screen adaptation of Miguel Delibes's novel.

In 1987 Camus adapted Federico García Lorca's *La casa de Bernarda Alba*, which did not fare as well.

Vicente Aranda, another director who favored screen adaptations of literary works, filmed Manuel Vázquez Montelbán's *Asesinato en el Comité Central* (1982), introducing to the big screen Pepe Carvalho, an iconoclastic literary character of the transition period. In 1985 Aranda filmed an adaptation of Luis Martín Santos's existential novel *Tiempo de silencio*, a difficult task given the novel's narrative complexity. *Si te dicen que caí* (1989) is based on a Juan Marsé postwar novel.[77] *El Lute, camina o revienta* (1987) and *El Lute, mañana seré libre* (1988) are films about Eleuterio Sánchez, "El Lute," a famous outlaw whose life served as a backdrop for Aranda's explorations of Franco's Spain. *Amantes* (1991) is a story of passionate love, violence, and murder set in the immediate postwar years amidst 1940s scarcity and the *estraperlo* (black market). During his prolific career Aranda successfully combined his two interests, screen adaptations and historical films. His cinema is recognizable for its inventive visual style and critical revisions of the Spanish past, explored through the intersection of the personal, sexual, collective, and political.

Apart from some successful screen adaptations, such as Camus's and Aranda's, the genre in general was criticized for being pretentious and unimaginative. Often perceived as dull copies of "originals," many screen adaptations had neither the commercial success nor the aesthetic distinction they claimed. Furthermore, exorbitant sums of state funds were spent on this type of cinema, accentuating problems of cronyism in the film industry during the socialist period, which was colonized by a highbrow, privileged minority that came into power with the change in the political system.

Another thematic tendency of the transition period was to take a critical look at the past and explore the socio-political collusion that made Francoism possible, a preoccupation that continued in the post-Franco era. By the 1980s, however, the return to history was more of a "nostalgic" gesture, where it was relegated to the anecdotal, primarily becoming the film's colorful background. This commercialization of the past often resulted in light comic films that lacked the more profound historical inquiry that characterized the previous period. Luis García Berlanga filmed *La vaquilla* (1984), the first Civil War comedy, in which the two warring sides, the Nationalists and the Republicans, survive economically by exchanging goods (cigarettes for lighters, for example), and socially by playing soccer matches during the ceasefire. Fernando Fernán Gómez continued directing as well. *Mambrú se fue a la guerra* (1986) is the story of a man, hidden since the

Civil War, who does not believe that Franco has actually died. Another Fernán Gómez film, *El mar y el tiempo* (1989), is also inspired by the past, this time in the form of bittersweet memories of political exile, set in Spain during the 1960s.

Carlos Saura, known for his explorations of the legacy of Francoism, turned his gaze to earlier historical periods in the 1980s. *¡Ay, Carmela!* (1990) is the story of a theater troupe that performed throughout the Civil War. The film explores the links between art and political engagement, and was a considerable commercial success, signaling Saura's comeback *El Dorado* (1988) questions Spain's colonial legacy through the figure of a fanatical, rebellious conquistador, Lope de Aguirre,[78] and *La noche oscura* (1988) looks at San Juan de la Cruz – the great mystic and church reformer – to examine complex religious issues in the Spain of Felipe II. Jaime Camino continued the thread of his successful *Las largas vacaciones del '36* (1976) with *El largo invierno* (*The Long Winter*, 1991). The "long winter" of the title refers to the first winter of the Francoist dictatorship. The film, set in Barcelona, explores the turmoil of the Spanish Civil War through the prism of Catalan culture and history. Jaime Chávarri's *Las bicicletas son para el verano* (1984), an adaptation of Fernando Fernán Gómez's work, follows a Republican family in Madrid during the Civil War. Chávarri's next film, the commercially successful musical drama *Las cosas del querer* (1989), is an homage to Miguel de Molina, a celebrated singer and performer who was persecuted during the postwar years because of his homosexuality and Republican leanings, and was finally forced into exile in 1942 (he took refuge in Argentina). José Luis Borau, the director of *Furtivos*, one of the most powerful films of the mid-1970s, made another masterpiece, *Tata mía*, in 1986. The story's protagonist, Elvira, returns to secular life after 17 years in a convent, and the film centers on her (in)ability to integrate into the new Spain of the 1980s. The movie is a comical allegory of sexual repression, identity, and gender issues, prompted by women's changing roles in contemporary Spain. The film also explores the process of historical revision. Elvira's struggles are tied to an attempt to assert the place of her father (a deceased right-wing general) within Spain's collective history and memory.[79]

Fernando Colomo and Fernando Trueba, the most prominent representatives of New Madrid Comedy, discussed in chapter 7, continued with very successful careers. During this decade they became masters of the comic genre, which continued to bring them commercial success and a strong following. Fernando Colomo made *La línea del cielo* in 1983, followed by

La vida alegre in 1987. Fernando Trueba's *Sé infiel y no mires con quien* (1985) was a box-office hit, followed by *El año de las luces* (1987). The latter film's 1940s postwar setting, combined with the young protagonist Manolo's coming-of-age story, was the precursor to *Belle Epoque*, Trueba's most successful film and the critical and artistic culmination of his career. *Belle Epoque* (1992) received an Oscar for Best Foreign Language Film in 1994. It is a glossy period film set in the spring of 1931, during the fall of the Spanish monarchy. Trueba presents the Second Republic, which follows the fall of the monarchy, as a utopian space of sexual and social liberation. Historical events are the backdrop for a light mixture of politics, love, erotic adventure, and intrigue. The success of the film was partially due to a great crew: Rafael Azcona wrote the script and Jorge Sanz, a rising sex symbol, was cast as the lead actor. *Belle Epoque* is tied both thematically and formally to *El año de las luces*, as Sanz also played Manolo in the later film. Above all, Trueba's triumph with *Belle Epoque* was due to the director's skillful manipulation of the "right formula" for a successful European comedy, already well established in the international market.

Basque filmmakers continued to explore the intersection of regional and national politics and identity, themes already examined in the previous decade. Imanol Uribe delivered on the promise of his earlier work by making one of his most acclaimed films of the eighties, *La muerte de Mikel* (1983), which problematizes the junction between nationalism (Basque) and homosexuality. Eloy de la Iglesia also expanded on his earlier themes – the world of delinquency, margins, prostitution, homosexuality, and violence – in *Colegas* (1982), *El pico* (1983), and *El pico II* (1984). Montxo Armendáriz's *Tasio* (1984) portrays the life of a Basque coal-miner and poacher, forced to abandon his native land in search of survival.

A promising new voice emerged in Catalonia with Majorcan filmmaker Agustí Villaronga, who debuted with *Tras el cristal* (1986), a morally ambiguous and profoundly unsettling story of a former Nazi death camp "doctor" named Klaus. One of the doctor's former victims and witness to his countless atrocities ends up nursing Klaus when he is confined to an iron lung. The film is a disturbing exploration of power struggles, sadism, psychological warfare, and role reversal between victim and victimizer. Even though *Tras el cristal* is set in the Nazi milieu, it explores themes pertinent to Spain, especially through the intersection of authority and mimesis. Bigas Luna, another Catalan voice, successfully ventured into the horror genre with *Angustias* in 1987. The film's hybrid setting – situated in Los Angeles and filmed in Barcelona – is an interesting example of the filmmaker's cross-cultural sensibility. *Las edades de Lulú* (1990) is Bigas Luna's adaptation of Almudena Grandes's celebrated pornographic novel of the same title. The novel's focus on sadomasochism, power struggles, fetishism, and "perverse" sexuality fit well with Bigas Luna's own obsessions. In the following decade, Bigas Luna would focus more on Catalan and Mediterranean themes.

As seen from these examples, both Basque and Catalan filmmakers are difficult to classify as such. While interested in issues of national identity as well as the intersections of national and regional political concerns, they also embarked on subjects too complex and diverse to be reduced to identity politics and national identity. These directors also had to contend with the reality that filming in a language other than Castilian radically decreased their audience, commercial appeal, and national visibility. Thus many of their films explore Catalan or Basque specificity, but are filmed in Castilian and marketed to a more general Spanish public.

Finally we turn to Pedro Almodóvar, a counter-cultural icon and a singular phenomenon in 1980s Spanish cinema. Almodóvar was ambiguously tied to the Socialists in power and he profited economically from state patronage. However, he embraced an aesthetic that was opposed to the artsy, glossy, and ultimately homogeneous European look that was favored by the politics of Pilar Miró.[80] Almodóvar's films provide testimony to Madrid's *la movida*, an effervescent cultural movement of the late 1970s and early 1980s that can be interpreted as a reaction to 40 years of oppressive dictatorship. *La movida* drew on the music and lifestyles of European and American punk and new wave, and revived an interest in the visual arts.[81]

A prolific film director, Almodóvar made eight feature films in the 1980s, each one progressively more visually and thematically sophisticated than its predecessor. In 1988 he exploded onto the international stage with *Mujeres al borde de un ataque de nervios*, which was nominated for an Oscar for Best Foreign Language Film. Thus, for the international audience, the Spanish cinema of the 1980s, despite its heterogeneity, is above all a cinema of Pedro Almodóvar.

Given Almodóvar's significant international impact, we chose his two films *Pepi, Luci, Bom y otras chicas del montón* (1980) and *¿Qué he hecho yo para merecer esto!* (1984) for this chapter. Both works capture the radical changes taking place during Spain's post-Franco period. *Pepi, Luci, Bom y otras chicas del montón* is a frenetic and exhilarating testimony to *la movida*. While its irreverent tone is tied to graphic comic-book aesthetics and punk music, the film's bizarre story revolves around drug use, illicit sex, and scatological humor. The film breaks the boundaries of high and low taste, finds pleasure in kitsch, gives a housewife the same access to pleasure as a drag queen, and delights in the impertinent fusion of post-modern sensibility and Spanish tradition. Nevertheless, *Pepi, Luci, Bom* was dismissed by critics and rebuked for its thematic and formal inconsistency, technical flaws, incoherent script, and poor performances.

The second film chosen for this chapter is *¿Qué he hecho yo para merecer esto!*, released in 1984. It is considered Almodóvar's crossover film and the beginning of his passage to broader international recognition. With *¿Qué he hecho yo para merecer esto!* Almodóvar left behind the low budget, frivolity, technical imperfections, and specialist audiences that characterize his earlier films.[82] *¿Qué he hecho yo para merecer esto!* is a grotesque neo-realist melodrama with strong social overtones. It focuses on the figure of the housewife, already explored in *Pepi, Luci, Bom*. The film portrays a marriage, motherhood, and family reduced to commercial transactions. With his (anti)heroine, the withered housewife Gloria, Almodóvar depicts a working-class, contemporary, dystopian Spanish family. In doing so, he performs a grotesque rewriting of the Francoist ideological glorification of the housewife, and mercilessly juxtaposes marriage and prostitution. In addition, Almodóvar also focuses on other social issues, such as immigration and the failed Francoist modernization politics of the 1960s.

1   *Pepi, Luci, Bom y otras chicas del montón* (Pedro Almodóvar, 1980)

Context and Critical Commentary

Production credits

Director: Pedro Almodóvar
Production: Pepón Corominas; Félix Rotaeta; Fígaro Films, S.A.
Cinematography: Paco Femenia
Screenplay: Pedro Almodóvar
Music: Alaska y los Pegamoides
Genre: Comedy
Country: Spain
Runtime: 80 minutes

Cast

Carmen Maura	Pepi
Olvido "Alaska" Gara	Bom
Eva Siva	Luci
Félix Rotaeta	Police officer/Twin brother
Kiti Manver	Model and singer
Julieta Serrano	Actress, woman dressed as Scarlett O'Hara
Concha Gregori	Charito, Luci's neighbor
Cecilia Roth	Girl in the "Bragas Ponte" commercial
Fabio de Miguel (Fanny McNamara)	Roxy
Cristina Sánchez Pascual	Bearded woman

Synopsis

The film's three protagonists, Pepi, Luci, and Bom, live strange and extravagant lives: Luci is a self-sacrificing housewife, Pepi is her "pop" neighbor, and Bom is a sadistic rocker. Their unlikely friendship results from a failed revenge attempt. After being raped by her neighbor, a policeman and Luci's husband, Pepi decides to seek retribution with the help of Bom and her punk band, Los Bomitoni. They cook up a plan to beat up the rapist, but accidentally attack his twin brother instead. Pepi and Bom's alternative plan is to get closer to the offender through his wife, Luci. Pepi arranges to take knitting classes from the dejected housewife, with the intent of establishing a relationship with her. Pepi's plan works, but only to the extent that she and Luci become friends. Luci confesses that she is a masochist and becomes a Los Bomitoni groupie and the punk singer Bom's slave.

The three women, immersed in Madrid's frenetic *la movida* scene, frequent outrageous parties, live with their punk and gay friends in the house of the painters Costus, and go to wild concerts. Their lives revolve around creating their own publicity firm, making a film about themselves, entitled precisely *Pepi, Luci, Bom y otras chicas del montón*, and experiencing modern life in Madrid. However, this life of leisure and excess is interrupted by another instance of revenge, this time at the hands of Luci's husband, the policeman/rapist. He snatches Luci from a club on one of her nights out with the girls, then rapes and beats her. The violent night lands Luci in the hospital, where Pepi and Bom visit her. They quickly realize that they have lost Luci, who has decided to go back to the person that can mistreat her the best – her husband. As they leave the hospital, Pepi comforts Bom, who has just lost her masochistic partner, and convinces Bom to leave the past behind and become a bolero singer.

Critical commentary

Pedro Almodóvar's first feature-length film, *Pepi, Luci, Bom y otras chicas del montón*, premiered in 1980 during the early, more spontaneous phase of *la movida*, a Madrid-based cultural movement whose creativity, excess, and postmodern aesthetics are vibrantly reflected in the film. Defying traditional beliefs about gender, the body, and sexuality, this creative movement anticipated the hedonism of the Spanish youth culture of the 1980s. A group of musicians, painters, designers, filmmakers, and journalists tied to *la movida* were immersed in a wide range of innovative cultural projects. In this context, *Pepi, Luci, Bom y otras chicas del montón* is a particularly valuable document that not only depicts but also contributes to the cultural history of 1980s Madrid. The use of authentic underground Madrid locations includes the real-life residence of the gay pop-art painters Costus (Juan Carrero and Enrique Naya), where Luci and Bom set up their home and play out their sadomasochistic fantasies. They frequent El Bo, the emblematic nightclub of the moment, and attend Los Bomitoni concerts, featuring Fanny McNamara, a singer, painter, and *la movida* icon. Critics such as Kathleen Vernon and Barbara Morris see Almodóvar's early films as more than a simple document of *la movida* cultural history, affirming that "both *Pepi, Luci, Bom* and *Laberinto de pasiones* constitute a chronicle of *la movida* as well as an almost utopian rendering of Madrid as locus amoenus, a space of infinite possibilities" ("Introduction: Pedro Almodóvar, Postmodern Auteur," p. 8).

Pepi, Luci, Bom y otras chicas del montón, Almodóvar's first film, introduced many themes now recognizable as typically Almodóvarian: friendship between women and female intimacy, sexual heterodoxy, violence, pornography, drug addiction, and hysteria. Among the film's most noteworthy characteristics are its much-debated frivolity, the insistence on the affirmation of libidinal economy, the use of kitsch and camp, and a love of pop culture, often fused with traditional Spanish cultural forms. Almodóvar explored new types of representation, attempting to redefine the political and cultural spaces left open after the demise of the dictatorship. Fanny McNamara's song "Murciana," featured in the film, is a characteristic piece of counter-cultural production, with its cult of bad taste, obscenity, and absurdity: "I love you because you are a filthy whore from Murcia. I love you, Murciana, because you're a pig."

The film both offended the sensibilities of the mainstream audience and was accused of political indifference. Hostile film critics objected specifically to the film's frivolity, while others argued that the same frivolity could also be read as a political posture. In spite of Almodóvar's famous affirmations that "we had no memory and we imitated everything we liked" (Almodóvar, *Patty Diphusa y otros textos*, p. 7) and "I make films as if Franco had never existed," (Besas, *Behind the Spanish Lens*, p. 216), the film takes an unmistakably critical position against the dictatorship from which the country had just emerged. *La movida*'s frivolity was a strategic tool its participants used against the oppressive discourse and traditions of a Francoist past: "Frivolity was a question of terrorism. You had to do it, because culture, at that time, was permeated with transcendence. The best way to attack it was to be frivolous, profane the altar of transcendence a little by placing frivolity above it" (Gallero, *Sólo se vive una vez*, p. 334). Postwar political strategies were pragmatic and exceedingly utilitarian; be it Franco's recreation of the Spanish empire, the 1960s generation's Marxist discourse, or the *ultras*'[83] desire to return to the betrayed "essence" of Francoism. Therefore, *la movida*'s frivolity is a political stance that both rejected Francoism's propriety and separated the movement from the direct involvement and sobriety of the political progressives.

In sum, *Pepi, Luci, Bom y otras chicas del montón* became an immediate emblem of *la movida* for its idiosyncratic aesthetic and provocative topics, and it propelled Almodóvar from the underground world into a more visible cultural space. From this moment on, Almodóvar dedicated himself exclusively to producing and directing films, leaving behind his work at the National Spanish Telephone Company, which had partially inspired some of his first productions.

Film Scenes: Close Readings

Scene 1   Domestic perversions

After her neighbor, a police officer, rapes her, Pepi is determined to settle the score with him. To get the revenge she craves, Pepi decides to befriend Luci, the policeman's wife, by taking knitting lessons from her. The scene opens with a cartoon intertitle that reads, "The next morning, Pepi has her first lesson." Luci teaches Pepi to knit, while Pepi teaches Luci about sadomasochism. Every time Pepi, the pupil, makes a mistake, they agree that she will actually punish Luci, the teacher. Luci derives considerable enjoyment from this dynamic, revealing her true masochistic tendencies. The scene gets even more shocking with the introduction of the third key character of the film, Bom, the singer of the punk band Los Bomitoni. At Pepi's suggestion, Bom urinates on Luci, an act that transposes the sexually marginal practice of "watersports" or "golden showers" into the domestic space and onto the figure of the housewife. The dialogue between Pepi and Bom is campy and outrageous. Bom enters the scene saying, "I have to pee really bad." Pepi responds, "Wait. Take advantage of Luci and pee on her. She's hot and it'll refresh her." Bom says, "It'll be a little difficult, but worth the trouble." Pepi responds again, "Wait, I'll help you. Stand on the table. Lift your leg."

This peeing scene is therefore simultaneously capricious, entertaining, and hilarious, as well as offensive, excessive, and disturbing. However, it is also provocative in the sense that it compels the audience to think about the cultural expectations and limitations placed on the housewife. Thus, and as Paul Julian Smith remarks, "it is around Luci that the film's parodic discourse on feminism circulates" (*Desire Unlimited*, p. 11). Luci's deviant sexual practice is comically juxtaposed with her domestic life. Just moments before she goes to Pepi's house for the "sadomasochistic session" she is seen complaining about the rising price of potatoes with her neighbor. Moreover, knitting, a traditional social activity for women, leads to an alternative, and what some would call deviant, social activity between women: sadomasochism. This humorous and provocative association is deliberately reinforced through close-up shots of one activity, knitting, followed by the other, peeing. The director subverts the sacred figure of the housewife, so exalted during the Franco dictatorship; in Almodóvar's universe, even the housewife is incited to participate in the hedonism of the 1980s. He provides a housewife the same access to pleasure and unrestrained fantasy as a punk singer or drag queen. In a sui generis fashion, Almodóvar thus comments on the complexities of the socio-political situation following the death of Franco. This includes the rapidly changing role of women in general, and the housewife in particular, in the transition from dictatorship to democracy.

Finally, the tone of the scene illustrates Almodóvar's love for the impertinent fusion of Spanish tradition with postmodern sensibility. This effect

Figure 8.1   Domestic perversions (*Pepi, Luci, Bom y otras chicas del montón,* 1980)

is achieved through a sharp contrast and incongruous juxtaposition of Luci, the typical housewife shopping in her domestic "uniform" (her hair is covered with a scarf, she wears a homemade sweater, and pulls a grocery cart like an old woman), with Luci, the masochist, who moments later is willingly being pissed on by a sadistic punk.

As Carmen Maura stated, "The peeing scene didn't seem at all odd to Alaska [Bom]. Nobody thought it was strange, not Pedro [Almodóvar], not Alaska, not Eva [Luci], as if they had been peed on all their lives" (Vidal, *El cine de Pedro Almodóvar*, p. 18). Thus, the scene of "domestic perversion" in *Pepi, Luci, Bom* demonstrates Almodóvar's irreverent spirit, in relation to both obsolete Francoist values and the seriousness that, in the director's opinion, characterized leftist politicians. Almodóvar, as can be seen, created a sensibility that dissociates *la movida* from the serious and repressed world that came before it.

Scene 2   Wear Panties: "Whatever you do, wear panties"
(Bragas Ponte: "hagas lo que hagas ponte bragas")

Pepi gains economic independence from her father – a nagging voice on the telephone who badgers her to get a "real job" – by becoming the manager of Bom's punk band and forming her own advertising agency. The products she markets, such as a menstruating doll and masturbatory underwear, represent a punk perversion of consumerism. This is reinforced by the unusual and excessive commercials Pepi also films to present these products to investors, one of which demonstrates the uses for "Bragas Ponte," a multifunctional pair of underwear that absorbs urine and rolls into a dildo.

The advertisement consists of two parts whose aesthetics differ radically. In the first commercial we see a woman in a polka-dot sun dress (Cecilia Roth) running through the park and trying to find a place to pee. The tone is burlesque and comic, accompanied by jittery music and the noise of the cars and buses in the background. She converses with a male voice that seems to originate from the viewer's point of view. The woman looks directly into the camera, in the direction of the viewer, as the male voice tries to calm the woman by explaining how "Bragas Ponte" ("Wear Panties") can resolve her uncomfortable situation because they are specially made to absorb urine. In a parody of television commercial techniques, the segment ends with a close-up of the product: yellow "Bragas Ponte" that turn green as they absorb urine.

The second segment has a romantic undertone. We see the same woman (Cecilia Roth), now laying on a wicker chaise longue and caressing herself through her silky nightgown. She is surrounded by plants, soft light illuminates the interior, and in the background we hear tranquil, romantic music. A soothing male voice explains, "There are moments when solitude

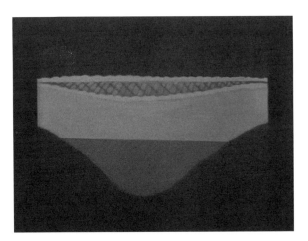

Figure 8.2   Wear Panties: "Whatever you do, wear panties" (*Pepi, Luci, Bom y otras chicas del montón*, 1980)

is our greatest enemy. 'Bragas Ponte,' when carefully rolled up, acquire a consistency that, in the absence of something better, can perform the same function as a passionate companion."

Almodóvar clearly emulates the television advertisement genre in each of these segments, reflecting the growing consumer culture of the 1980s, and commenting on the role of the media in post-Franco Spain. The intertextual advertisements also function as a distancing device, pointing to the artifice of cinematic narrative and probing the reality and mechanism of cinematic representation. Finally, in addressing the taboo issues of menstruation and masturbation, Almodóvar breaks the silence around female bodies and pleasure, so suppressed in the official discourse of Francoist ideology.

Scene 3   General erections

Luci and Bom, who at this point in the film are a sadomasochistic couple, go with Pepi to a raucous party. This scene attests to the documentary nature of *Pepi, Luci, Bom* and can be read as Almodóvar's visual testament to *la movida*, Madrid's subculture, Spain's modernity, and the hedonistic post-Franco youth. The theme of the party is the "general erections," a competition that Almodóvar – inserting himself into the scene – presides over, where the man with the "biggest, most svelte, most inordinate penis" wins the opportunity to "do what he wants, how he wants, with whomever he wants" (*Pepi, Luci, Bom y otras chicas del montón*). Significantly, the name of the contest, "general erections," is clearly a parodic rendering of the first general elections held in Spain in 1977, just about the time when Almodóvar was writing his script for *Pepi, Luci, Bom.*

Almodóvar's parody of the general elections, Spain's political milestone, is thus accompanied by an assertion of sexuality and a utopian celebration of pleasure in his typically outrageous fashion. This blatant affirmation of pleasure over politics prefigures a broader trend of postmodernity and its reconfiguration of the political realm. Additionally, as in the previously analyzed scene "Domestic perversions," in Almodóvar's universe, the housewife actually has a role in the hedonism of the 1980s. Moncho, the winner, picks Luci, the ex-housewife, to "suck it," making Luci the most envied woman at the party. Again Almodóvar resignifies the character of the housewife, liberating her from the traditional role of woman and sacrificial mother so typical of the Franco period, and turning her into a protagonist of postmodernity.[84]

In this scene, the use of music, mise-en-scène, and modes of perform-ance are representative of formal inconsistencies and technical problems apparent throughout *Pepi, Luci, Bom*. For example, the image of Almodóvar's head is cut off during the first few takes of the "general erections" party presentation, clearly a technical flaw resulting from inexperience. This error is even more perceptible because Almodóvar is frantically talking in the scene, but his voice seems to materialize from his neck and the microphone. The camera pans shakily over the audience and the quality of the image is inconsistent. Nevertheless, the scene is also delightfully campy and features traits that will become signatures of Almodóvar's style, even after his film-making matures. The elaborate and stylish costumes, especially Pepi's pop outfit and Bom's punk attire, are colorful and fantastic, characteristic of Almodóvar's cinema of visual pleasure.

Moreover, this scene is crosscut with the monologue of a bearded woman (played by Cristina Sánchez Pascual) complaining to her husband for neglecting her sexually, while he is peeping through the window at the "general erections," which we later find out have been organized for his voyeuristic pleasure. This element is a stylized, burlesque rendition of Tennessee Williams's *Cat on a Hot Tin Roof*, pointing to another Almodóvar trademark – the incorporation of intertextual references, especially of films and novels, in his cinema.

2   *¿Qué he hecho yo para merecer esto!* (Pedro Almodóvar, 1984)

Context and Critical Commentary

Production credits

Director: Pedro Almodóvar
Production: Kaktus Producciones Cinematografic, S.A.; Tesauro, S.A.
Cinematography: Ángel Luis Fernández
Screenplay: Pedro Almodóvar
Score: Hans Fritz Beckmann; Wizner Boheme; Bernardo Bonezzi; Ramón Perelló
Genre: Comedy/drama
Country: Spain
Runtime: 102 minutes

Cast

Carmen Maura	Gloria
Ángel de Andrés López	Antonio
Verónica Forqué	Cristal
Juan Martínez	Toni
Chus Lampreave	Abuela
Fabio de Miguel	
(Fanny McNamara)	Woman in "La bien pagá" performance
Pedro Almodóvar	Singer in "La bien pagá" performance
Miguel Angel Herranz	Miguel
Kitti Manver	Juani
Sonia Anabela Hoffman	Vanessa
Luis Hostalot	Inspector Polo
Gonzalo Suárez	Lucas
Amparo Soler Lael	Patricia
Javier Gurruchaga	Dentist

Synopsis

Gloria is a housewife who lives in a cramped apartment with her two sons, her taxi-driving husband Antonio, her mother-in-law Abuela, and a lizard named Dinero ("Money"). Between cooking and cleaning for her family and her second full-time job as a cleaning woman, Gloria does not have one free moment to herself. To make it through her 18-hour day and stifle her own hunger so she can feed her family instead, she has become addicted to pharmaceutical speed. She is enslaved by a domesticity that is draining her of life, while everyone around her ignores her suffering. To make matters worse, her dysfunctional family suffers from a lack of communication, with the exception of the oldest son Toni and his grandmother, who share a room and an endearing friendship. Further souring Gloria and Antonio's relationship is the ghost of a German singer, Ingrid Muller, whom Antonio has been in love with since he was her driver in Berlin 15 years earlier. Cristal, the prostitute who lives next door, earns much more money than Gloria and seems to be much happier. Similarly, Gloria's teenage son Toni has a lucrative business selling drugs, while her youngest son Miguel sells his body to his smarmy dentist.

One evening Antonio comes home and orders Gloria to iron one of his shirts so he can pick up Ingrid Muller at the airport. Gloria refuses, and Antonio reacts by slapping her. Gloria defends herself with the first thing she finds, a ham bone hanging in the kitchen. She hits him so hard on the head that she kills him, and then makes a stock with the bone to erase all traces of the murder weapon. A couple of incompetent policemen come to investigate the death, ruling it an accident when they can't find any evidence. After Antonio's death, Gloria's oldest son Toni and his grandmother decide to move back to the village that Abuela has idealized throughout the film. Paradoxically, although Gloria is finally free from the confines of her family, she feels lonely. She is just at the point of throwing herself off of her grim, high-rise balcony when her youngest son returns. Bored with the dentist he was living with, Miguel has decided to return home because, as the pre-teen, gay prostitute says to Gloria, "this house needs a man."

Critical commentary

Although *¿Qué he hecho yo para merecer esto!* marks the end of Almodóvar's underground period, this film still show traces of the *la movida* sensibility. It is Almodóvar's fourth feature-length film, but the first to benefit from a considerable budget and to attract international attention. Moreover, it is with this movie that Almodóvar began focusing on more socially conscious themes, acknowledging a past that he had intentionally circumvented in his previous films. *¿Qué he hecho yo para merecer esto!* is groundbreaking, both for its technical innovations and for its treatment of vital social issues such as poverty, rural migration, prostitution, and drug abuse.

The film also attests to Almodóvar's postmodern fusion of genres, ranging from neorealism, in his depiction of Gloria, the working-class mother, to hyperrealism, embodied in Vanessa, a mistreated girl who has developed telekinetic powers (an homage to Brian de Palma's *Carrie*). Almodóvar's skillful blend of comic and tragic elements in *¿Qué he hecho yo para merecer esto!* makes it a tribute to Spanish neorealism of the late 1950s and 1960s, typified by masterpieces like *El pisito*, *El cochecito*, *El extraño viaje*, and *El verdugo*, films that in the director's words were "more ferocious, more entertaining, and less sentimental" than their Italian counterparts (Vidal, *El cine de Pedro Almodóvar*, p. 116).

This black tragicomedy comments on three major issues: gender roles, social class, and urban poverty. The film's antiheroine, Gloria, is an over-worked, underappreciated, and depressed housewife. Because she is invisible to the rest of the family, the electrical appliances seem to be the only witnesses to her daily struggles. However, it is exactly this seeming invisibility that ironically saves Gloria from the law when she kills her husband with the Serrano ham bone hanging in the kitchen. The murder weapon literally disappears in that night's dinner and in the normalcy of her domestic function as a housewife. Almodóvar highlights the misery of the housewife's identity, constantly lost in a domesticity in which she is not recognized, but paradoxically on which she depends to establish her as a social subject. Gloria fights with herself and others to not turn into "that" which she has already become. Yet, when she manages to break free through her husband's death and her son and mother-in-law's reverse migration to the village, she doesn't know what to do with herself. As Almodóvar notes, "she killed her husband and nothing happened; she's alone without anything to do because everything is already clean. This is her loneliest moment. The worst is that she didn't have the time to realize that she didn't even have her own life. In this moment, she is a free woman, but she has no internal desires" (Vidal, *El cine de Pedro Almodóvar*, p. 146).

This film illustrates the deception that characterizes the lives of an entire class of people who emigrated from rural Spanish villages to the urban capital in search of a better future. Instead, what they found was the reality of Franco's failed modernization project of the 1960s – the prison-like high-rises of the working-class neighborhood of La Concepción, encircled by a monstrous beltway, the M-30 freeway. Thus, and as Almodóvar himself has noted, Gloria's neighborhood of La Concepción becomes another character in the film: "It is a very eloquent symbol of the deceptive comfort to which the Spanish public had conceded in the 1970s" (Vidal, *El cine de Pedro Almodóvar*, p. 124).

Gloria is confined to her daily existence in the working-class La Concepción, yet she is still exposed to the comfort of more privileged social classes, whose houses she cleans in order to survive economically. Almodóvar's focus on socio-economic issues in *¿Qué he hecho yo para merecer esto!* is reinforced through the film's technical aspects. The claustrophobic socio-economic confinement in which Gloria's family lives is strengthened by mise-en-scène, modes of performance, and camera work. As Almodóvar himself points out, "the film is very sober, with the camera almost always taking a medium shot. The characters constantly enter and leave the frame, and this gives it a feeling of dryness, so everything happens right in front of the viewer, without adornment. The camera changes height according to the mood and point of view, raising or lowering to give the sensation of oppression or the discovery of the ground" (Vidal, *El cine de Pedro Almodóvar*, p. 119). In sum, *¿Qué he hecho yo para merecer esto!*, with its focus on social issues and its technical innovations, became a crossover success with mainstream distribution and an international audience. This film, which marks the end of the director's early, more experimental phase, brought Almodóvar increasing visibility and indicated the beginning of his international career as one of the most important contemporary film auteurs.

Film Scenes: Close Readings

Scene 1   Consuming the consumer

Out of an entire life of abuse at the hands of her husband and family, the worst for Gloria, the protagonist, has been the invisibility of her domestic life. Objects and home appliances become the only witnesses to her misery. One of the film's more effective formal innovations is Almodóvar's placement of the camera inside domestic appliances like the refrigerator, the washing machine, and the oven. As the filmmaker has explained, "I put myself inside the objects because the appliances are the only witnesses to this woman's life. She is scrubbing, cleaning all the time, and nobody sees her but these objects. In this way I invert the propaganda surrounding these marvelous domestic objects" (Vidal, *El cine de Pedro Almodóvar*, pp. 119–20). Gloria cooks, cleans, and mops the floors wearing old sweaters and unstylish dresses covered by worn-out aprons, in front of a backdrop of outdated, loud wallpaper that covers every inch of her tiny, claustrophobic apartment. Gloria, in all her plainness, is "absorbed" by the interior decoration, becoming indistinguishable from the kitschy wallpaper and the prints that surround her.

Gloria's enslavement to appliances and objects of supposed modern luxury culminates in this scene, which opens with her and her neighbor Juani window-shopping in their marginal neighborhood of La Concepción.[85] In this scene, Gloria covets an electric hair-curling iron that she cannot afford. According to Almodóvar this scene, an impossible traveling shot inside the stores ("un travelling imposible de las tiendas"), was one of the most technically challenging in the film (Vidal, *El cine de Pedro Almodóvar*, pp. 121, 122). It is an ingenious inversion of a tracking shot where normally the camera would be moved on a dolly and would smoothly follow Juani and Gloria as they stroll past shop windows. However, Almodóvar reverses the perspective and Juani and Gloria are seen from inside the shops, from the point of view of objects, where the camera is located. The scene consists of four shots edited together to simulate continuity. This inversion suggests how these objects determine Gloria, and helps articulate Almodóvar's critique of consumerism. As he explained, "She would like to integrate herself into consumer society, but she only manages to consume herself, day after day" (Vidal, *El cine de Pedro Almodóvar*, p. 132).

Moreover, Almodóvar's interest in the housewife's subjectivity is reflected by his and the cinematographer Angel Luis Fernández's experimentation with illumination, "The images have a tension close to fear . . . the film had to have the opposite lighting of a Doris Day film; everything that was pastel there had to be dark here, everything that was friendly in those films had to be an aggressive force here" (Vidal, *El cine de Pedro Almodóvar*, p. 120). Hence Gloria, Almodóvar's antiheroine and the antithesis of Doris Day, bears witness to the material conditions of working-class women's oppressive limits and lack of choices. It is important to note that Gloria is finally able to purchase the desired curling iron only after she sells her son Miguel to an extravagant gay dentist. The material need (to have one less mouth to feed at home, and to partake in consumerism) takes priority over maternal love or ethical integrity.

Figure 8.3   Consuming the consumer (*¿Qué he hecho yo para merecer esto!*, 1984)

Scene 2   La bien pagá

In this scene Almodóvar contrasts the figure of Gloria with that of Cristal, a prostitute who seems to have a much better life in economic and emotional terms. In what will become a signature of Almodóvar's style in his later films, he uses a well-known Andalusian song, "La bien pagá," to ironically compare Gloria's role as a housewife to Cristal's as a prostitute. Although the role of mother and housewife is sanctified by Francoist ideology, Almodóvar suggests that in reality Gloria's life is worse than that of her friend and neighbor Cristal's.

In this scene Abuela and Toni are watching a television show in which Almodóvar lip-synchs a popular couplet, "La bien pagá" ("The well-paid woman"), to Fanny McNamara, who is dressed as Scarlett O'Hara. Meanwhile in the adjacent bedroom, Antonio gratifies his sexual desires with a totally passive and unsatisfied Gloria. However, she uses the situation to her advantage to ask Antonio for money to take their youngest son to the dentist. The scene's irony is announced in the lyrics of the song, which can be heard from the other room:

> Well-paid woman,
> yes, you are a well-paid woman
> because I bought your kisses,
> and you knew how to give them to me
> for a fistful of money.
> Well paid, well paid, well paid
> you were, woman.

Parallel to this grotesque exchange, and underlining the tragicomic tone of the scene, the grandmother innocently comments, "The songs of my era were so beautiful." Abuela's nostalgic comment has the opposite effect to that she intends, though, highlighting for the viewer the song's ideological context and retrograde message.

In addition to making a statement about male domination and female passivity Almodóvar's gesture, lip-synching to the voice of Miguel de Molina, is a symbolic homage to the singer and the ideals that he represented.[86] Molina was a popular Republican singer who often interpreted songs associated with and sung by women. As Paul Julian Smith remarks, "it is in such unlikely moments that Almodóvar's intervention into history and politics are to be found" (*Desire Unlimited*, p. 54). In sum, through a

Figure 8.4   "La bien pagá" (*¿Qué he hecho yo para merecer esto!*, 1984)

complex layering of musical citation and historical references, Almodóvar draws parallels between prostitution and marriage, though Gloria, unlike the well-paid woman in the song, is barely paid, if at all. The scene's irony becomes even more biting in a subsequent scene that takes place in the dentist's office. Because she doesn't have any money to pay for her youngest son Miguel's visit, she gives the pre-teen to the pedophilic dentist as payment instead.

Scene 3   Splendor in the grass

Among all of the difficulty associated with living in the marginalized, working-class neighborhood of La Concepción, we also witness a family with serious communication and affective problems. Nevertheless, the grandmother and her eldest grandson Toni form a curious friendship. In addition to sharing a room where the figure of Saint Anthony coexists with heavy-metal posters, the grandmother and her grandson share a tendency to idealize the village from which the family emigrated. This is seen in their film taste, the animals they rescue, and their walks in the scant green space that surrounds their concrete neighborhood.

In this scene we see Tony and his grandmother watching Elia Kazan's 1961 film *Splendor in the Grass*. We first hear a line spoken by the male voice, "I would like to work on that ranch you own outside of town." The announcement is followed by the close-up of Toni and Abuela in the flickering light of the movie theater, mesmerized by the big screen and the dialogue. Toni immediately identifies with the main character of *Splendor in the Grass*, the rebellious son Bud Stamper (played by Warren Beatty), who against his father's wishes does not want to study on the East Coast, but instead would like to remain in their small Kansas town. Toni leans over and says to Abuela, "Maybe I'll set up a ranch in the village," and she enthusiastically agrees.

From their disparate perspectives, the grandmother and grandson converge in their desire to return to the village. While the grandmother, displaced in the hostile urban environment, constructs the village as a type of idyllic paradise drawn from her own nostalgic memory, Toni fabricates the same ideal from his urban experience and from Hollywood films like the one they are watching in this scene. Almodóvar's cinematic reference is not gratuitous, but political and strategic. His use of Hollywood cinema allows him to articulate the working-class family's struggle for survival and their failed emigration from the countryside to the capital city. Hollywood cinema thus opens up a space for a common fantasy, a place where Toni and Abuela can reimagine and reconfigure their lives. In addition, the density of the scene's intertextual allusion points to Spanish cinematographic history as well. Almodóvar references classic themes of Spanish cinema – country versus city, tradition versus modernity, and failed rural-to-urban migration – subjects explored in Spanish masterpieces like Florián Rey's *La aldea maldita* (1930) and José Antonio Nieves Conde's *Surcos* (1951).

It is also important to point out that this scene connects thematically to one of the most moving moments of the film, when Gloria actually sees Abuela and Toni off as they board the bus to return to the village. Gloria is solemn as she clutches her plastic shopping bags, her hair is wet, and she appears tattered. As they say good-bye, Toni gives her the money he earned as a drug dealer and advises her to stop taking pharmaceutical drugs. Ironically, Gloria, who had sacrificed so much and migrated from the village to the city in search of a better life for her children, sees her oldest son off as he returns to the village that she had escaped. As the grandmother and Toni wave from the departing bus, the camera follows the now distressed and tearful Gloria. This emotional close-up is reinforced by the melodramatic background music. Gloria returns home, where her solitude is emphasized with a subjective 360-degree pan shot of her empty home.

In sum, this complex scene crystallizes for the viewer the socio-political issues determining these characters' lives and the decisions they make. Through the intertextual use of a Hollywood film, Almodóvar touches on important themes such as failed rural integration, the alienation of marginal social classes in the big city, intergenerational bonding, domestic angst, poverty, and solitude.

Director (Life and Works)

Pedro Almodóvar (b. Calzada de Calatrava 1949)

Pedro Almodóvar was born in Calzada de Calatrava (Ciudad Real) in 1949. After moving to Extremadura with his family, he studied at the school of the Salesian Fathers of Caceres. At the end of the 1970s he escaped the confines of his provincial town and moved to Madrid, where he worked as an administrative assistant at the Compañía Telefónica Nacional de España (National Spanish Telephone Company). During that time he also became increasingly involved in theater and in Madrid's underground art scene, *la movida*. Almodóvar, a self-taught filmmaker, began his cinematographic career with a series of low-budget, creative, and irreverent short films: *Dos putas, o historia de amor que termina en boda* (1974), *La caída de Sodoma* (1974), *Homenaje* (1975), *El sueño o la estrella* (1975), *Sexo va, sexo viene* (1977), *Salomé* (1978), and *Folle folle, fólleme Tim* (16 mm, feature-length, 1978). Almodóvar's first feature film, *Pepi, Luci, Bom y otras chicas del montón* (1980), became an instant icon of *la movida* due to its peculiar aesthetic and provocative topics. From this moment on, Almodóvar dedicated himself exclusively to producing and directing films, leaving behind his work at Telefónica, which had partially inspired some of his first productions. The next film, *Laberinto de pasiones* (1982), is another testimony to *la movida* and explores similar topics, in addition to sharing some of the same problems of thematic and formal inconsistency, technical flaws, incoherent scripts, and poor performances as *Pepi, Luci, Bom*.

After this initial, more experimental phase, Almodóvar made *Entre tinieblas* in 1983, and in 1984 he filmed *¿Qué he hecho yo para merecer esto!*, a film that had mainstream distribution and brought him international recognition. Moreover, with *¿Qué he hecho yo para merecer esto!*, Almodóvar began distancing himself from the more "frivolous" themes typical of the *la movida* period and started to engage with Spain's past in a more explicit and critical fashion. He explored bullfighting in his next film, *Matador* (1985), which can be seen as a subversive reinscription of some of Spain's most rooted cultural symbols. In 1986 he directed *La ley del deseo*, a film that not only centered explicitly on homosexual passion, but also reappropriated Catholic iconography to explore the limits of love and desire.

His 1988 box-office hit *Mujeres al borde de un ataque de nervios* brought Almodóvar international success (a crucial breakthrough in the very competitive US market), was nominated for an Oscar, and became one of the most commercially viable films in Spanish history (it had 3,300,000 spectators).[87] The film introduced themes now recognizable as typically Almodóvarian, such as his focus on female characters and their newfound agency in post-Franco Spain; his delight in comic confrontation; and a playful re-elaboration of hysteria and neurosis.

Almodóvar's following three films, *¡Atame!* (1990), *Tacones lejanos* (1991), and *Kika* (1993), comprise what many consider his most problematic period, due to their controversial reception and the critique from inside and outside Spain, which revolved around the rape and violence depicted in these films. In the 1990s he returned with full force to the international film scene, beginning what Paul Julian Smith has called his "blue period" (replacing the previous "pink period") with films like *La flor de mi secreto* (1995), *Carne trémula* (1997), and *Todo sobre mi madre* (1999).[88] During this mature, blue period "the early focus on sexual dissidence is replaced by a new attention to the problems and pleasures of heterosexuality; an early spontaneity, even improvisation, of narrative and dialogue gives way to a much more self-conscious literarity and appeal to texts as precedents; and finally, an optimistic vision of the city as setting for desire gives way to a more pessimistic view of urban life as the location of alienation, violence and AIDS" (Smith, *Contemporary Spanish Culture*, p. 150). *Todo sobre mi madre* won the Oscar for Best Foreign Language Film and won Almodóvar the award for Best Director at the Cannes Film Festival.

Almodóvar's next film, *Hable con ella* (2002), was another international success that focuses on solitude, faith, rape, friendship between men, lack of communication between couples, and cinema as a subject of conversation. In *La mala educación* (2004) Almodóvar returns to explore homosexual passion, law, literature, friendship, and betrayal. The story incorporates a semi-autobiographical figure of the director himself, which he had included in the earlier film *La ley del deseo*. With his latest film to date, *Volver* (2006), Almodóvar returned to the "women's film" for which he is so well known, where the plot's central motivators are women. The mostly female cast includes his signature actresses, Carmen Maura and Penélope Cruz, and is partially set in the matriarchal, rural environment seen in some of his earlier films, and where the director himself grew up.

9

Contemporary Trends (1992 to the Present)

1 *Vacas* (Julio Medem, 1992)
2 *Carícies* (Ventura Pons, 1997)
3 *Flores de otro mundo* (Icíar Bollaín, 1999)
4 *The Secret Life of Words* (*La vida secreta de las palabras*) (Isabel Coixet, 2005)

Historical and Political Overview of the Period

As analyzed in the previous chapter, Spain's culturally prestigious year of 1992 – in which Barcelona hosted the Olympics, Seville was the setting for the celebration of the World Exposition Seville, and Madrid was proclaimed the European City of Culture – marked the beginning of the decline of the ruling Spanish Socialist Workers' Party (PSOE) in the political arena. These celebrations were obscuring the profound social crisis, political disenchantment, and economic recession that eventually led to a change of government in 1996. The country's economic recession was paradoxically a result of Spain's entry into the European Community (EC) in 1986, after which the national economy was subordinated to the EC's demands and had to endure often-unfavorable trade practices that led to an increase in unemployment. Nevertheless, Spain was becoming an elite member of the EC (and of the European Union or EU after it was established in 1992) and a major political power in the 1990s, despite the problems its ruling party faced at home.

This final chapter looks at contemporary Spain: the socialist governments until 1996, the ascension of the center-right PP (Partido Popular or Popular Party) to power that lasted for eight years, and finally the country's latest political reversal as the Socialists returned to power with José Luis Rodríguez Zapatero in 2004. José María Aznar was the prime minister of Spain from 1996 to 2004. After a hard-fought campaign that focused on some of the corruption scandals in Felipe González's socialist government, Aznar won the March 3, 1996, general election with 37.6 percent of the vote. With 154 of the 350 seats (the PSOE had 141), Aznar had to reach agreements with three nationalist parties: Convergence and Unity (Catalan), the Basque Nationalist Party, and the Canary Islands Coalition, in order to govern. His first term in power was characterized by major economic reforms and negotiations with nationalist parties.

In the 1990s the traditional left and right parties' agendas were blurred within the Spanish national political space, as evidenced by the almost indistinguishable cultural programs of the two most important parties (the PSOE until 1996 and the PP thereafter). Therefore, Spain's major political reversal with the PP coming to power in the spring of 1996 impacted the film industry and infrastructure less significantly than originally predicted. Already in the later part of the first socialist period in power, Prime Minister Felipe González was pressured to stop subsidizing industries that were not self-sufficient. During this time, the Socialists' radical cultural politics and extravagant film subsidies of the early 1980s were replaced by an attempt to institute a more self-regulating industry in the early 1990s. In a similar manner, once in power the PP was unable to implement some of the radical measures that it had announced in 1996. José María Aznar's government's proposal to abolish the protective state policies (screen quotas and dubbing licenses), supported by the Spanish secretary of culture Miguel Angel Cortés and by the director of the Institute for Cinema and the Audiovisual Arts (ICAA) José María Otero, elicited strong protest from filmmakers and the film industry in general. As a result these drastic proposals were never implemented and the PP's cultural and economic politics ended up closely resembling those of their socialist predecessors. José Luis Rodríguez Zapatero's PSOE won the general election on March 14, 2004. The Socialists' most recent accession to power indicated a return to more radical leftist cultural politics, exemplified by the withdrawal of Spanish troops from Iraq and the legalization of same-sex marriage.

Spain's domestic political dynamic was further complicated by its repositioning within the larger European geopolitical space in the 1990s. The fall of the Berlin Wall in 1989, the break-up of the Soviet Union, the breakdown of Yugoslavia, the unification of Germany, and the continuous expansion of the EU radically altered the physical and political territory of Europe. The continent was reshaped and its cultural imaginary redrawn. Spain's membership in the EU changed the status of Spanish film, both inside the EU and outside of its borders. Film became an object of economic exchange and movies made within the EU became a single trade category, as opposed to those made outside of it. However, the transnational European market, bound to various trade agreements, was also tied to larger global trade accords. The main threat came from the United States. Already a dominant force in the global mediascape, the US insisted on the international free-trade accord (General Agreement on Tariffs and Trade, GATT, 1993) in which audio-visual products would simply be treated like any other commercial goods. Eventually, films and television programs were exempted from free-trade measures, though the politics and economics of the global audiovisual sector remain a contentious and unresolved issue.

In the 1990s film markets around the globe developed new distribution and exhibition structures. They relied on the festival-fueled circuits of inter-national art cinema, television funding, and increased co-productions, and were characterized by a blurring of the divide between art film and com-mercial cinema. These changes prompted complex cultural and industrial strategies within the Spanish film industry, particularly vulnerable in this competitive transnational media space, where Spain is the fifth largest market for Hollywood films. In the face of this rapidly changing globalized film industry, in the 1990s both the PSOE's and the PP's cinematographic policies adopted more aggressive market criteria. Most of the new meas-ures stimulated commercial products, rewarding the highest-grossing films most generously. State subsidies, now mostly tied to box-office success, encouraged the production of more marketable films. In the late 1980s and early 1990s, several other sources of funding consisted of subventions from the regional governments, resources from selling broadcast rights to television networks, distribution advances, home video, advanced sales of foreign distribution, official bank loans, and private financing. The most significant impact on the film industry was the growth of private-sector television networks. Spain's television industry transformed radically, from a national monopoly with only two public stations to new, powerful, private-sector networks with multinational interests and capital. Besides creating a new cultural and media landscape, along with a global audience unified by satellite transmission, TV also became one of the main film industry clients: currently 35 percent of a film's budget comes from (pre-)sales of films to television.

Multinational investment, especially in the media, is a powerful new element in this global restructuring of film industries. PRISA, Spain's most influential multimedia conglomerate, encompasses various branches that operate across different media: la cadena SER, Canal Plus, *El País*, and publishing houses Santillana-Alfaguara, Aguilar, and Taurus. PRISA has multinational accords with Warner, and Sogecable is a film production and distribution subsidiary of PRISA, divided into Sogecine (production), Sogepaq-Warner Sogefilms (distribution of cinema, TV, and video), and Warner Lusomundo Sogecable (exhibition).

Despite all these changes, state subventions continue to be a major source of funding at the national level. However, state subventions are supplemented by two other protection mechanisms: screen quotas and dubbing licenses, which have been sources of funding since the 1940s, although in different forms. As Peter Besas points out, these mechanisms "have been and continue to be the three financial crutches that have enabled the Spanish 'industry' to survive" ("The Financial Structure of Spanish Cinema," p. 249).[89] Co-productions with other countries from the EU have been another sizeable source of funding ever since the creation of pan-European grants set up by the Council of Europe in 1989.

This complex, global, "borderless" context prompted the re-articulation of "national cinema," including that of Spain. The new political framework of the EU, the pan-European market, and the infrastructural and structural changes driven by the globalization of media called for a rethinking of the status of cinematic institutions in the age of globalized cultural production. National cinema, still seen as cultural capital, national patrimony, and a unique cultural product tied to national identity, is nevertheless forced to rethink and renegotiate certain "outdated" notions of Spanishness and national specificity. This context prompted a creative repackaging of the representation of Spanish national culture for the global audience and the world market.

De-territorializing, global forces that restructured the film industry have drastically reshaped Spain's political, social, and cultural landscape as well. Among the most important factors of change was an influx of immigrants into post-Franco Spain, especially since Spain's 1986 entry into what was then the EC. This new socio-political situation urged a more carefully conceptualized politics of immigration, only slightly addressed a year earlier with the Ley de Extranjería or Law on the Rights and Freedoms of Foreigners in Spain (1985). While the first wave of immigrants came mostly from the Maghreb and sub-Saharan Africa, the second wave saw an increase in Latin American immigration and an influx of people from Eastern European countries. Besides its socio-political dimension, the impact of immigration was also symbolic, radically altering Spain's collective imagination. While Spain has become more culturally and racially diverse, the country is also facing many issues that have arisen alongside the recent wave of immigration, including racism, questions of social welfare for immigrants, and the complexities of cultural integration.

In addition to immigration issues, at the beginning of Aznar's presidency Spain also faced high unemployment, a price the country has paid for modernization and Europeanization (the unemployment rate was approaching an alarming 25 percent in 1995). Ironically, the job cuts that led to the high unemployment rate, along with the restructuring of the primary sector, sustained an economic boom. Furthermore, despite democratic changes, plurality, and prominence in the EU, Spain was still facing its old demons, namely the return of nationalisms. However, old cultural, social, regional, and political tensions were being re-articulated and distributed along different lines. The dismantling of the oppressive, authoritarian, centralist nation-state after Franco's death gave way to a series of autonomies with regional governing bodies.

Spain's regionalization (1978–83) and integration into Europe reshaped notions of cultural difference and understandings of cultural identity, which is now intertwined with issues of immigration, hybridity, the multinational economy, and demographic global realignments. Spanish society of the twenty-first century is in flux and its porous socio-political fabric is in the process of steady restructuring.

Spanish contemporary film tendencies are inseparable from these socio-political changes and from the increasingly domineering yet fragmented global mediascape. Within the diverse and complex film panorama that saw the debut of over 200 new directors between 1990 and 2001, there are some well-defined trends: the emergence of the so-called *hijos bastardos de la postmodernidad de los ochenta* ("bastard children of 1980s postmodernism") generation;[90] a return to engaged cinema and "social realism"; historical period films; a boom of women directors; and veteran filmmakers who have reinvented themselves in the new global socio-political and cultural context.

These trends often overlap; Icíar Bollaín, one of the most prominent women directors, also made a pioneer film on immigration, while Alejandro Amenábar's postmodern explorations did not preclude his venture into social themes. Before outlining these trends in more detail it is important to mention that present-day Spanish cinema emerged from a profound industrial crisis, most palpable in 1992, in which year only 35 Spanish films were produced. Despite its precarious beginnings, Spanish cinema of the 1990s garnered two Oscars for Best Foreign Language Film: *Belle*

Epoque (Fernando Trueba, 1992) and *Todo sobre mi madre* (Pedro Almodóvar, 1999), an achievement that Spain had not enjoyed since José Luis Garci's *Volver a empezar* (1982). Alejandro Amenábar, who won an Oscar for Best Foreign Language Film in 2005 for *Mar adentro*, emerged on the Spanish film scene in 1996 with his first feature film, *Tesis*. This international industry recognition signaled the end of the cultural isolation of Spanish cinema. The Oscars for best films were accompanied by the transnational success of Spanish actors. Victoria Abril and Carmen Maura achieved international celebrity status, especially in France, and Spanish stars Antonio Banderas and Penélope Cruz have both made a successful crossover to Hollywood.

A new generation of filmmakers took over the Spanish film scene in the mid-1990s. Leaving behind classical references (novels and films), these films reflected a shift toward mass culture films, television, advertising, and video. These films pushed to the limits some of the well-known postmodernist narrative forms, such as intertextuality, hybridity, and quotation. Exploring narrative mechanisms and playing with generic conventions were more prevalent than engaging with cultural, social, or political realities. The lack of a material place and time was accompanied by an affirmation of the cinema as spectacle.

Two Spanish films symptomatic of this radical postmodern tendency are Santiago Segura's *Torrente: el brazo tonto de la ley* (1998) and its sequel *Torrente 2: Misión en Marbella* (2001). Astutely aware of structural changes in Spain's contemporary entertainment industry (*la industria de ocio*), the director and actor Santiago Segura made the first film into a mass media event. *Torrente* illustrates the radical transformation of Spain's audio-visual cultural industry. Linked with other forms of entertainment, it is a product that fits in perfectly with the consumption practices of Spanish youth (named *los amiguetes*, or "playmates," by Segura), whose objects of consumption are primarily comic books, hard rock, and videogames. The first *Torrente* was a resounding box-office success that grossed more in Spain than the American blockbusters showing at that time,[91] and the second *Torrente* had an unprecedented five million spectators. Together with its commercial triumph, the film also became a late-1990s socio-cultural phenomenon.

Critics proclaimed that *Torrente* was vulgar, reactionary, and in bad taste (*gamberra, cutre, casposa*), questioning its aesthetic "quality" and the ambiguity of its political and social messages. The film's protagonist, Torrente, a repulsive, racist, misogynist, and corrupt ex-policeman, was not seen as

a parodic incarnation of a fascist (*un facha*) but rather as a dangerous celebration of this stereotype. However, the film was also perceived as ingenious
for its deliberate stupidity. Furthermore, *Torrente* was celebrated for its
re-evaluation of popular film genres that were previously repudiated, such
as *españoladas* – popular lowbrow films from the 1960s and 1970s.[92] Through
his films, Segura resurrected and vindicated "has-been" cultural icons such
as the 1970s star Tony Leblanc.

Some of the other films that form part of this *hijos bastardos del postmodernismo* tendency are Juanma Bajo Ulloa's *Airbag* (1997), Alejandro
Amenábar's *Abre los ojos* (1997), Mateo Gil's *Nadie conoce a nadie* (1999),
David Serrano's *Días de fútbol* (2003), and Alex de la Iglesia's *El día de
la bestia* (1995), *Muertos de risa* (1999), and *La comunidad* (2000). These
filmmakers have significant generational and global ties with other directors
of post-postmodern cinema, or this "cinema of image," such as Quentin
Tarantino, David Fincher, Danny Boyle, Tom Tykwer, Jean-Pierre Jeunet,
and Mathieu Kassovitz.

Rather than focusing on the lack of "aesthetic values" and the absence
of an ethical stance of which these films are accused, it might be more
productive to look at this tendency as signaling the restructuring of film
practices, illustrating that it is impossible to talk about the film industry
without considering the wider contexts of the cultural industry, communication media, and marketing strategies. Like the *Torrente* phenomenon,
these films also have to be seen in the context of the global economy and
the development of new technologies of communication, where culture is
linked to leisure and the selling of experiences and lifestyles. Nevertheless, it is important to point out some of the legitimate criticism leveled
against this culture of image. As Vicente Sánchez-Biosca has perceptively
written, this tendency's most crucial problem is that "absolutely everything is passed through television's grinder. This produced a genuine and
unexpected centralization of referents: the television is the exclusive instrument of historicization" ("Paisajes, pasajes y paisanajes de la memoria:
la historia como simultaneidad en la comedia española de los noventa,"
p. 66).[93] Furthermore, Sánchez-Biosca claims that these tendencies lead
to the obliteration or gross misrepresentation of the past because "the
practice of recycling is characterized by a cleaning of the past's surface,
stripping it of its dirt, its materiality, its historical patina, designing it and
uniting its form with that of the present" (pp. 63–4).

The counterpoint to the excessive cinema of the *hijos bastardos del
postmodernismo* is a cinema engaged with social themes, ranging from

unemployment, immigration, and sex tourism to euthanasia, child abuse, and domestic violence.[94] These issues often intersect, and many of the films attribute the source of Spain's contemporary social ills to the traditional patriarchal structures. As a solution, a striking number of such movies propose models for alternative families based on affective, rather than biological, ties.[95] Benito Zambrano's *Solas* (1999) dissolves a family structured around a violent patriarch and proposes new forms of social cohesion. In Pedro Almodóvar's *Todo sobre mi madre*, encounters between characters lead to "cohabitation without limits" and "dependence on the kindness of strangers" (Smith, *Desire Unlimited*, p. 193). Achero Mañas's *El bola* (2000) provides an alternative family for a child who was traumatized and abused by his biological one. Fernando León de Aranoa's *Familia* (1996) cleverly deconstructs the oppressive structures of the nuclear family. His second film, *Barrio* (1998), centers on marginalized adolescents, their strategies for survival, and their "adoptive" families, while his third film, *Los lunes al sol* (2002), focuses on unemployment. Icíar Bollaín's *Te doy mis ojos* (2003) is a profound drama of domestic abuse and its repetitive cycles.

Labor issues are another theme that preoccupies many filmmakers, from Benito Zambrano's *Solas* to *El pájaro de la felicidad* (Pilar Miró, 1993), while prostitution is a theme of both *Nadie hablará de nosotras cuando hayamos muerto* (Agustín Díaz Yanes, 1995) and *Princesas* (Fernando León, 2004). Immigration, racism, cultural integration, and multiracial/cultural families are themes addressed in Montxo Armendáriz's *Las cartas de Alou* (1990), Felipe Vega's *El techo del mundo* (1995), Imanol Uribe's *Bwana* (1996), Manuel Gutiérrez Aragón's *Cosas que dejé en La Habana* (1997), Llorenç Soler's *Said* (1998), and Icíar Bollaín's *Flores de otro mundo* (1999). Films centered on immigration are growing in number and complexity, leaving behind the type of reductive depictions that tended to portray the immigrant simplistically, primarily as the victim of an unjust system.[96]

These two cinematic tendencies bring us to Alejandro Amenábar, an exceptional talent of recent Spanish cinema who successfully combines a postmodern sensibility with "social realism." In his first feature film, *Tesis*, one of the characters claims that "film is an industry and you have to give the public what it wants." Accordingly, Amenábar skillfully combines his unique authorial voice with the commercial demands of the film industry. Through snuff videos, films whose "appeal" lies in the supposed use of real violence, Amenábar explores the limits of violence and its representation. Amenábar's second film, *Abre los ojos* (1997), explores the creation of new spatial and temporal dimensions in a virtual sphere, and can be read as an affirmation of the cinematic image as a substitution for reality. The film was a great box-office success, making 751 million pesetas and drawing 1,200,000 spectators (after *Torrente* it was the second-largest-grossing film in Spanish history). Amenábar's third film, a Gothic tale titled *Los otros* (2001), starring Hollywood's Nicole Kidman, was filmed in English but geared toward a foreign market. With six million spectators, *Los otros* is exemplary of Amenábar's smooth integration into the Hispano-Hollywood formula. Amenábar's last film to date, *Mar adentro* (2004), a docudrama of a real-life paraplegic, Ramón Sampedro, and his fight for the right to die, was Amenábar's incursion into social themes. Even though it won an Oscar for the Best Foreign Language Film in 2005, it was nevertheless accused of realism "a la Spielberg."[97]

The 1990s also initiated a boom in historical period films that has extended to the present. Francisco Regueiro centers on Francisco Franco in *Madregilda* (1994), and Manuel Iborra's *El tiempo de la felicidad* (1997) depicts Ibiza during the 1960s. Fernando Trueba's *La niña de tus ojos* (1998) and David Trueba's *Soldados de Salamina* (2003) focus on the Spanish Civil War period, as does the Mexican Guillermo del Toro's *El espinazo del diablo* (2001) and *El laberinto del fauno* (2006), both Mexican/Spanish co-productions. José Luis Cuerda's *La lengua de las mariposas* (1999) explores the period immediately preceding the Spanish Civil War and José Luis Garci's *Canción de cuna* (1994), *La herida luminosa* (1997), and *You're the One* (2000) examine the immediate postwar period and Francoist political and cultural repression. Martínez Lázaro's *Carreteras secundarias* (1997), set in the mid-1970s, allegorizes the agony of dictatorship through a father-and-son relationship. Vicente Aranda's *Juana la Loca* (2001) is a remake of Juan de Orduña's 1948 epic, set in sixteenth-century Spain (Castile and the Flemish region). *Teresa, el cuerpo de cristo* (2007) by Ray Lóriga is the story of Santa Teresa of Ávila, the prominent Spanish mystic, writer, and monastic reformer. With regard to historical cinema, the superproduction *Alatriste* (Agustín Díaz Yanes, 2006), about Captain Diego Alatriste, a heroic figure from the country's seventeenth-century imperial wars, also stands out.

Most of the historical films produced in this time period have high production values and center on period details, opulent wardrobes, and lush landscapes. They romanticize the past through visually rich styles, songs, period costumes, and other aesthetically pleasing material details. The representation of history in these films is often anachronistic and commercialized. Parallel to this tendency to "de-dramatize history" (Sánchez-Biosca, "Paisajes, pasajes y paisanajes de la memoria: la historia como simultaneidad en la comedia española de los noventa"), women filmmakers who had historically been excluded from the industry finally claimed a more central role. Until the end of the twentieth century, Spanish films made by women were, as Susan Martin-Márquez claims, a "sight unseen," for reasons ranging from a lack of women in the profession and poor dissemination of their works to patronizing dismissals and analytical oversights of important films.[98] Even as recently as the transition period there were only three major women directors: Cecilia Bartolomé, Josefina Molina, and Pilar Miró. However, the 1990s witnessed a boom in women's filmmaking in Spain, with some twenty new female directors making their feature debut. Sadly, though, women's filmmaking also experienced a significant loss in that decade. Pilar Miró, one of the most renowned veteran directors (discussed in chapter 7), unexpectedly died in 1997. Her last film, *El perro del hortelano* (1996), received several Goya awards in 1997.

Miró's 1993 film *El pájaro de la felicidad* exemplifies the contradictions and difficulties facing women directors in the Spanish film industry. A highly personal film, *El pájaro de la felicidad* revolves around its female protagonist's professional and personal emotional crisis. Motivated by a robbery and an attempted rape, the protagonist takes off on a self-reflective journey. The film follows the central character's slow disengagement from the fetters of society, family, and gender expectations. While Miró's work in general, and this film in particular, explore crucial feminist issues such as gender, space, and maternity, she nevertheless vehemently opposed the "feminist" or "woman filmmaker" label throughout her career. Miró's posture is indicative of a broader rejection of feminism by Spanish women filmmakers. Many Spanish film historians and critics have accused feminism of separatist tendencies, which may contribute to certain women filmmakers' resistance to being classified as such. Furthermore, women filmmakers themselves conceive of the making of "women's films" as a self-imposed limitation geared toward a ghettoized female audience. While women directors should not simply be conflated with feminist cinema, its consistent disavowal points to the tense cohabitation of woman directors and the film industry in Spain.

Within this context it is not surprising that only recently has there been a more overt feminist sensibility in Spanish cinema. In addition to gender issues, woman-authored cinema of the 1990s and up to the present day also explores other significant subjects, most notably ethnicity, race, class, and the experiences of Spain's rapidly growing immigrant population.

This new generation is comprised of women with varied backgrounds and experience; some studied formally in Spain and abroad, while others worked their way up through the audiovisual industry (from apprenticeships as assistant directors in television and film to directing commercials, shorts, and videos). Their heterogeneous work ranges from explicitly feminist topics, social issues, and experimental filmmaking to more general subjects, pure entertainment, and more predictable commercial genres. In addition to its thematic variety, the women's film scene is also characterized by a notable regional diversity; they work in Castile, Catalonia, the Basque Country, Galicia, and Andalusia. They film in the various languages of Spain as well as in English, working on international projects and co-productions.

The women directors and films highlighted in this section are only somewhat representative of the notable and ever-growing presence of women in today's film industry, including Dunia Ayaso, Marta Balletbò-Coll, Ana Belén, Icíar Bollaín, Elizabet Cabeza, Isabel Coixet, Ana Díez, Cristina Esteban, Ángeles Gonzalez-Sinde, Chus Gutiérrez, Mónica Laguna, Arantxa Lazcano, Eva Lesmes, María Miró, Silvia Munt, Dolores Payàs, Mirentxu Purroy, Gracia Querejeta, Azucena Rodríguez, Pilar Sueiro, Helena Taberna, and Rosa Vergés, among others.[99] Among the most acknowledged and prolific women directors are Icíar Bollaín, Chus Gutiérrez, Gracia Querejeta, and Isabel Coixet. Successful both artistically and commercially, Icíar Bollaín has made three feature-length films to date: *Hola, estás sola?* (1995), *Flores de otro mundo*, and *Te doy mis ojos* (2003), all with her own production company Producciones La Iguana S.L., established in 1991 with Santiago García and Gonzalo Tapia. *Hola, estás sola?* is a girl's coming-of-age road movie that explores issues of maternity, abandonment, the reconstitution of the family, lack of education, and labor exploitation. *Flores de otro mundo*, Bollaín's pioneering film on immigration, is analyzed in detail later in this chapter. For her third film, *Te doy mis ojo*, an intense drama of domestic violence and abuse, Bollaín received Goyas for Best Director and Best Original Script. Chus Gutiérrez, both a director and screenwriter, debuted with *Sublet*, produced by Fernando Trueba in 1992. The film is largely based on Gutiérrez's experience in New York, where she studied cinema and was part of a band called Xoxonees. In 1994 she made a successful documentary, *Sexo oral*, followed by *Alma gitana* in 1995. Other films by this prolific filmmaker are *Insomnio* (1998), *Poniente* (2002), and *El calentito* (2005). Gracia Querejeta, daughter of Elías Querejeta, the crucial anti-Francoist film producer from the 1960s and 1970s, filmed her first feature-length film, *El último viaje de Robert Rylands*, in 1996, based on the well-known novel

Todas las almas by Javier Marías. Querejeta's second film is *Cuando vuelvas a mi lado* (1999). *Héctor* (2004), her last film to date, is a moving story of a few days in the life of an adolescent who faces drastic life changes after losing his mother. Isabel Coixet, a TV veteran known for her work on commercials, made her first feature film *Demasiado viejo para morir joven* in 1988. Her second film, *Things I Never Told You* (*Cosas que nunca te dije*), was released in Spain in 1996 and in the US two years later. These films were followed by *A los que aman* (1998), *My Life Without Me* (*Mi vida sin mí*, 2003), and *The Secret Life of Words* (*La vida secreta de las palabras*, 2005), which received Goyas for Best Director and Best Original Screenplay, among others. Coixet combines an independent, auteur aesthetic with a commitment to socio-political issues to make complex films that are still accessible to viewers from multiple cultural contexts.

There are several other noteworthy projects, such as Arantxa Lazcano's *Los años oscuros* (1993), which centers on the Basque Country during the postwar period under Franco. The film explores the socialization of a young girl, torn between her Basque family tradition and language, and the outside world, symbolized by the compulsory Castilian customs and language enforced during the repressive times of the dictatorship. María Miró's *Los baúles del retorno* (1995) looks at Morocco's occupation of the Western Sahara and calls for Saharawi self-determination. Miró's film is fictional, but the on-location shooting gave it a strong documentary effect. Marta Balletbò-Coll's romantic lesbian comedy *Costa Brava* (1995) won the audience awards for best picture at the Los Angeles and San Francisco Gay and Lesbian Film Festivals. Helena Taberna's *Yoyes* (1999) is based on the true story of the life of a former ETA member who was assassinated by her former terrorist group members after returning from exile in Mexico. Azucena Rodríguez's first feature film, *Entre rojas* (1995), centers on a women's prison, Yeserías, and the role of working-class women in the political struggle against dictatorship. Dunia Ayaso has worked in both television and cinema and is a successful screenwriter who specializes in comedy. All of her films are a collaborative effort with Félix Sabroso; they include *Quítate tú pa' ponerme yo* (1982), *Perdona bonita pero Lucas me quería a mí* (1996), *El grito en el cielo* (1998), and *Descongélate* (2003). Finally, it is important to note that several of the above-mentioned women filmmakers participated in collaborative projects. Ana Simón Cerezo and Marta Balletbò-Coll teamed up on *¡Cariño, he enviado los hombres a la luna!* (1997), while one of the best-known collective projects, *El dominio de los sentidos* (1996), was directed by five Catalan directors: Isabel Gardela,

Judith Colell, María Ripoll, Nuria Olivé-Bellés, and Teresa Pelegri. Each woman directed one episode, focusing on each of the five senses.

While some veteran filmmakers continued working in their established domains, others like Pedro Almodóvar reinvented themselves within the new global socio-political and cultural context. After a period of crisis epitomized by the condemnation and censure – in the form of a damning X-rating from the Motion Picture Association of America – of *¡Atame!* (1990), the fiasco of *Kika* (1993), and the lukewarm reception of *Tacones lejanos* (1991), Pedro Almodóvar returned, regenerated and revitalized, with *La flor de mi secreto* (1995). With *Todo sobre mi madre, Hable con ella* (2002), and *Volver* (2006), three spectacular commercial and critical successes, Almodóvar reclaimed his worldwide audience, receiving Oscar, Globe, César, and Goya awards. Almodóvar's frivolous and extravagant "rose" period was long left behind, giving way to a more austere, mature, and formally complex "blue" one (Smith, *Contemporary Spanish Culture*, pp. 150, 152). While Almodóvar continues with his trademark incorporation of marginal bodies and subjects, especially sexual minorities such as gays, lesbians, and transsexuals, his late "open heart cinema" (Smith, *Desire Unlimited*, p. 193) is currently marked by a newly radical humanism, best seen in his re-inscription of maternity: hybrid, plural, regenerative, performative, and not limited to biological mothers or even necessarily to women.[100] His last two features to date, *La mala educación*, chosen to open the 2004 Cannes Film Festival, and *Volver*, represent the culmination of Almodóvar's directorial style and show that he is unequivocally one of the world's most acknowledged contemporary filmmakers.

Among other veterans, Mario Camus, who focused in the 1980s on literary adaptations, has embarked on a refreshing new cycle of films dealing with political disenchantment, xenophobia, and terrorism, in *Después del sueño* (1992), *Sombras en una batalla* (1993), and *Amor propio* (1994). Bigas Luna also continues to be commercially successful. His eighth film, *Jamón, jamón* (1992), looks at how the traditional Spain of the interior was rapidly transformed by modernization, economic prosperity, and consumerist lifestyles. *Jamón, jamón*, the first film of a trilogy of Iberian portraits, featuring Spanish sex symbol Javier Bardem, grossed six million dollars on European screens, and was followed by *Huevos de oro* (1993) and *La teta y la luna* (1994). As in Bigas Luna's previous films, in this trilogy political and economic factors are tied to sexuality through icons and clichés of Spanish culture: hams, tortillas, bullfighting, and the sentimental ballad singer Julio Iglesias.

Víctor Erice, one of the most complex, least prolific, and least classifiable Spanish directors, filmed *El sol del membrillo* (1992), an intimate portrait of the painter Antonio López. Contemplating the intersection of art, death, and (artistic) creation, *El sol del membrillo* is suspended between documentary and fiction and engages with the notion of film language and representation. Ever since his groundbreaking film *El espíritu de la colmena* (1973), Erice has continued to create a singular, highly personal, and cryptic cinematic universe.

Pablo Llorca's avant-garde cinema is minimalist and experimental; his films include *Venecias* (1989), *La cocina en casa* (1990), *Jardines colgantes* (1993), *Una historia europea* (1994), *Todos hieren* (1998), *La espalda de Dios* (2001), *Pizcas de paraíso* (2003), *Las olas* (2004), *La cicatriz* (2005), and *Uno de los dos no puede estar equivocado* (2007). The dark, complex world of Llorca can be traced back to the Escuela de Barcelona, a Catalan art-film movement of the 1960s.[101] Another director of similar singularity is Marc Recha, with his *Le ciel monte* (*El cielo sube*) (1991), *L'arbre de les cireres* (*El árbol de las cerezas*) (1998), *Pau y el seu germà* (*Pau y su hermano*) (2001), and *Les mans buides* (*Las manos vacías*) (2003).

The four films included in this chapter are Julio Medem's *Vacas* (1992), Ventura Pons's *Carícies* (1997), Icíar Bollaín's *Flores de otro mundo* (1999), and Isabel Coixet's *The Secret Life of Words* (*La vida secreta de las palabras*) (2005). *Vacas*, Julio Medem's first feature film, obliquely explores the complexity of Basque identity and history. It won the 1993 Goya Award for Best New Director. Set in a small Basque valley (the Guipúzcoa region), *Vacas* follows the fate of three generations of feuding families, the Irigibels and the Mendiluces, from the midst of the Third Carlist War (1875) to the beginning of the Spanish Civil War (1936). The complex visual style of *Vacas* and its non-linear narrative established Medem as one of the most original Spanish directors to emerge in the 1990s. *Vacas* was followed by *La ardilla roja* (1993), *Tierra* (1996), *Los amantes del círculo polar* (1998), *Lucía y el sexo* (2001), *La pelota vasca: la piel contra la piedra* (2003), and *Caótica Ana* (2007).

Like Julio Medem, Ventura Pons has also achieved considerable commercial success without sacrificing his highly idiosyncratic personal vision. After a decade directing theatre, Ventura Pons made his first film in 1977. *Ocaña, retrat intermitent*, a documentary about Andalusian drag queen and artist José Ocaña, brought Pons a cult following. With 17 feature films Pons has become one of the best-known Catalan film directors. He makes films in Catalan, a language that serves as one of the markers of his cinematic identity, yet is not viable in commercial terms.[102] Despite economic, aesthetic, and political challenges, Ventura Pons, working with his own production company Els Films de la Rambla (founded in 1985), makes some of the most original contemporary Spanish films. Pons's cinema, like Medem's micro-regional cinematic tradition, coexists with global tendencies.

His 1997 film *Carícies*, based on the prestigious play by esteemed dramatist Sergi Belbel, effectively combines its high-culture references with an innovative visual style. *Carícies* is set in a Barcelona that is both familiar (the Plaça de Catalunya) and abstracted (a chaotic metropolis at the end of millennium). Through 11 intense but fleeting vignettes Pons insists on the impossibility of communication while still holding out hope for momentary love and a few caresses (*carícies*). *Carícies*, like Pons's other films, is recognizable for his theatrical and experimental cinematic technique: minimalist settings, explosive and hurried dialogues, prolonged silences, and claustrophobic interiors contrasted with expansive city landscapes seen through fast-motion subjective shots and rapid editing.

Icíar Bollaín's *Flores de otro mundo* is a story of three female protagonists – the Basque Marirrosi, Dominican Patricia, and Afro-Cuban Milady – brought to the depopulated ghost town of Santa Eulalia (Castile), to be matched for marriage to local single men. Through an exploration of race and gender dynamics, issues at the heart of the film, Bollaín explores questions of social and cultural anxieties brought on by immigration and hybridization. *100 Years of Spanish Cinema* ends with Isabel Coixet, who like Medem, Pons, and Bollaín, is a highly personal filmmaker who represents a new way of making film, where national boundaries make way for the common territory of human emotion.

1   *Vacas* (Julio Medem, 1992)

Context and Critical Commentary

Production credits

Director: Julio Medem
Production: José Luis Olaizola; Fernando de Garcillán
Cinematography: Carles Gusi
Screenplay: Julio Medem; Michel Gaztambide
Score: Alberto Iglesias

Genre: Drama
Country: Spain
Runtime: 96 minutes

Cast

Emma Suárez	Cristina
Carmelo Gómez	Manuel/Ignacio/Peru Irigibel
Ana Torrent	Catalina
Txema Blasco	Manuel
Cándido Uranga	Carmelo/Juan Mendiluce
Pilar Bardem	Paulina
Karra Elejalde	Ilegorri/Lucas
Miguel Angel García	Peru
Ana Sánchez	Cristina, as a child

Synopsis

Across three generations, two families (the Irigibels and the Mendiluces) from a small valley in the Basque Country maintain a cyclically tortuous relationship marked by passion and rivalry. The story begins in Guipúzcoa (Basque Country) in 1875. Manuel Irigibel and Carmelo Mendiluce, neighbors and rival *aizkolari* (wood-splitters), find themselves in a trench during the Third Carlist War.[103] Carmelo dies in battle, and Manuel escapes from the war by smearing Carmelo's blood on his face and pretending to be dead. Manuel is carried off of the battlefield on a cart of corpses, into the woods, where he encounters a cow, which will become an obsession for Manuel and his family throughout the film. Beginning with this incident, the film recounts the rivalry and forbidden love that persists between the two families for three generations. The film ends in 1936 at the start of the Spanish Civil War.

Critical commentary

After directing nine short films, Julio Medem made his first feature-length film, *Vacas*, in 1991. Due to the film's setting, a small Basque valley (the Guipúzcoa region), and its theme, a series of rivalries and love affairs between three generations of feuding families, Spanish critics hailed Medem as a new promise for Basque cinema. The lives of the three feuding generations of *Vacas* are inseparable from the historical framework that defines them: the narrative spans the period 1875–1936. However, these precise historical dates coexist with mythological time, equally important in the film. This coexistence is illustrated by the film's four chapters: 1875; 30 years later, in spring 1905; 10 years later; and summer 1936, introduced by the following intertitles, respectively: "I. The Coward Woodcutter"; "II. The Axes"; "III. The Burning Hole"; and "IV. War in the Forest."

The historical dimension of *Vacas* is symbolized by *aizkolaris* (woodcutters), guns, uniforms, horses, and cars, while the mythological one is embodied by women, cows, and the forest. Moreover, mythology coexists with advanced technology, another dominant element of Medem's cinematic universe. The film's apparently pastoral setting is contaminated by war, history, madness, incest, claustrophobia, and family feuding. *Vacas*, in addition to being Medem's first film located in and referencing the Basque Country, introduces a series of recurrent topics and narrative structures seen in the director's later films: travel, chance (*azar*), flight (*huida*), and "the coincidence and capricious turns of a blind destiny that hits, sometimes miserably, its characters" (Fernández Valentí, "Julio Medem: el cine de azar," p. 49). In addition, Medem's film, obsessive and repetitive, centers on themes of love, death, and nature. Using a series of elements and symbols taken from nature in particular, Medem constructs his own peculiar universe. His signature mark is bestowing a subjective point of view on animals (cows) and on inanimate objects (flying axes).

The film's formal aspects reinforce *Vacas*'s thematic complexity. The subconscious and the unseen become the organizing and underlying principles that structure the narrative, which is fragmented and difficult to access. There are other formal peculiarities such as the reappearance of the same actors in different roles, which conveys a sense of repetition and cyclicality. Thus, the grown-up Peru is indistinguishable from his father Ignacio and his grandfather Manuel (the same actor, Carmelo Gómez, plays all three characters). The intricate visual style of *Vacas* – the circularity of the narrative, hallucinations, the blending of real and fantastic elements, meticulous framing, and radical juxtapositions of time, place, and perspective – established Medem as one of the most innovative Spanish auteurs to emerge in the 1990s.

Finally, Medem's film, set in the Basque Country – framed by historical references and plagued by war, violence, and death – has often been read as a political and a national allegory of the Civil War, the dictatorship, or Basque separatism. However, overtly forceful political readings are pre-empted by Medem's ambivalent relationship to his homeland. The film, made in Castilian by a Basque director, explores issues of national and cultural identity as it mockingly draws attention to its own recycling of stereotypes and myths of origin.[104] Furthermore, *Vacas* was able to success-fully market signifiers of the regional and the local in the global arena. Medem thus represents both "Basque cinema" and a more transnational global tradition and has succeeded in developing an auteurist vision as well as garnering commercial success.

Film Scenes: Close Readings

Scene 1   Cow's eyes

Cows appear as the ubiquitous witnesses of the story from the very begin-ning of the film, where we see Manuel Irigibel trying to flee the madness of the Third Carlist War. He is precisely the coward that the first intertitle ("I. The Coward Woodcutter") of the film refers to. Manuel, the most famous *aizkolari* of the region, is unable to respond to gender expectations; his celebrated masculinity fails him at the war front. Significantly, he is saved thanks to the death of his neighbor and rival *aizkolari*, Carmelo Mendiluce. Smearing himself with the blood of his opponent and pretending to be dead, Manuel is taken for another lifeless body and carried off the battlefield.

As the cart drives away we see Manuel struggle to emerge from the heap of corpses piled on top of him. After he hits the ground, there is a prolonged close-up of his bloody face and naked body as he painfully drags himself away from the moving cart. The sound of a bell outside of the frame is followed by a low-angle shot of a white cow, filmed from Manuel's sub-jective perspective. As the camera focuses on its eyes, the cow seems both mysterious and almost human. The cow's eye becomes the threshold of the subconscious throughout the rest of the film. Medem uses Manuel's fade-in to the cow's eye as a transition between sequences, suggesting lapses of time and changes of space. Next, he reappears, 30 years later, in his family *caserío* (hamlet).

Still profoundly affected by the war 30 years later, Manuel never re-enters the masculine space that he had been traditionally and culturally assigned.

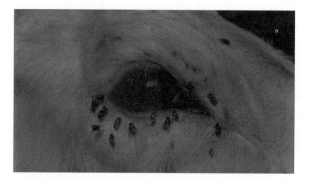

Figure 9.1   Cow's eyes (*Vacas*, 1992)

For the rest of the film, he will inhabit a different universe, one tied to madness, femininity, and marginal space. But above all, he is most intimately connected to La Txargorri, La Pupille, and La Blanca, the three generations of cows that become the witnesses to the feuds between neighbors and to the family's history. Through the peculiar relationship that Manuel establishes with the cows, his granddaughter Cristina, and his grandson Peru – Catalina and Ignacio's illegitimate son – the film narrates the secrets of the forest and the mysteries of nature that always seem to foreshadow what happens to the family. Manuel's renunciation of the patriarchal and masculine universe grants him access to the mysterious temporal and spatial interconnections of the mythical and natural world. The cow's eyes and the mysterious hole in the tree stump (the *agujero encendido* or burning hole of the third intertitle) are used as recurrent metaphors that code the grandfather's gaze, which is privileged by the director.

Scene 2   The challenge

The patriarch of the Irigibel family, Manuel, was a champion of the traditional Basque sport of splitting tree trunks with an ax (*aizkolari*), before he went to war and suffered a leg wound. His son, Ignacio, has followed in his footsteps, just as his neighbor, Juan Mendiluce, has carried on the same tradition in his own family. In this scene the rival neighbors compete for 700 reales in a traditional Euskadi (Basque) activity in which they must chop 10 tree trunks in half as quickly as possible. Both men compete not just for money, but also for the respect of the town, the women, and their family's honor.

The moment Ignacio makes the final chop to win the competition, a piece of wood goes flying through the air and falls directly into the apron of Manuel's younger sister, Catalina, a visual metaphor that suggests she will later become pregnant by Ignacio. Catalina and Ignacio, members of the rival families, are attracted to each other, much to the discontent of Ignacio's wife and Catalina's brother, who never approve of their love. When Ignacio wins the competition, Juan begins to go crazy, moved by his anger. Conversely, as the Mendiluce family begins to suffer from Juan's insanity, the Irigibel family begins to enjoy Ignacio's success as the *aizkolari* champion.

This scene is symbolic of much wider issues in *Vacas*. Firstly, the protagonism of *aizkolaris* points to the film's cultural specificity, its unique Basque universe. However, Medem simultaneously cautions against incestuous territories and the insularity of the valley. The two characters from the scene, Ignacio and Catalina, are precisely those that eventually manage to escape the constraints of their homeland, fleeing to America. Secondly, the scene clearly points to the gender expectations and limitations linked to women. Catalina is linked to pregnancy, reproduction, and natural cycles, all additionally symbolized in the film by the cows (*vacas*) of the title, the gaping hole in the tree stump (*el agujero encendido*), and the forest. Ignacio, on the other hand, embodies activity and motion, his ax inexorably tied to his masculinity.

This division is reinforced visually. The long sequence alternates shots of Juan with those of Ignacio, focusing on their sweating bodies, the strenuous movements of their arms, and their intense physical exertion. Most of the sequence is filmed in low-angle shots, directly from below, giving the men an imposing presence and making them appear larger than life. Meanwhile, the women are mere spectators. Catalina and Ignacio's wife are clearly competing for Ignacio, but solely through the jealous looks they exchange throughout the sequence. The sound is equally important. As Juan and Ignacio compete, the sound of the ax rapidly cutting through wood adds to the sense of awe, but also heightens the ominous and foreboding tension felt throughout the film. The minimalist yet dense atmosphere of the contest is suddenly interrupted when a piece of wood flies into the air, filmed with an abruptly tilted camera, and by the soaring music of Alberto Iglesias.

Also significant is the fact that the woodcutting contest and feud between the Irigibels and Mendiluces are framed by two civil wars: the Third Carlist

War and the Spanish Civil War. Thus, axes are replaced by guns; the rivalry between the two families transcends the boundaries of their neighboring farms and is expanded to a larger scale, that of the nation's tragic and fratricidal confrontations.

Scene 3   *Peru and Cristina*

Ignacio leaves his lawful family behind, taking Catalina and their illegitimate son Peru to America. After their departure, Ignacio's daughter Cristina and the grandfather Manuel continue to live almost suspended in time on the family estate, while Peru, as communicated through the letters and photos he sends, seems to live a very different and active life. Cristina and Peru correspond between Spain and America until the outbreak of the Spanish Civil War, when Peru returns as a war photographer for an American newspaper. Cristina stumbles upon Peru in the forest of their childhood. They have not seen each other in more than a decade, but the intensity of their connection has not faded. Carmelo Gómez, the same actor that plays the role of Cristina's father Ignacio in the film, plays the adult Peru, further intensifying the incestuous nature of Cristina and Peru's relationship.

Inseparable from then on, Cristina and Peru are soon caught in the battle between the villagers and the National army that has invaded the valley. In this scene they are in the dense forest, the natural and mysterious world so familiar to them from their childhood, but now disturbed by menacing gunshots, dying soldiers, and villagers' corpses. As Cristina and Peru wander through the forest trying to escape the battle and the valley, the same white cow that Manuel, their grandfather, had seen when he fled from the Third Carlist War in the first scene of the film reappears. However, this time the cow also appears with a horse whose rider has been killed. These two animals are charged with symbolism; the cow is tied to femininity and the earth, while the horse symbolizes masculinity and mobility. After the meeting of traditions symbolized by these two animals, the cow retreats passively. The horse then becomes the only means of escape from the war for Cristina and Peru, who commandeer it with the intention of taking refuge in France.

Cristina and Peru's reunion, his reincarnation in his father's body, and their "escape" from the valley of their childhood can be interpreted in multiple ways. On the one hand, Medem's gesture points to the endogamous limits of the local community. The reincarnation of characters points to the continuation of the family history, which seems destined to repeat itself. On the other hand, Peru is clearly tied to his grandfather Manuel and the cows, as he has chosen a camera over both his father and uncle's axes and guns. Peru and Cristina's decision to move to France and flee the endogamous claustrophobia of the valley can be seen as moving away from the space of myth to that of history. Yet again, while they ride away on the horse, leaving their native valley, the cows, and the forest behind, they pass by the *agujero encendido* (the burning hole) and are pulled into it with the film's final fade-to-black. We only hear their voices from the utter blackness of the hole:

CRISTINA: I have been waiting my whole life to love you.
PERU: I'm never going to let go of you.
CRISTINA: We're arriving now.

Thus, *Vacas* ends on an extremely ambiguous note, since Cristina's "We're arriving now" does not necessarily entail their arrival in France. Therefore, the move toward history and away from the endogamous valley, implied earlier in the scene, is undone through the move toward the black hole of the tree stump and the myth. With this ending, Medem leaves the spectator with questions about the nature of history and myth, culture and nature, the cycles of regeneration and continuation, and the restrictive notions of nationhood and Basque national identity.

Director (Life and Works)

Julio Medem (b. San Sebastián 1958)

Julio Medem Lafont was born in San Sebastián (Basque Country) on October 21, 1958. After spending part of his childhood in San Sebastián, he moved with his family to Madrid. Later he moved back to San Sebastián to study medicine and surgery at the Universdad del País Vasco. His medical and psychiatric training influenced his later creative interests, characterized by his inquiry into the human mind, his metaphysical and psychological queries, and the exploration of the unconscious and alternative realities. He is a filmmaker of intimate, inner landscapes.

Once back in San Sebastián, he made contact with the professional film world through his stint as a film critic for the daily newspaper *La Voz de Euskadi*, while training himself by making short films and writing scripts. He traveled to Madrid to pitch *Vacas*, but every producer he approached rejected the project. Medem returned to San Sebastián and began to work on *La ardilla roja*, a screenplay that was more industry-friendly. As he was working on the second film, he received a call from the recently established producer Sogetel, who decided to produce *Vacas*. The film was instantly acknowledged as a critical and box-office success and Medem began to be recognized as an inheritor of such uniquely Spanish perspectives as those of Luis Buñuel, Iván Zulueta, and Víctor Erice, for his formal and stylistic innovations and unique cinematic universe.

After his second feature film, *La ardilla roja* (1993), starring Emma Suárez and Nacho Novo, his professional life changed completely. On the recommendation of Stanley Kubrick (who was an admirer of Medem's work), Steven Spielberg asked Medem to direct *La máscara del Zorro*. However, after reading the screenplay, Medem turned down the offer and continued with his own projects in Spain. He made *Tierra* (1996), which he had to postpone numerous times as he waited for Antonio Banderas, his first choice to play the male lead, Ángel. Eventually he placed Carmelo Gómez, his lead actor in *Vacas*, in the role. In 1998 *Los amantes del círculo polar*, another success, confirmed his status as one of Spain's greatest cinematic assets. Medem became a controversial voice in contemporary Spanish cinema. He rejects the label of Basque filmmaker, while persistently addressing questions of political and national identity. As seen throughout his cinematic trajectory, and pointed out by Isabel Santaolalla, Medem progressively distanced himself from his homeland: "from the Basque-Navarran forests of *Vacas*, down to the Riojan countryside for *La ardilla roja*, to the Aragonese parched vineyards in *Tierra* and to the edge of the globe in *Los amantes del círculo polar*" ("Julio Medem's *Vacas* (1991): Historicizing the Forest," p. 312).

In 2001 Medem made *Lucia y el sexo*, his most widely distributed movie up to that point. In 2003, in the Sección de Especiales Zabaltegui of the San Sebastián International Film Festival, Medem premiered *La pelota vasca: la piel contra la piedra*, a polemical documentary about the political and social problems in Euskadi (Basque Country). With his latest film to date, *Caótica Ana* (2007), Medem returns to his characteristic examination of the complexities of human psychology.

2   *Caricies* (Ventura Pons, 1997)

Context and Critical Commentary

Production credits

Director: Ventura Pons
Production: Els Films de la Rambla
Cinematography: Jesús Escosa
Screenplay: Sergi Belbel; Ventura Pons (based on the play by Sergi Belbel)
Score: Carles Cases
Genre: Drama
Country: Spain
Runtime: 94 minutes

Cast

David Selvas	Young man
Laura Conejero	Young woman
Julieta Serrano	Elderly woman
Montserrat Salvador	Old woman
Agustín González	Old man
Näim Thomas	Kid
Sergi López	Man
Mercé Pons	Girl
Jordi Dauder	Elderly man
Roger Coma	Boy
Rosa Maria Sardà	Woman

Synopsis

Caricies is comprised of a cyclical chain of 11 vignettes, with the city of Barcelona as their postmodern urban backdrop. Each scene features two nameless characters that desperately try and then fail to communicate with each other, with all but one dialogue resulting in a violent action – be it physical or mental. A frenetic montage of Barcelona streets at night, taken from the perspective of the passenger seat in a speeding car, opens the film. This type of subjective shot links and is juxtaposed with each static, minimalist scene, highlighting the diversity of Pons's cinematic technique. Through a chain-linked narrative structure, each scene relates to the next through the reappearance of one of the characters from the previous vignette.

A violent encounter between an unhappily married couple starts the chain reaction, which continues with pairings of a daughter and mother, elderly former lesbian lovers, an estranged brother and sister, a beggar and a hooligan, a father and son, a man and his mistress, a father and daughter, an old man and a male prostitute, then the prostitute and his mother. The end of the film circles back around to link to the beginning, when the husband, bloody from the brutal beating he has just taken from his wife, rings the doorbell of his neighbor (the prostitute's mother) to ask for a cup of olive oil. She brings him in and tells him that she will treat him better than a mother. It is here that the only non-violent "caresses" of the ironically titled film occur, though they occur between two strangers. The characters' inability to communicate with each other or express themselves – be it because of general postmodern alienation, oppressive family structures, or the interrelation of the two – results in physical or verbal violence being their only form of expression. At the end of the film, the viewer has been exposed to people talking circles around each other, throwing punches and food, and spreading a violent form of "communication" that perhaps only stops once the family circle is broken.

Critical commentary

Caricies, filmed in 1997 and based on a play by contemporary Catalan playwright Sergi Belbel, is a visually, formally, and thematically ambitious film that received both critical and popular acclaim, despite the fact that it is heavily dialogue-based and filmed in a less accessible language, Catalan. The influences of Pons's theatrical background and the play from which the movie was adapted are most apparent in the dialogue and its delivery. Characters often seem to speak in code, and although each scene is technically a dialogue, the protagonists talk in the direction of the other rather than actually to each other. In this way, they carry on disjointed monologues that further confuse meaning and make communication that much more untenable. In one scene between a mother and daughter, language breaks down completely, bringing the dialogue to a close with: "Mother, you should have aborted" to which the mother responds, "I'll like it," in reference to the nursing home she is about to move in to.

Pons successfully creates a tone of disenchantment, anger, and claustrophobia by paring what one critic, Alex Gorina, called "cubist"[105] dialogue with tightly framed shots and cramped locations. The compact and claustrophobic framing of many scenes – squeezing two characters into a tight shot in which one person is in sharp focus, while the other becomes a blur that looms over the foreground; or eliminating one person from the frame altogether – succeeds in heightening what Nuria Bou and Xavier Perez call the "dramatic temperature" of the scene.[106] They suggest that the visually minimalist style allows the emotional content of the film to take center-stage.

When the characters are not arguing in physically constricted spaces, such as the bathroom, bedroom, or kitchen, they are on the unmistakably urban streets of Barcelona. The particularity and recognizability of Barcelona highlight what various critics have indicated is the unique mix of the peculiarity of place and culture with the universality of the film's main themes: the impossibility of communication, violence, disenchantment, familial dysfunction, and postmodern alienation.

Paul Julian Smith points out that "Belbel's and Pons's employment of an international idiom (minimalism) is curiously contaminated by localist vernacular (the former's idiosyncratic Catalan, the latter's unmistakable metropolis). . . . [I]t is precisely this particularity of reference that both promotes and restricts the cross-over potential of independent film" (Smith, *Contemporary Spanish Culture*, pp. 136–7). Given the relative national and international success of *Carícies* and his subsequent films, Ventura Pons seems to negotiate this paradox to his advantage.

Film Scenes: Close Readings

Scene 1   *Salad of love*

A study of the impossibility of communication, domestic violence, cruelty, and vulnerability, this first scene is the most physically brutal and encompasses many of the thematic issues that dominate the film. In general, the scene also presents the film's characteristic absurd combination of violent actions or intent that are disconnected from the conversation or dialogue being delivered, a technique that emphasizes the alienation and solitude from which these characters are suffering. The action starts with the young man returning home from work. He enters the apartment where the young woman is sitting on the couch, reading. They exchange no greetings. He goes to the window and looks out to a completely desolate street corner – which visually symbolizes the emptiness we soon learn he feels in the relationship. The alienated silence is broken when he tells her they no longer have anything to say to each other.

The scene progresses with quick shot/reverse-shot edits that tightly focus on their frustrated, angry voices as they argue. The shots are wide at first, and then get increasingly tighter as the argument gains speed – provoking a feeling of anxiety, dread, and claustrophobia in the spectator. As the argument escalates, he tries to interrupt her and she does not stop talking. The shot then widens again to encompass them both, as he begins to slap her brutally, knocking her to the ground and drawing blood. If verbal language has lost all meaning and function, it is through violence that they establish the only form of "communication."

The woman picks herself up, seemingly unperturbed. She unexpectedly changes her tone and cordially asks him what he would like for dinner, reflecting the normality that can coexist with domestic abuse. In the kitchen, the young woman mechanically catalogues the food they have, as she uses a paper towel to wipe the blood off of her face. The tension slowly begins to rise again as she enumerates the ingredients of a tropical salad, and boils to the surface as they each emphasize which dessert they will have. Then, just as unexpected as her numb reaction to being beaten, she launches a counter-attack. Using the salad bowl as a weapon, aided by her high-heeled shoes, she delivers an even more brutal beating than she received minutes earlier. The young woman's weapons, along with her insistence on asking him what food he prefers as she beats him, highlight the violence that lies just below the surface of domestic complacency and oppression.

The character that was at first the victim then quickly becomes the aggressor, a dynamic that we see repeatedly throughout the film. The inverisimilitude in which this scene eventually results characterizes the majority of the film. The absurd in conjunction with the very actorly or "cubist" dialogue creates the necessary distancing effect that enables the viewer to be viscerally affected by the scenes portrayed, while at the same time recognizing the very conscious treatise on violence and communication that the director and screenwriter are presenting.

Scene 2   Memory, tango, and rock

This scene, which takes place in a nursing home for elderly people, begins when two women (the elderly woman – mother of the young woman in the first scene – and the old woman) are finishing dinner. The ensuing dialogue quickly diverges from the expected dinner-table discussion. Instead of the anticipated dialogue, the scene actually manifests in two mono- logues through which each woman reveals the defining moments of her life. The elderly woman, a lover of rock-and-roll in her youth, narrates her frustration at having to abandon her great passion once she got pregnant. She recounts how, unwed and still living at home at the time of her pregnancy, she was locked in her house and forbidden to dance. Instead of expressing the normal maternal instincts the viewer expects to hear, the elderly woman describes the hatred she felt for the child that was growing in her womb. She describes the baby as a "monstrous creature" and a "stupid parasite." Furthermore, the elderly woman is dressed as if she were trapped in the era of rock-and-roll, or the time of her youth. Her fixation on the most traumatic moment of her life also seems to explain the difficulty she has relating to the world, herself, and her daughter.

The old woman then reveals the core of her identity, which, like the elderly woman's, is linked to the music that she loves: tango. As she recounts the moments when she danced, we learn of her distaste and even hatred for men; in tango, it is always the man that leads, denying her control and autonomy and reinforcing a dynamic of female submission and male dominance. Although she loved tango, she was prevented from dancing it because of the strict gender roles inherent in the dance.

In the final part of the scene, the two women kiss on a couch as other residents of the nursing home dance. They get up and start dancing with each other to the music, but then abruptly separate to dance alone. The camera alternately cuts to each woman, as the extra-diegetic music alternates between rock-and-roll and tango. The two bodies that at first seemed to unite through dance paradoxically end up experiencing extreme aliena- tion once again. This failed encounter culminates in the final dialogue, in which the elderly woman who loves rock expresses her happiness at having found the old woman again, implying that they had been either past lovers or friends. The old woman matter-of-factly responds, "I don't remember you."

Scene 3   Barcelona as perpetrator and confessor

This scene not only continues the exploration of the film's main themes, but also demonstrates how Barcelona is, as Pons has indicated, one of the main characters of the film. In the short montage preceding the scene, the homeless old man is filmed in accelerated time from the front, riding his shopping cart in the middle of the street as if it were a motorcycle. We also see the city from his point of view, with the sequence finally ending in a profile shot of him pushing his cart along a graffiti-covered wall. The frenetic representation of the city is therefore directly associated with a character, his movement, and his perspective, highlighting a subjective connection to the urban environment.

The camera pans down a wall graffitied with an image of Mick Jagger, and settles on a wide shot of the old man sleeping on the sidewalk in front of the wall. An adolescent punk, the kid, enters the frame and wakes up the old man to rob him. However, instead of attacking the old man, the kid ends up telling him a long story about his exploits on the streets, revolving around drug acquisition and delinquency. Pons uses a flashback with a grainy, security-camera quality to visually depict the story that the kid narrates, taking the viewer to various sites throughout the city, all of which harbor one self-destructive, violent act after another. The conversation strangely escalates once the kid begins talking about his dead brother, and then turns violent as the kid repeatedly kicks the old man and steals his prized wedding ring. The kid's unprovoked, schizophrenic rambling to a homeless man that he has just attempted to rob implies that he is seeking out anyone to express himself to. His interlocutor is a complete stranger, yet the recipient of his most intimate, personal confession. As in almost every scene in the film, the communication that almost seems within reach ultimately breaks down and leads to violence.

This scene also highlights the dispossession of identity that the nameless characters seem to suffer from, which is compounded by their failed attempts to actually articulate their fractured identities to someone. This scene aptly illustrates the desperate search for identity, and the self-destruction that results from these characters' failed attempts. For the kid, this self-violence seems to stem from his desire to locate an identity that has been usurped by the city streets and the legacy of his dead brother. The kid ends up releasing his frustration on the old homeless man, who pays a high price for listening to the kid's confession. Just as quickly as the kid appeared on the scene, he disappears into the middle of the night, into the arms of the hostile city.

Figure 9.2   Barcelona as perpetrator and confessor (*Carícies*, 1997)

Director (Life and Works)

Ventura Pons (b. Barcelona 1945)

Born in Barcelona in 1945, Ventura Pons entered the world of theater at the age of 20, and then in 1967 directed his first play, *Els diàlegs de Ruzante*. During one week in the summer of 1977 he filmed what would be the first of dozens of films, a documentary titled *Ocaña, retrat intermitent*, about José Ocaña, a cross-dressing Andalusian artist known for his performances on the famous Ramblas of Barcelona. The film was selected for the "Un certain regard" program at the Cannes Film Festival in 1978, where it was very well received. Beginning with this first film, Pons has maintained a balance between serious, studied films and riotous comedies, with both genres dealing with issues like homosexuality, prostitution, solitude, and family. Pons's next film, *El vicari d'Olot* (1981), is a satirical comedy that deals with Catholicism and sex.

In 1985 he started his own production company, Els Films de la Rambla, and in early 1986 he filmed *La rossa del bar*, with help on the screenplay from Raul Nuñez. It was the novel by Rafael Arnal and Trinitat Latorre that inspired Pons to make his next film, *¡Puta miseria!* (1989), a tragi-comedy set in Valencia. He followed that with another comedy, *Que t'hi juques, Mari Pili?* in 1990. On his next film, *Aquesta nit o mai* (1991), he worked with the same screenwriter, Joan Barbero. Two years later he released yet another comedy, *Rosita please*.

After more than a decade of making comedies, Ventura Pons felt the need to do a more personal project, so he filmed *El perquè de tot plegat* (1994), an adaptation of the book of the same title by Quim Monzo. It was a great success, winning among other awards the Premio Nacional de Cultura de la Generalitat Catalana. He then made *Actrius* (1996), an intimate character study of four fictional actresses, adapted from a play by Josep Maria Benet i Jornet. Continuing with adaptations of contemporary Catalan plays, Pons then released *Carícies*, based on a popular work by Sergi Belbel.

The next summer, in 1998, he continued with his stage-to-screen interpretations by asking Josep Maria Benet i Jornet for an adaptation of his work *Testamento*. The result is the critically acclaimed *Amic/Amat*, in which Pons deals with the themes of friendship, love, death, and the uncertainty of the future. In 1999 Ventura Pons received two homages to his work, the first at the Institute of Contemporary Arts (ICA) in London and the second in New York's Lincoln Center. Also during that summer he filmed *Morir (o no)*, a fable about life and death told through a passionate game of words.

During the summer of 2000 he filmed an adaptation of Lluís-Anton Baulenas's *Bones obres* called *Anita no perd el tren*, a bittersweet comedy starring such established Spanish film actors as Rosa Maria Sardà, Jose Coronado, and Maria Barranco. With a non-linear narrative structure, the film delves into one of Pons's favorite themes – human relationships and the need for affection and communication – through the life of Anita, a movie-ticket seller.

Pons's next film, *Food of Love* (2001), is based on the novel *The Page Turner* by David Leavitt. Filmed in both the US and Barcelona, this minimalist gay tragicomedy of manners was well received both nationally and internationally. His next film, *El Gran Gato* (2002), is a musical documentary that explores the life and works of famous Catalan composer, lyricist, and singer Javier Patricio "Gato" Pérez. Two years later, in 2004, Pons released *Amor idiota*, based on the Catalan novel *Amor d'idiota* by Lluís-Anton Baulenas. Pons's next film, *Animals ferits* (2005), is another literary adaptation, this time based on stories from *Animals tristos* by Jordi Puntí. In 2006 Pons released *La vida abismal*, which spans the life of a man who makes money gambling on his own life by playing Russian roulette.

Pons's most recent film to date is *Barcelona (un mapa)* (2007), based on the play of the same name by Lluïsa Cunillé. It features many of the renowned Spanish actors that have graced his previous films, including the versatile Rosa Maria Sardà, and touches on his signature themes of sexuality, solitude, and death. Ventura Pons is one of the most ambitious and prolific contemporary Spanish directors, with an impressive 19 films made throughout his 30-year career.

3   *Flores de otro mundo* (Icíar Bollaín, 1999)

Context and Critical Commentary

Production credits

Director: Icíar Bollaín
Production: Producciones La Iguana S.L.
Cinematography: Teo Delgado
Screenplay: Julio Llamazares
Score: Pascal Gaigne
Genre: Drama
Country: Spain
Runtime: 108 minutes

Cast

José Sancho	Carmelo
Lisette Mejía	Patricia
Luis Tosar	Damián
Marilyn Torres	Milady
Elena Irureta	Marirrosi
Rubén Ochandiano	Oscar
Chete Lera	Alfonso
Amparo Valle	Damián's mother

Synopsis

The film begins with the arrival of a bus full of women responding to a call placed by single men in the rural, depopulated town of Santa Eulalia looking for women interested in marriage. The town holds a welcome party, where the viewer is introduced to two of the film's main protagonists: Patricia, a Dominican woman searching for stability for herself and her children, in addition to fleeing from her situation as an undocumented immigrant in Madrid; and Marirrosi, an older nurse from Bilbao who is lonely now that her son has grown up and left home. Alfonso and Damián, the single men from Santa Eulalia who pair up with the women, share their solitude. The third protagonist we meet is Milady, a young Cuban woman whose boyfriend Carmelo brings her from Havana to live with him in the small Spanish town. The film depicts each woman's experience in the town, as they negotiate cultural and gender differences, misunderstandings, and prejudices. Eventually Milady escapes the town and her abusive boyfriend Carmelo with the help of a shy young man who has taken an interest in her. But once he has helped her leave, Milady abandons him as well and goes to the city on her own. Marirrosi returns to Bilbao, and Patricia stays married to Damián, making a home for herself and her children once she finally overcomes her mother-in-law's initial rejection.

Critical commentary

Flores de otro mundo is the second film that Icíar Bollaín directed after her successful directorial debut, *Hola, estás sola?*, which tells the story of two young girls who leave their dysfunctional homes and their tight family circles to take a journey of self-discovery. With *Flores de otro mundo*, Icíar Bollaín continued with her examination of female subjectivity, in this case, that of immigrant women. The plot, in which women answer a call by the single men of a rural town who are looking for wives, is based on a true story. In 1992, the depopulated Spanish town of Plan (the fictional Santa Eulalia in the film) made an official call through the media to women all over the country interested in meeting small-town men with intentions to marry. They organized a caravan of buses that descended on the town from various regions of Spain and Latin America, converging at a welcome party in the town square, an event that is depicted in the first scene of *Flores de otro mundo*.

   Flores de otro mundo is a story about three female protagonists – Marirrosi, Patricia, and Milady – who become involved with Alfonso, Damián, and Carmelo, the single men from Santa Eulalia. Through a triple narrative construction that focuses on the three main characters' experiences of acceptance and exclusion, Bollaín depicts the various ways "otherness" is constructed, as traditional Spanishness confronts that which is foreign; urban culture meets the rural lifestyle; and female self-determination faces off with traditional masculinity. The film reflects the immigrant existence by representing these women's internal doubts and preoccupations. Furthermore, by focusing on female subjectivity, the director questions traditional gender dynamics and expectations through her protagonists – women who rebel against submission and patriarchal dominance. This element is underlined further through the film's narrative; ultimately it is the women who control the rhythm of the narration and assert themselves as self-determining subjects: Marirrosi decides to leave Alfonso and return to the city; Milady abandons Carmelo; and Patricia, who has developed her own identity and role in the town on her own terms, decides to stay with Damián.

Bollaín explores questions of social and cultural anxieties, specifically in the rural sphere, brought about by immigration and hybridization, exploring both the socio-political and symbolic dimensions of the phenomenon. The film illustrates how Spain has become more culturally and racially diverse, but as a result, is also dealing with issues that arise from immigration, such as racism, the complexities of cultural integration, and the reversion to certain nationalistic tendencies that include the exaltation of Spanishness and intolerance toward immigrants. In addition, the film also focuses on economic recession, illustrating how it can be fertile ground for cultivating racism, xenophobia, intolerance, and political demagoguery. Therefore, Bollaín celebrates the possibilities of a more hybrid Spain while also examining the complexities that arise or are provoked by immigration in the "host" country.

Flores de otro mundo advocates for the rights of immigrant women in Spain, depicting their battle with exploitation and their struggle for assimilation. Furthermore, as Susan Martin-Márquez perceptively argues, the films of Icíar Bollaín capture the cultural turn in which "the treatment of notions of home, of displacement, and of cultural difference emerges from contemporary contexts of globalization rather than from the traumas of the post-Civil War period" ("A World of Difference in Home-Making: The Films of Icíar Bollaín," p. 257). *Flores de otro mundo*'s closing message, perhaps overtly optimistic and utopian, could be summarized through the lyrics of the song "Contamíname" ("Contaminate me"), which serves as a leitmotif throughout the film: "contamíname / mézclate conmigo / que bajo mi rama tendrás abrigo" ("contaminate me / mix with me / under my branch you have protection").

Film Scenes: Close Readings

Scene 1   The caravan of women

The film begins with the image of a bus full of women on its way to the town of Santa Eulalia, in response to a call from the town's single men in search of women interested in marriage. The opening shots of the landscape show an environment that is dry, empty, almost barren, and enveloped in silence. The sepia landscape resembles an old photograph, emphasizing the feeling of stagnancy, of a place that has been trapped in time. This muted landscape contrasts with the mix of intense colors and sounds inside the bus. Bollaín's first cut is from a tracking shot from the wide-open exterior to the lively interior of the bus, implying a change in perspective; inside the bus one of the women gets up from her seat to tell a joke to the rest of the women about deriving sexual pleasure from a gynecological exam. Laughter breaks out while the camera pans back over the still, sepia landscape outside the bus windows.

In the rural world that the bus is approaching, women have traditionally been subordinate to patriarchal power, and relegated to the reproductive and domestic role. The culturally sanctioned objectification of women, and the control over the female body that a gynecological exam can signify in certain contexts, is inverted with the humorous joke about the gynecologist. Female sexual pleasure is reclaimed through this linguistic re-appropriation, symbolizing the retaking of control over one's body and sexuality. This scene lends itself to multiple layers of interpretation. In addition to juxtaposing the biological and the cultural, nature and nurture, it also codes Spain as barren and the foreign as fertile. Moreover, Bollaín makes the spectator aware of other cultural stereotypes, such as Caribbean exaggerated sexuality juxtaposed with a supposed Castilian chastity. The scene also advocates female (and immigrant) agency as well as cultural and linguistic self-mastery, which are tied to the film's overall message of self-determination and independence. This is reinforced by the fact that all of its main female protagonists, Patricia, Marirrosi, and Milady, finally make their own decisions and take control of their own lives.

Scene 2   Contaminate me, mix with me . . .

In this scene the women step out of the bus and are greeted with the sounds of music in the small town's main plaza. The women are of diverse racial and social backgrounds, in contrast with the homogeneous Castilian town. The mayor gives a welcome speech, ending with "may you all meet each other and enjoy yourselves." This expression of acceptance of the foreigners is reinforced by the variety of international flags adorning the plaza. It is then that the music, a salsa, begins. These gestures are even more significant when examined in the context of rural Spain, stereotypically perceived as being culturally traditional and regressive. That the town is looking to "solve its problem of depopulation," as the mayor also indicates in his speech, by inviting foreigners signals a significant shift. The sound of a salsa rhythm filling the international-flag-adorned plaza also suggests to the viewer that Spain's apprehension of the foreign is changing. The camera frames the first contact and conversations between the townspeople and the recently arrived guests. It is at this moment that we hear the words of the song the band is playing: "Contamíname" ("Contaminate me").

"Contamíname" (Pedro Guerra), popularized at that time in Spain by the singer and actress Ana Belén, communicates to the viewer the film's central message: to reach a mutual understanding between the familiar and the foreign, "us" and "them," the indigenous and the immigrant. In the late-1990s Spain that the film depicts, the introduction of mass immigration, especially from Latin American countries, was the most significant and transformative socio-political phenomenon, with both positive and negative dimensions. Bollaín's film offers a case-study of

Figure 9.3   Contaminate me, mix with me . . . (*Flores de otro mundo*, 1999)

just a few of the many ways immigration is playing out in contemporary Spain; as the country benefits from increased cultural and racial diversity, it also suffers from resulting racism and problems of integration. The "contaminate me, mix with me" of the song, however, shows above all the supposed acceptance of the new multicultural composition of contemporary Spanish society. It exemplifies Bollaín's optimistic, yet somewhat utopian proposition.

Scene 3   Dance the pasodoble!

Carmelo has brought his young "girlfriend" Milady from Cuba to his small Spanish town. She installs herself in Carmelo's house, and spends her days dreaming of Cuba and her Italian boyfriend, as she dances to rhythms of salsa and *son*. But in this scene, Carmelo turns up the volume of the radio in the kitchen; he is listening to a pasodoble, a traditional Spanish partnered dance, and he wants Milady to dance it with him. A few days earlier, Carmelo had beaten Milady for going to the city. Milady, forbidden to listen to the music from her own country, is now forced to dance to a foreign rhythm. In this context, the pasodoble becomes a subjugating instrument that dominates and excludes the other.

Through Milady's subjective gaze, we see an indifferent Carmelo happily marking the pasodoble rhythm. Bollaín's filmic technique, the use of a subjective shot, both implicates the spectator in the narrative and makes it clear that Milady's point of view is being privileged in this scene. The viewer thus empathizes with the pain she feels at Carmelo's rejection of her own culture and personality. Carmelo, the prototype of the arrogant Spaniard, who tells his friends he brought Milady to Spain so "she could see a little bit of the world" but actually keeps her locked in his house, represents a provincialism that shows an intolerance for immigrants and their cultural difference. Carmelo imposes his music on Milady and forces her to dance to a rhythm she doesn't like; as he says, "with a couple of kids running around here, you won't have time to get bored." Through the exaltation and imposition of his own cultural values, in this case the traditional pasodoble, Carmelo rejects all that is different. Bollaín effectively conveys Milady's feeling of subjugation and repression to the spectator. This scene thus enables an affective identification with film's female protagonist.

Director (Life and Works)

Icíar Bollaín (b. Madrid 1967)

Born in Madrid in 1967, Bollaín is the daughter of a Basque businessman and a music professor. She made her film debut as the protagonist in Víctor Erice's *El Sur* (1983) at the age of 15, to favorable reviews. While continuing to act, Bollaín began studying fine arts at the Universidad Complutense de Madrid in 1985. The following year she was in the film *Las dos orillas*, under the direction of her uncle Juan Sebastián Bollaín. Later she worked on *Mientras haya luz* (1987) by Fernando Vega and one year later she appeared in José María Forqué's television series *Miguel Servet: sangre y cenizas*. While she was filming the television series, she co-starred with Miguel Molina in the film *Malaventura*, directed by Manuel Gutiérrez Aragón. Bollaín's career unfolded rapidly thereafter; she was in *Doblones de oro* (Andres Linares, 1991), and the following year she was the lead protagonist in *Sublet*, the debut film by woman director Chus Gutiérrez, which narrates the adventures of a Spanish woman in New York. Bollaín was also in the film *Un paraguas para tres* (Felipe Vega, 1991) and then in 1992 she acted in *Dime una mentira*, again under the direction of Juan Sebastián Bollaín. It was then that she began directing her own short films, of which *Los amigos del muerto* (1993) stands out. In 1994 she acted in a film by the well-known English director Ken Loach, *Tierra y libertad*, where she plays Maite, a militia member in the Spanish Civil War. The following year she made her first feature-length film, *Hola, estás sola?* co-written with Basque director Julio Medem. The film, a critical and popular success, stars the actresses Candela Peña and Silke, and tells the story of two young friends who abandon their home city of Valladolid to go on a journey of self-discovery.

Since 1991 Bollaín has been involved with the production company Producciones La Iguana S.L., which she took control of in 1994. Producciones La Iguana S.L. financed and produced her second film, *Flores de otro mundo*, which brought Bollaín considerable national and international attention. In 2000 she began acting again in the film *Leo*, directed by José Luis Borau, and the following year she was also in *La balsa de piedra*, directed by George Sluizer and based on the novel of the same name by José Saramago. The film depicts the fictional separation of France and the Iberian peninsula, which breaks away and floats in the direction of Latin America.

In 2003 Bollaín secured her place as an important contemporary Spanish director after the success of her film about domestic violence, *Te doy mis ojos*, which won numerous Goyas, including the award for Best Director. The most recent film she has directed to date is *Mataharis* (2007), about three women detectives who are better at investigating other people's lives than their own.

4   *The Secret Life of Words* (*La vida secreta de las palabras*) (Isabel Coixet, 2005)

Context and Critical Commentary

Production credits

Director: Isabel Coixet
Production: El Deseo with Mediapro (Esther García; Agustín Almodóvar; Jaume Roures)
Cinematography: Jean Claude Larrieu
Screenplay: Isabel Coixet
Score: Patrick Ghislain
Genre: Drama
Country: Spain
Runtime: 122 minutes

Cast

Sarah Polley	Hanna
Tim Robbins	Josef
Javier Cámara	Simon
Sverre Anker Ousdal	Dimitri
Eddie Marsan	Victor
Steven Mackintosch	Dr Sulitzer
Julie Christie	Inge
Daniel Mays	Martin
Dean Lennox Kelly	Liam
Danny Cunningham	Scott

Synopsis

Hanna, a lonely and partially deaf woman from the former Yugoslavia, is forced to take a two-week vacation from her monotonous work in a textile factory in Northern Ireland. Not knowing what to do with her free time, she takes a temporary job as nurse on an offshore oil rig, taking care of a man, Josef, who has been temporarily blinded and badly burned in an oil fire. Josef's blindness and his need for constant care make him particularly dependent on Hanna, linking them in a strange intimacy of secrets, truths, lies, humor, and pain, from which neither of the two will escape unchanged. Because of the gravity of his wounds, Josef is airlifted to a hospital. A few hours before they leave the oil rig, Hanna confesses the truth about her tormented past in the Balkan Wars, where she was raped and tortured with a group of women, of which she is one of the only survivors. Once the helicopter lands, Hanna leaves without saying anything to Josef and returns to her monotonous life in the textile factory. Josef is cured and recovers his eyesight, but he can't stop thinking about Hanna. He decides to look for her with the clues he gleaned from their conversations and a back-pack she left behind. He makes his way to Copenhagen, to a hospital for victims of war crimes, where he meets with Hanna's former psychologist. He manages to gets the address of the textile factory in Northern Ireland and waits there for Hanna to get off work. Hanna, who barely shows any emotion when she sees Josef, tries to run away, but he catches her and convinces her that he is in love with her. Presumably a few years later, we see Hanna at home with two children, waiting for Josef to return home.

Critical commentary

Coming from the world of audiovisual advertising, Isabel Coixet managed to become one of the most thriving film directors of her generation. *The Secret Life of Words* (*La vida secreta de las palabras*) is the Catalan director's fifth feature-length film, following *Demasiado viejo para morir joven* (1988), *Things I Never Told You* (*Cosas que nunca te dije*) (1996), *A los que aman* (1998), and *My Life Without Me* (*Mi vida sin mi*) (2003). Additionally, she has co-directed pieces in two collective films: *Paris je t'aime* (2006) and *Invisibles* (2007). Coixet's work fits into a new current of international film-makers, like Alejandro Iñarritu, who are experimenting with new methods of narration, untangling films from their national context to privilege the universal essence of the individual: emotions, feelings, and existential conflict. Coixet's films *Things I Never Told You*, *My Life Without Me*, and *The Secret Life of Words* are co-productions filmed in English, with international actors who are mostly located in Canada and the United States. As the director commented in an interview, "Each story, each screenplay, has its own language and habitat. It's difficult for me to imagine this story [*My Life Without Me*] in Spain. The rootlessness of North America, both in Canada and the United States, helps me believe the characters . . . It is a story that belongs to that world."[107]

In this way the path is cleared for thinking about national film from different perspectives. The director can operate from a place of absolute freedom, no longer tied to the traditional "isms": nationalism, localism, or feminism. Thus liberated to tell stories that venture beyond her own "isms," Coixet took on the task of directing *The Secret Life of Words*, about the pain and trauma of a survivor from the former Yugoslavia. The characters in this film find themselves desperately alone, stranded in the middle of an ocean where the only landscape is a boundless sea. The character of Hanna, the film's emotionally damaged protagonist, particularly speaks to the impossibility of forgetting the past, in spite of her attempts to monotonize her life. Nevertheless, the hope of finding love and friendship emerges in what seems like an impossible place, given the hostility of the environment: an offshore oil rig. As in all of her earlier films, Coixet is interested in demonstrating the process by which each character survives, in spite of themselves, moments of pain and trauma.

The Secret Life of Words could be considered Coixet's most somber film to date; the absence of land, the gray oil rig, the rain, the smoke, and the ocean seem necessary to unleash a true introspection in the characters. Paradoxically, it is this atmosphere that allows the emergence of friendship and love through the healing power of personal stories. More than narrating a story, this film provides an intense example of how one might survive, overcome, and live with a traumatic and painful past, even if it is impossible to completely forget. Coixet's film posits an irresolvable tension between communication and silence, between speaking and concealing. The words and stories that were hushed, repressed, or lost have their own secret life and an uncanny power to re-emerge.

Tim Robbins, the well-known American actor, and Canadian actress Sarah Polley, who starred in Coixet's earlier film *My Life Without Me*, were widely praised for their interpretations of the complex and damaged characters. *The Secret Life of Words* received significant recognition from the Spanish film industry in 2006, winning the Goyas for Best Director, Best Original Screenplay, Best Production, and Best Picture. It was the first time in Spanish film history that an English-language film, made outside of the country, was recognized as the best Spanish film.

Film Scenes: Close Readings

Scene 1   *The austere "comfort" of mundanity*

In this scene Hanna returns home from work and opens the door to reveal a strikingly austere apartment. A close-up shot follows her to the bathroom, where, from a tower of soap, she takes a fresh bar to replace one that has barely been used, suggesting a phobia of sorts. The camera cuts to another close-up of the inside of Hanna's nearly empty refrigerator, where we see two identical plates of food – lunch and dinner – carefully wrapped in plastic, emphasizing the monotony of Hanna's diet. The food she eats at home appears to be exactly the same as the lunch she ate in the textile factory where she works. The mechanical, repetitious gestures required by her job, depicted in the previous scene, are now replicated while she eats in what is supposed to be the comfort and intimacy of her home. After she finishes her austere supper, we see her robotically embroidering in a way that seems more therapeutic than enjoyable. Thus, the spectators intuit that Hanna's need to impose a perfect outer order and her tendency to repetition must counterbalance some intense inner turmoil.

Hanna is always seen alone, never communicating with her puzzled and eventually insulted co-workers. Hanna's only attempt to reach out is after her solitary dinner, when she picks up the phone and calls a woman who appears to know the origin of her traumatic silence. But even then Hanna is incapable of speaking; she hangs up the phone without uttering a word, leaving the person on the other end of the line to puzzle over the eerie sound of the dial tone. The only words spoken that evening are those of the mysterious, disembodied voice-over of a young girl, who announces, "She told me stories tonight. They were a bit scary," as the protagonist lies in bed with her eyes wide open.

The scene's intensity lies in the alternation of close-up shots that detail the protagonist's unusual and monotonous habits with medium

Figure 9.4   The austere "comfort" of mundanity (*The Secret Life of Words*, 2005)

shots revealing her barren apartment, effectively framing Hanna's solitude and discomfort in her own space. This intimate look at Hanna's peculiar existence leads the viewer to assume that this character's life is overly determined by her past.

Scene 2   *Hanna comes back to life*

Hanna's austere and monotonous life, depicted in the previous scene, is disrupted on the oil rig. A medium long shot shows Hanna feeding Josef, who clearly enjoys the food that the ship's gourmet Spanish chef has prepared. Josef asks Hanna about her favorite foods. Until this moment Hanna has barely spoken to her patient and has preferred to not get involved with him, to the point that she goes by a fictional name – Cora – that Josef invented for her. Josef begins listing his favorite foods, and Hanna responds that she only eats chicken, rice, and apples. A long shot then shows Hanna returning with Josef's half-finished tray of Italian food (gnocchi, veal, and mascarpone ice cream) to the kitchen. Unexpectedly she pauses on the stairs and at first she timidly picks at the foreign food. The camera then zooms in quickly on Hanna, as she voraciously devours Josef's leftovers, whose flavors seem to awaken something in the reserved nurse. The pleasure of eating, something that she hasn't allowed herself to enjoy for years, seems to bring her back to life. But together with the pleasure that the eating obviously brings, we also see Hanna's face, distorted in pain and close to tears. The close-up of her grimace is hard to interpret, and it provokes a great feeling of discomfort in the spectator, who intuits that Hanna's strange relationship to food stems from some deep, unresolved trauma. As the scene fades, Hanna's gesture – almost stabbing at the food with her fork – becomes both more frantic and more automated, highlighting the de-humanizing and internalized effects of the mechanized gestures already perceived at Hanna's workplace, the textile factory, as well as at her home.

Scene 3   Hanna's new life

The final scene of the film appears to inject a renewed sense of hope into the story. After learning about Hanna's brutal suffering, Josef decides to go looking for her. A wide shot shows the workers leaving the textile factory, and Josef standing there waiting. Hanna starts walking home when she hears Josef's voice calling her name. He gives her the backpack she had left behind in the helicopter the last time they saw each other, and confesses his love for her. Hanna tries to flee, but then eventually lets Josef embrace and kiss her.

The next take is another wide shot of Hanna drinking water in the kitchen, sitting at a small table in what we assume is her house. The apparent coziness of Hanna's new household is disturbed by the return of her automatism. Moments before, we saw her turn on the faucet, fill the glass, and mechanically drink water. The automatic gestures are followed by a close-up shot that lingers on her absent look. The disturbing emotional vacuity her facial expression communicates is reinforced by a voice-over that accompanies the scene. It is the same young girl's voice, the voice of trauma that opened the film, stating, "I left a long time ago. . . . [But] these cold and sunny winter mornings when she has the house to herself, then she feels strange and fragile and empty, and for a moment she doesn't know if all has been a dream. Then I come back to her." Hanna, although no longer isolated in the middle of an ocean, is still as solitary as she once was. However, the girl's voice-over also tells the viewer that Hanna now has two kids, and the camera pans toward the window, through which we can see the shadows of two children noisily coming in from the garden. This ambiguous ending points to Coixet's interest in exploring the human condition, where secret words hide in a consciousness that seems to be as impenetrable and as deep as an ocean.

Director (Life and Works)

Isabel Coixet (b. Barcelona 1962)

Isabel Coixet was born in 1962 in Barcelona, where she went on to study history at the Universidad de Barcelona. She then worked on the magazine *Fotogramas*, for which she interviewed a variety of national and international film personalities. This multifaceted filmmaker (she directs, writes, produces, and acts) is considered one of the key figures of contemporary Spanish film. She began her career filming commercials and then released her first feature-length film, *Demasiado viejo para morir joven* – a story about three aimless friends, Equis, Taxi, and Evax – in 1988. Coixet's talent was recognized, as she was nominated for a Goya for Best Director for her first film.

In 1996 she directed *Things I Never Told You* (*Cosas que nunca te dije*), her first movie filmed in English with Canadian and US actors. It tells the story of Ann, an employee in a photo shop who suffers from depression and attempts suicide. The film was nominated for a Goya for Best Adapted Screenplay. In 1998 Coixet filmed in Spanish again, releasing *A los que aman*, which narrates the passionate story of a doctor who falls in love with a woman who eventually dies after he is unable to cure her.

In 2003 Coixet went to Canada to make the film that has brought her the most critical and public attention to date: *My Life Without Me* (*Mi vida sin mi*), based on a short novel by writer Nanci Kincaid. In this film, Ann, a young, 23-year-old mother, lives a complicated and grim life in the suburbs of Vancouver. After a medical check-up, Ann learns that she has terminal cancer, but decides not to tell her family. She tape-records messages for her children to listen to on each of their birthdays when she is no longer living, and decides to have an affair for the first time. Ann also starts looking for a new wife for her husband. The film was nominated for three Goyas, and won the award for Best Adapted Screenplay. The film also won the Premio Nacional de Cine y Audiovisual de Cataluña, and the Premio Ojo Crítico for the sensibility of its cinematic language.

In 2005 Coixet continued making films in English and released her most internationally successful film, *The Secret Life of Words* (*La vida secreta de las palabras*). In 2006 Coixet contributed to the film *Paris, je t'aime*, directing the segment "Bastille." In 2007 she collaborated on a segment for the film *Invisibles*, titled "Cartas a Nora." At the time of writing, her film *Elegí* is in postproduction.

In addition to making films, Coixet has been closely tied to commercial, documentary, and video production. In 2000 she created the production company Miss Wasabi Films. Like other contemporary filmmakers, Isabel Coixet has bridged the gap between the artist and her public by creating an alter ego, Miss Wasabi, who blogs on her official web site, inaugurated in July of 2003.

Glossary of Film Terms

aerial shot: A camera shot filmed in an exterior location from far above the camera's object; from a bird's-eye view.

angle of framing: The position of the camera in relation to the object that it shows. There are multiple angles (looking up from below – a low angle, normal or straight on, and oblique or tilted), each defined by the field and the vertex of the take.

art-house film: In contrast to commercial films, art-house films are often low-budget, foreign-language, "independent," or non-mainstream films that are considered to have artistic, conceptual, or aesthetic merit and/or pretensions; mostly shown in specialized theaters.

audio bridge: A sound, dialogue, or sound effect in one scene that continues over into a new image or shot.

auteur (or auteur theory): Literally, the French word for "author." Used in film criticism, the term attributes personal vision, identifiable style, thematic aspects, and techniques of the film to its director (auteur), rather than to the collaborative efforts of all involved. It was introduced in the 1950s by Francois Truffaut and the editors of the celebrated French film journal *Cahiers du Cinéma*.

avant-garde film: A type of film, often experimental and abstract, that self-consciously emphasizes technique over substance and challenges conventional filmmaking.

black/dark comedy: A type of comedy film, first popular during the late 1950s and early 1960s, in which normally serious subjects are treated with macabre humor.

camera angle: The angle chosen from which to film a shot. The most common angles are looking up from below – a low angle, normal or straight on, and oblique or tilted, each defined by the field and the vertex of the take. Directly related to the angle of framing.

cinematic identification: The process through which the spectator personally identifies with a character's situation or experience.

cinematographer: The person expert in and responsible for filming or photographing moving images.

cinematography: Activities and elements related to the making and study of film. Specifically refers to the art and technique of film photography, the capture of images, and lighting effects.

close-up: A close-range view, particularly of a person or object, that details expression. The scale of the object is magnified, appears relatively large, and fills the entire frame. The most common close-ups are of a character's head from the neck up.

closure: The degree to which the film closes and ends the film's narrative.

continuity editing: The systematic procedure of editing cuts to preserve the continuity, space, and time of the action.

crane shot: A shot filmed from a mechanical apparatus called a crane. The crane moves the camera and the cinematographer (in some cases the director) in different directions. Crane shots usually provide an overhead view of a scene.

crosscutting: Alternating shots of two sequences in different locations, often occurring simultaneously.

cut (or cutting): An abrupt or sudden change in camera angle, location, placement, or time, from one shot to another; consists of a transition from one scene to another (a visual cut) or from one soundtrack to another (a sound cut).

depth of field: The depth of composition of a shot, comprised of several planes: foreground, middle-ground, and background. Depth of field specifically refers to the area, range of distance, or field (between the closest and farthest planes) in which the elements captured in a camera image appear in focus.

diegesis: A film's fictionalized, narrative world. Designates the action, occurrences, events, and spaces that constitute the film's story.

diegetic sound: Any kind of sound (voices, sound effects, background music, etc.) that manifests in, constitutes, and originates from the film's universe.

direct sound: Sound effects, conversations, music, or noise that are recorded simultaneously as the film is being shot.

dissolve: In the transition between takes, the superimposition of one image on another. The second image appears superimposed over the first, which slowly disappears.

dolly (shot): A moving shot taken from a camera that is mounted on a hydraulically powered wheeled camera platform (sometimes referred to as a truck or dolly), pushed on rails (special tracks) and moved smoothly and noiselessly during filming while the camera is running.

dubbing: Replacing the voice from an original dialogue with another. This process can serve to correct recording errors, but it mainly functions to present the dialogue in the spectator's native language.

editing: The technical and logistical composing of the film. This process joins shots and orders the film's story and its visual and sound elements.

ellipsis: A temporal jump or omission of a period of time in the film's narration. This jump is indicated either visually, or simply through character dialogue.

elliptical editing: Shot transitions that omit part of the events, causing an ellipsis in the plot and story.

establishing shot: Usually a long (wide-angle or full) shot, almost always the first in an edited sequence. Taken from a considerable distance, the shot establishes the spatial relations between the important figures, objects, and setting of the film's scene.

extra-diegetic sound: Sound, such as mood music or a narrator's commentary, represented as coming from a source outside the space of the narrative.

extreme close-up: A shot in which a small object (like a body part or an insect) occupies the entire frame.

fade-in: The gradual brightening of a dark screen, from complete black to full exposure, as an image or shot appears. Also refers to a gradual change in the intensity of sound.

fade-out; fade-to-black: The gradual darkening or disappearance of an image or scene. Also refers to a gradual change in the intensity of sound.

frame: A single image, the smallest single piece that makes up the film's structure. A series of frames juxtaposed and shown in rapid succession make up a motion (or moving) picture.

framing: The space demarcated by the edges or limits of the camera, which is used to select and compose the visual picture.

freeze (or freeze-frame): An optical printing effect in which a single frame image is identically repeated or replicated over several frames when projected; gives the illusion of a still photograph.

graphic match: A visual correlation between the compositional elements of two successive takes.

high-angle shot: A shot in which the subject or scene is filmed from above; contrast with the low-angle shot.

jump-cut: A cut in film editing that joins two similar shots together, causing a jump in continuity, camera position, or time.

long shot: A camera view of an object or character from a considerable distance so that it appears relatively small in the frame. A long shot often serves as an establishing shot.

long-take: A shot that continues longer than normal without an edit.

low-angle shot: A shot in which the subject is filmed directly from below, making the subject appear larger than life; contrast with the high-angle shot.

match on action: A cut between two shots of the same action taken from two different positions in order to achieve the illusion of simultaneity.

medium long shot: A shot in which a fairly large object (like a human body seen from the ground up) fills the entire screen.

medium shot: A shot between a close shot and a long shot. Roughly half of a fairly large object (like a human body from the waist or knees up) fills up the screen.

mise-en-scène: A term for referencing all of the elements placed in front of the camera to be photographed and included in the sequence: settings and props, lighting, costume, make-up, and the action of the characters.

montage: 1. A French word literally meaning "editing," "putting together," or "assembling shots." Refers to a filming technique, editing style, or form of movie collage consisting of a series of short shots or images that are rapidly connected into a coherent sequence to create a composite picture. 2. A particular style of editing developed by Russian filmmakers during the 1920s that emphasizes dynamic discontinuities, the relationship between takes, and the juxtaposition of images to create new visual concepts in the film.

offscreen sound: Simultaneous sound that comes from a source that is assumed to be within the space of the scene but in an area outside of the visible space of the screen. The classic example of this is the voice-over (which in some cases assumes the role of narration).

pan (or panning shot): An abbreviation of "panorama shot"; the horizontal scan, movement, rotation, or turning of the camera in one direction (to the right or left) around a fixed axis while filming.

reverse angle shot: A basic camera angle composed of a shot photographed from the opposite side of a subject to provide a different perspective. The alternating pattern between two characters' points of view is known as shot/reverse shot.

scene: Usually a shot (or series of shots) that together comprise a single, complete, and unified dramatic event, action, unit, or element of film narration.

screen direction: The direction in which actors or objects appear to be moving on the screen from the point of view of the camera or the audience. Common screen directions include "camera left" (movement to the left) or "camera right" (movement to the right); a neutral shot is a head-on shot of a subject with no evident screen direction; a jump-cut often indicates a change in screen direction. The screen direction creates the continuity of the shot.

slapstick (comedy): A boisterous form of comedy involving exaggerated physical violence (usually harmless), activities, or pantomime.

sound: The audio portion of a film including dialogue, music, and sound effects.

subjective point of view (POV): The viewer seeing or interpreting events from the point of view of either a character or the author. Also refers to a film in which the narrator has a limited point of view regarding the characters, events, action, or places.

telephoto shot: An image shot with an extremely long lens, making distant objects appear nearer and thus larger.

tracking shot: A smooth shot that follows a line horizontal to the ground, alongside the subject. On the screen this produces a mobile frame that moves through the cinematic space, relative to the scene or action: forward, backward, or side-to-side.

voice-over: Recorded dialogue, usually narration, that comes from an unseen, offscreen voice, character, or narrator that can be heard by the audience but not by the film characters themselves. Voice-over often conveys a character's thoughts.

wide-angle lens: A lens with a focal reach of at least 25 mm used with 16 mm film, or of 50 mm used with 35 mm film. This lens produces a wider, or more extended, view than a normal lens.

wide-angle shot: A shot taken with a lens that is able to take in a wider field of view to capture more of the scene's elements or objects than a regular or normal lens.

zoom: The movement of a lens of variable focal length that can be changed during the shot. It enables a smooth transition from wide-angle to telephoto shots without actually moving the camera.

Historical Chronology

1895   Queen María Cristina, widow of Alfonso XII, marks her tenth anniversary as regent of Spain until her son comes of age. The Cuban War of Independence begins. José Martí dies in an ambush returning from exile in New York.

The Partido Nacionalista Vasco (Basque Nationalist Party) is founded.

The first private exhibition of the cinematograph is held.

1896   In May, the first public exhibition of the cinematograph is held in Madrid. Other cities also present cinematic devices.

Alexander Promio, a Frenchman, films a variety of scenes of daily life in Spain with a Lumière camera. In October, Eduardo Jimeno Correas films *Salida de la misa de doce del Pilar de Zaragoza*, the first Spanish-made movie.

1897   Fructuós Gelabert, from Barcelona, films *Riña en un café*, the first Spanish fiction film.

1898   The Spanish–American war begins. The United States declares war on Spain and supports Cuba, which has been fighting for its independence for three years. The Spanish army is defeated in Santiago de Cuba. The Treaty of Paris is signed and Spain loses its last colonies: Cuba, Puerto Rico, the Philippines, and Guam. The Spanish government is in crisis.

Spanish intellectuals, such as writers Unamuno, Galdós, Pio Baroja, and the philosopher José Ortega y Gasset, call for the reformation of the country's institutions and structure. This movement is termed "Regeneracionismo" or "Regenerationism."

1900   The Ministry of Public Instruction is created to help decrease the illiteracy rate.

Picasso's blue period begins.

1901   The Lliga Regionalista (Regionalist League), a conservative Catalan nationalist political party, is created.

Anticlerical protests are held across Spain.

1902   María Cristina's reign ends and Alfonso XIII ascends to the throne.

1903   A law establishing obligatory Sunday rest is passed.

1904   Hispano-Suiza, the first automobile factory in Spain, is inaugurated.

Pio Baroja writes *La lucha por la vida*.

The Valencian film production company Films Cuesta is created.

Picasso's blue period ends.

1906   A protectionist tariff law is passed.

The Barcelonan film production company Hispano Films is founded.

1909   The "Semana Trágica" (Tragic Week) takes place in Barcelona. The union Solidaridad Obrera (Workers' Solidarity) calls a massive general strike, and rioting anarchists, Socialists, and Republicans destroy churches, monasteries, and Catholic welfare institutions. Anarchist Francisco Ferrer is executed. Alfonso XIII removes president Antonio Maura from power.

1910   Women are allowed to study in universities. The prestigious college and cultural institution the Residencia de Estudiantes in Madrid opens.

The anarcho-syndicalist labor union Confederación Nacional del Trabajo (CNT, or National Confederation of Labor) is created.

Arte y cinematografía, the first Spanish film magazine, is founded.

1912   The Morroco Protectorate is created.

A royal decree regulating film censorship is approved.

1913   Antonio Maura resigns as president of the conservative party and creates the "maurismo" movement.

Playwright Adriá Gual, influenced by the positions of Film d'Art, creates the Catalan production company Barcinógrafo.

1914   World War I begins. Spain declares itself neutral.

The Mancomunidad Catalana (unifying the four provinces of Catalonia into one region) is created, with Prat de la Riba as president.

Juan Ramón Jiménez publishes *Platero y yo*.

1915   Álvaro de Figueroa de Torres, Count Romanones, is appointed president.

The Mutua de Defensa Cinematográfica (Mutual Film Defense), the profession's corporate organization, is created.

Juan Solá and Alfred Montanals found the Barcelona production company Studio Films.

Benito Perojo develops the Patria Films production company.

1917   The Bolshevik Revolution takes place in Russia.

In Spain, the liberal Manuel García Prieto is named president. The Juntas de Defensa (Army Committees) are created, which lead to the end of García Prieto's liberal government just two months after his appointment. Conservative Eduardo Dato becomes the new president. A general revolutionary strike is held throughout the entire country. The strike ends after the government's decision to declare a state of war. The army controls the streets and impedes marches.

1918   World War I ends.

The Basque Country and Catalonia demand autonomy.

The production company Cantabria Cines is founded.

Count Romanones is appointed president again.

1919   There are massive strikes and a surge in anarchist activism in Barcelona.

A law establishing the eight-hour working day is passed.

Antonio Maura replaces Count Romanones as president. Two months later Maura resigns and Joaquin Sánchez Toca becomes the temporary president until conservative Manuel Allende Salazar is appointed.

Spain enters the League of Nations.

The Madrid production company Atlántida S.A.C.E. is founded.

1920   The conservative Eduardo Dato is named the new president. The Ministerio de Trabajo (Ministry of Labor) is created.

1921   The Partido Comunista de España (PCE, or Spanish Communist Party) is founded.

Syndicalists from Barcelona assassinate conservative president Eduardo Dato. Allende Salazar replaces him.

The Spanish army is defeated in Annual (Morocco). There is a political crisis.

1922   García Prieto, a liberal, leads the new government.

1923   Syndicalist Salvador Seguí is assassinated. General Miguel Primo de Rivera leads a coup and imposes single-party rule by the Unión Patriótica (Patriotic Union). King Alfonso XIII accepts the dictatorship.

1924   The Compañía Telefónica Nacional de España (Spanish National
       Telephone Company) is created. Radio Barcelona, the first radio
       station in the country, is inaugurated.

1926   Colonel Frances Macía attempts a coup against Primo de Rivera's
       dictatorship. The coup fails.
       The war with Morocco ends with the withdrawal of Spanish troops.

1928   The First Spanish Film Congress is held, motivated by the magazine
       La Pantalla. Antonio Machado's *Poesías completas*, Federico García
       Lorca's *Romancero Gitano*, and *Cántico* by Nicolás Guillén are
       published.
       Josemaría Escrivá de Balaguer founds Opus Dei.

1929   Students riot against the dictatorship. Various university pro-
       fessors resign and the universities in Madrid and Barcelona close.
       The World Exposition is held in Barcelona. Seville hosts the
       Iberoamericana Exposition.
       The film *Un chien andalou*, Luis Buñuel and Salvador Dalí's
       surrealist cinematic masterpiece, premiers.
       The first Spanish sound film, *El misterio de la Puerta del Sol* by
       Francisco Elías, is released.

1930   Miguel Primo de Rivera resigns and goes into exile in Paris. General
       Berenguer replaces him.
       The philosopher José Ortega y Gasset publishes *La rebelión de las
       masas*.

1931   The Republican parties win the election and proclaim the Second
       Spanish Republic, with Niceto Alcalá Zamora as president and
       Manuel Azaña as premier. King Alfonso XIII flees the country.
       A new constitution is approved.

1932   There is a failed coup attempt by General Sanjurjo.
       The Ley de Divorcio (Divorce Law) and the Estatuto de Autonomía
       de Cataluña y el País Vasco (Statute of Autonomy of Catalonia
       and the Basque Country) are approved.
       The Ley de Reforma Agraria (Law of Agrarian Reform) is estab-
       lished; the state appropriates properties owned by the Catholic
       church and by some aristocratic families.
       The Compañía de Jesús (Company of Jesus) is prohibited and the
       Jesuits go into exile.
       Valencia production company CIFESA (Compañía Industrial
       Film Española S.A.) is founded.

The Orphea movie studio is inaugurated in Barcelona.

The magazine *Nuestro cinema* is first published.

1933   José Antonio Primo de Rivera founds the Falange Española (Spanish Falange). Alejandro Lerroux's centre-right party wins elections and he becomes president of the Second Republic.

Women vote for the first time.

The CEA Studios are inaugurated in Madrid and ECESA Studios in Aranjuez.

1934   Lluís Companys, president of the Generalitat de Catalunya (Government of Catalonia), declares independence.

Miners' strikes are brutally repressed.

The minister of agriculture, industry, and commerce creates the Consejo de Cinematografía (Film Council). The Ballesteros studios are inaugurated in Spain.

1935   Lerroux steps down as president. General elections are called.

1936   The Frente Popular (Popular Front), made up of distinct groups with leftist tendencies, wins the elections. Manuel Azaña is elected president of the Republic.

On July 18 General Francisco Franco leads a military coup. The Civil War begins. In September Francisco Largo Caballero is named the new president. Francisco Franco is proclaimed *generalísimo de los ejércitos* (general in chief of the armed forces).

José Antonio Primo de Rivera is executed in Alicante Prison.

Laya Films, the film section of the Comissariat de Propaganda de la Generalitat de Catalunya (Propaganda Commissariat of the Government of Catalunya), is created.

The production company Filmófono is created, where Luis Buñuel begins his activity as screenwriter and producer.

In Salamanca the Nationalist Oficina de Prensa y Propaganda (Office of Press and Propaganda) is created.

The anarcho-syndicalist labor union CNT creates the production company SIE-Films to make propaganda documentaries and fiction films.

1938   The first Nationalist Francoist government is constituted in Burgos.

The Departamento Nacional de Cinematografía (National Department of Cinematography), overseen by the Dirección General de Propaganda (General Directorship of Propaganda), is created. It will go on to produce *Noticiario Español*.

The German–Spanish co-production company Hispano-Film Produktion makes four folkloric feature films.

1939   The Civil War ends. Franco is named *jefe del estado* (head of state) and *caudillo de España* (leader of Spain). The Ley de Responsabilidades Políticas (Law of Political Responsibilities) is passed, allowing for the repression of anyone opposed to the new regime. Food rationing begins. Hunger and economic crisis spread throughout the country.

World War II begins. Franco's government declares Spain neutral.

1940   An interview takes place between Franco and Hitler in Hendaya (France).

The magazine *Primer Plano* is first published.

1941   King Alfonso XIII dies in exile in Rome.

The Ministry of Industry and Commerce makes it obligatory to dub into Spanish all foreign language films shown in the country.

1942   Adultery is included in the penal code.

The Cortes Españolas (Spanish Courts), the parliament designated by the Franco government, are created.

The Comisión de Censura Cinematográfica (Commission of Cinematic Censorship) and the Comité Nacional de Censura (National Censorship Committee) are created.

The Noticiario Cinematográfico Español is set up to make Noticiarios y Documentales Cinematográficos (NO-DO, or News and Documentary Films), which all cinemas throughout the country are required to project before every film.

Raza premiers, directed by José Luis Sáenz de Heredia and based on a script by Jaime de Andrade, a pseudonym for Francisco Franco.

1945   World War II ends. The United Nations (UN) denies entry to Spain because it perceives the country as governed by a fascist dictatorship.

The Riera laboratories catch fire, destroying numerous films.

1946   The UN approves diplomatic sanctions against the Franco regime.

The first edition of the magazine *Fotogramas* is published.

1947   The Instituto de Investigaciones y Experiencias Cinematográficas (IIEC, or Institute for Cinematic Investigation and Experimentation) is created.

The Ley de Sucesión en la Jefatura del Estado Español (Law of Succession of the Head of the Spanish State) is passed by referendum.

1948   In Madrid the first Hispano-American film competition, Certamen Cinematográfico Hispanoamericano, is held, during which the Unión Cinematográfica Hispanoamericana (Hispano-American Film Union) is created.

1950   The Oficina Nacional Permanente de Vigilancia de Espectáculos (Permanent National Office of Film Vigilance) is established, with ties to the Catholic church.

1951   The Ministerio de Información y Turismo (Ministry of Information and Tourism) is created to oversee film-related policies. Colonel José María García Escudero is named general director of cinematography and theater, though he will resign the following year.

1952   Food rationing and the *cartilla de racionamiento* ("ration card") end. Spain enters UNESCO.
The Junta de Clasificación y Censura de Películas (Film Ratings and Censorship Board) is created.
García Escudero is forced to resign as general director of cinematography and theater for being too liberal.

1953   The Filmoteca Nacional (National Film Archive) is established.
The first Semana Internacional de Cine de San Sebastián (International Week of Film in San Sebastián) is celebrated.
The film *¡Bienvenido Mister Marshall!* by Luis García Berlanga premiers.

1954   First color edition of NO-DO appears.

1955   Spain enters the UN.
The Conversaciones de Salamanca (Salamanca Conversations) take place, organized by the Cine Club de la SEU (Film Club of the Union of University Students). During these "conversations" the need to renovate Spanish film is recognized.

1956   Students protest at the University of Madrid against the Franco regime.
Televisión Española (TVE, or Spanish Television) broadcasts for the first time.

1959   The radical Basque nationalist organization ETA (Euskadi Ta Askatasuna, or Euskadi and Liberty) is formed by those critical of the mainstream Basque nationalist party, the PNV (Partido Nacionalista Vasco), for its stance on Franco.
The Ley de Orden Público (Law of Public Order) is passed, prohibiting street demonstrations.

The Valle de los Caídos (Valley of the Fallen), a monument to the Francoist victims of the Civil War, is finished.

President Eisenhower visits Spain.

Samuel Bronston, US film producer, films his first in a series of lavish superproductions in the country.

Uniespaña, a service for the diffusion of Spanish film abroad, is established.

1960   The Asociación Sindical de Directores-Realizadores Españoles de Cinematografía (ASDREC, or Association of Spanish Filmmakers and Directors) demands the abolition of censorship.

1961   The magazines *Nuestro cine* and *Cinestudio* are published for the first time.

Viridiana, Buñuel's first film following the Civil War, wins the Palme d'Or at the Cannes Film Festival. Nevertheless, Spain prohibits the film from being shown in the country.

1962   The Conferencia de Munich (Munich Conference) is held, during which Spanish politicians demand a return to democracy.

The IIEC becomes the Escuela Oficial de Cinematografía (EOC, or Official School of Cinematography).

García Escudero is named general director of cinematography and theater for the second time.

TVE broadcasts 62 hours per week and sales of television sets increase. The first films of the New Spanish Cinema genre are made.

1963   The Primer Plan de Desarrollo Económico (First Economic Development Plan) is constructed.

Institutions and international governments protest the execution of the militant communist Julián Grimau.

1964   The Franco regime celebrates its anniversary with the motto "25 years of peace." The communist-leaning union Comisiones Obreras (Workers Commissions), organize nationally as a permanent, though still illegal, labor organization.

1965   A second television channel broadcasts for the first time in Spain. The number of television sets has reached more than one million.

1966   The Ley de Prensa e Imprenta (Law of the Press and Print), drafted by Manuel Fraga Iribarne, minister of information and tourism, is passed. Obligatory censorship is abolished and replaced by "voluntary consultation."

1967   The Ley Orgánica del Estado (Organic Law of the State) is passed, reaffirming the Franco regime. University strikes and demonstrations in opposition to Franco are held. Admiral Luis Carrero Blanco is named vice-president of the government.
The Ley de Libertad Religiosa (Law of Religious Freedom) is passed as well.
The first Jornadas de Escuelas de Cine (Film School Symposiums) are held in Sitges. The conference's findings are prohibited and the police break up the meeting.

1968   The Segundo Plan de Desarrollo, or Plan Marshall (Second Development Plan, or Marshall Plan), is drawn up, with investments from the United States.
ETA assassinates a police commissioner.
Basque filmmakers Néstor Barrenetxea and Fernando Larruquert make *Ama Lur*, the first feature film in Euskera, the Basque language.

1969   Police repression gets more severe and the regime declares a state of exception (the second degree of a state of emergency) in January, imposing a curfew and stationing soldiers in the streets. Basque priests accused of supporting ETA are incarcerated en masse.
Prince Juan Carlos de Borbón, grandson of Alfonso XIII, is named successor to the head of state. His father, Infante Don Juan of Spain, remains in exile in Portugal demanding Spain return to democracy.
The Matesa (Maquinaria Textil del Norte de España) scandal breaks. Important political figures and Opus Dei are involved in political and economic corruption, specifically of misusing public funds.

1970   In December the Burgos trial of ETA members provokes widespread protest in Spain and abroad. Street riots and strikes increase. A state of exception is declared until 1971. Because of the riots and student protests, universities are closed for several weeks.
ASDREC demands freedom of expression and an end to censorship.

1971   As a result of the Burgos trial, nine ETA members are pardoned; the rest are sentenced to death. International organizations and governments condemn the measure.
The Assemblea de Catalunya (Assembly of Catalonia), a unifying platform for opposition to the Franco regime, is created.

1972   The Tercer Plan de Desarrollo (Third Development Plan) is created.
The magazine *Dirigido por . . .* is published.

1973   In July, Admiral Carrero Blanco is named president of Spain. ETA assassinates him in Madrid in December.
TVE and Radio Nacional de España (RNE, or National Spanish Radio) incorporate into the Servicio Público Centralizado RadioTelevisión Española (RTVE, or Spanish Radio-Television Centralized Public Service).

1974   Carlos Arias Navarro is named president. Prince Juan Carlos provisionally stands in as head of state for Franco, who is gravely ill.
The Junta Democrática de España (Spanish Democratic Junta), comprised of distinct opposition parties, is established.
Felipe González is named secretary general of the Partido Socialista Obrero Español (PSOE, or Spanish Socialist Workers' Party), in a congress held in exile in Suresnes (France).
Fascists attack a movie theater in Barcelona that is playing the film *La prima Angélica* by Carlos Saura.

1975   Five ETA militants are executed. The international community condemns the regime. Riots and protests in the streets increase.
In November Francisco Franco dies, following months of agonizing illness.
Juan Carlos I is proclaimed king of Spain.
Eduardo Savolta publishes his novel *La verdad del caso Savolta*. New film rating regulations (Normas de Calificación Cinematográfica) are issued.

1976   A political reform law (Ley para Reforma Política) is approved by the Spanish legislature and then passed by referendum. A democratic system is established. Arias Navarro resigns the presidency. The king appoints Adolfo Suárez as president.
The first post-Franco Catalan-language film, *La ciutat cremada*, is released.
NO-DO is no longer required to be shown in movie theaters.
The EOC is closed.

1977   Seven labor lawyers and members of the Communist Party are assassinated on Atocha, a popular street in Madrid. The PCE is legalized.
In June the first democratic elections since 1936 are held. Adolfo Suárez and his Unión de Centro Democrático (UCD, or Central Democratic Union) win.
Political crimes prior to 1976 are pardoned. Exiles return.
The Generalitat de Catalunya is re-established and Joseph Tarradellas assumes the presidency once he returns from exile.

Censorship is abolished.

Luis Buñuel's *Viridiana* is finally shown in Spain, after being banned since 1961.

1978   The democratic constitution is approved. The constitutional monarchy is recognized as the basic form of government.

Formerly "regions," the nationalities within unified Spain are declared *comunidades autónomas* (autonomous communities).

The I Congreso Democrático del Cine Español (First Democratic Congress of Spanish Cinema) is held.

1979   The UCD wins the general elections, though the PSOE begins to gain political power.

Catalonia and the Basque Country approve by referendum their Estatutos de Autonomía (Statutes of Autonomy).

Pilar Miró's film *El crimen de Cuenca* is confiscated and prohibited for being considered offensive to the army and the Civil Guard.

1981   Adolfo Suárez steps down as president. Colonels Antonio Tejero and Jaime Miláns del Bosch stage a coup, which fails. Riots are suppressed the following day, and Leopoldo Calvo Sotelo is appointed president.

Divorce is legalized through the passing of the Ley de Divorcio (Divorce Law). Picasso's *Guernica* returns to Spain.

The law protecting national cinematic production is approved.

Pilar Miró's *El crimen de Cuenca* is finally shown.

1982   The PSOE wins the elections with an absolute majority. Felipe González is appointed president.

Pilar Miró is named *directora general de cinematografía* (director general of cinematography).

Spain enters NATO.

The "X" rating is created, along with pornographic movie theaters.

1983   TV3, the autonomous Catalan television channel, broadcasts for the first time. The Ley Miró (Miró Law), regarding the protection and subvention of national film production, is established.

The film *Volver a empezar* by José Luis Garci wins the Oscar for Best Foreign Language Film.

1985   The Ley de Extranjería (Law on the Rights and Freedoms of Foreigners in Spain) is passed to regulate immigration into Spain. The law will go on to be revised multiple times throughout contemporary Spanish history.

1986   Spain joins the European Community.

           The PSOE wins general elections again. Felipe González's presidential mandate is reinforced.

           Pilar Miró resigns as director general of cinematography. She is then named director general of RTVE.

           The Academia de las Artes y las Ciencias Cinematográficas (Academy of Cinema Arts and Sciences) is created.

1988   Pedro Almodóvar's *Mujeres al borde de un ataque de nervios* is released internationally.

           The Miró Law regarding film production subventions is revised.

1989   The PSOE wins general elections for the third time. Parliament approves the admittance of women into the army.

           Writer Camilo José Cela wins the Nobel Prize for Literature.

           Mujeres al borde de un ataque de nervios is nominated for the Oscar for Best Foreign Language Film.

1990   RTVE and the Instituto de Cinematografía y las Artes Audiovisuales (ICAA, or Institute for Cinema and the Audiovisual Arts) reach an agreement to support Spanish film production. An agreement is also reached between the ICAA and the Banco de Crédito Industrial (Industrial Credit Bank) about supporting national film production.

           A national plan for the promotion of the audiovisual industry is approved.

1991   Madrid hosts the Middle East Peace Conference.

           Theater and film actors hold a general strike against the government's subvention policies.

           The Instituto Cervantes (Cervantes Institute) is founded.

1992   The five-hundredth anniversary of the "discovery" of America is celebrated.

           The World Exposition begins in Seville.

           Barcelona hosts the Olympic Games.

           Madrid hosts the Iberoamerican Conference.

           Madrid is declared the European City of Culture.

1993   Elections are held early and the PSOE wins again, though not with an absolute majority. Widespread corruption leads to an economic and political crisis.

1994   The new Ley del Cine (Film Law) is passed, limiting subventions for new filmmakers and promoting subventions based on the marketability of films.

In Madrid ECAM, the Escuela de Cinematografía y del Audio-visual de la Comunidad de Madrid (Cinematography and Audiovisual School of Madrid) is founded, and in Barcelona the Escola Superior de Cinema i Audiovisuals de Catalunya (Film and Audiovisual College of Catalonia) is also founded, both at university level.

The film *Belle Epoque* by Fernando Trueba wins the Oscar for Best Foreign Language Film.

1995   Barcelona hosts the "100 Years of Spanish Cinema" conference.

1996   The conservative Partido Popular (PP, or Popular Party) wins general elections. José María Aznar becomes president.

The Film Law is reformed and official subventions are cut.

1997   Latin American, Central European, and African immigration grows progressively.

Ibermedia, an organization that promotes cinematic co-productions between Spain and Latin America, is created.

1998   Pedro Almodóvar wins the Medalla de Oro al Mérito from Bellas Artes.

2000   The PP wins general elections again and Aznar continues as president.

Along with the other countries in the European Union, Spain begins to use the euro as currency, taking the peseta out of circulation.

Almodóvar's film *Todo sobre mi madre* wins the Oscar for Best Foreign Language Film.

2003   President Aznar supports US president George W. Bush in the invasion of Iraq. Massive demonstrations are held in protest. Political crisis ensues.

2004   In March, Al Qaeda commits a terrorist attack in Madrid, kill-ing 191 people. Aznar's government initially accuses ETA of the attack. The country reacts with social mobilization in opposition to the government. Three days after the attack the PSOE wins the general elections. José Luis Rodríguez Zapatero becomes president. In June, Zapatero orders the withdrawal of all Spanish troops from Iraq.

2005   A law permitting same-sex marriage is passed.

Almodóvar rejects the Academia de las Artes y las Ciencias Cine-matográficas voting system and leaves the prestigious institution.

Alejandro Amenábar's film *Mar adentro* wins the Oscar for Best Foreign Language Film.

2006   In March, ETA declares a conditional ceasefire after negotiations with the Spanish government. The conservative PP opposes the talks, and massive demonstrations take place. On December 30, ETA detonates a bomb in Madrid's Barajas airport. Though ETA does not officially declare it, the government considers this to be the end of the ceasefire.

Isabel Coixet becomes the Spanish director to win the most Goya Awards with her film *The Secret Life of Words* (*La vida secreta de las palabras*), the first non-Spanish-language film to be considered a national production by the Academia de las Artes y las Ciencias Cinematográficas.

2007   ETA officially declares an end to the ceasefire. The president (*lehendakari*) of the Basque government, Juan José Ibarretxe, calls for a referendum to be held in 2008 on Basque independence. The Spanish government rejects the plan.

Spain becomes the European country with the highest percentage of immigrants (10 percent of its total population).

The Ley de la Memoria Histórica (Law of Historical Memory) is passed, annulling all judicial sentences and symbols of Francoism. Some conservative sectors oppose the measure.

The Valle de los Caidos officially becomes a monument dedicated to all victims of the Spanish Civil War.

2008   The PSOE wins the general elections and Zapatero begins his second term as president.

Notes

1 "Papier-mâché cinema" refers to larger-than-life historical epics and superproductions.

2 Throughout this book we have presented innovative readings on the periodization of Spanish film, while taking care to include Spain's canonical films. Therefore, the materials that we analyze remain accessible to readers and students outside of Spain.

3 Martin-Márquez takes as her point of departure a recent feminist cinema encyclopedia's erroneous claim that Spanish cinema lacks a "feminist voice." For a more detailed analysis see her *Feminist Discourse and Spanish Cinema: Sight Unseen.*

4 For example: *Spanish Cinema for Conversation*. Eds. Mary McVey Gill, Deana Smalley, and María-Paz Haro. Newburyport, MA: Focus Publishing, 2002; John H. Underwood's *Hablando de cine; Conversación avanzada*. Boston: McGraw-Hill, 2003; *Más allá de la pantalla: El mundo hispano a través del cine*. Eds. Fabiana Sacchi, Silvia Pessoa, and Luis Martín-Cabrera. Boston: Thomson Heinle, 2006.

5 Some of the journals include *Arte y cinematografía, El cine, Cinema variedades, Fotogramas*, and *Popular Film*. The Filmoteca Nacional in Madrid was only established in February 1953, providing an institutional framework for film preservation.

6 Marvin D'Lugo affirms that during the early twentieth century, Spain's attempts to modernize were not as successful as those of other developed countries, resulting in persistent cultural and political underdevelopment (*A Guide to the Cinema of Spain*, p. 1).

7 See Fernando García de Cortázar and José Manuel González Vesga's *Breve historia de España*, pp. 534–6.

8 On a theatrical stage, the proscenium arch is a large archway at or near the front of the stage, through which the audience views the play.

9 As Augusto Torres points out: "In June, 1929, *The Jazz Singer* is premiered in Madrid. It is the first American sound motion picture, but the film is first

seen without sound since there are no movie theaters equipped with sound projection. The American talkie *The Innocents of Paris* starring Maurice Chevalier is premiered in Barcelona that same year, but only the part sung is exhibited with sound and the rest of the picture is shown silently since it is in English" ("1896–1929," pp. 26–7).

10 Kinder specifically ties it to "Olga Preobranskaia's *Women of Liaison* (1927), also known as *The Village of Sin*, which was shown both in Spain and in Paris, where Florián Rey spent time in the 1920s" (*Blood Cinema*, p. 457).

11 The critical commentaries for *El ciego de aldea*, *Amor que mata*, and *Don Pedro el Cruel* are combined and given after the discussion of all three films, due to the short length of the silent films and because only one scene from each film is discussed.

12 We were unable to find cast information for *El ciego de aldea* (Ángel García Cardona, 1906) and *Don Pedro el Cruel* (Ricardo Baños, Albert Marro, 1911).

13 Birth and death information for Ángel García Cardona and Antonio Cuesta are not known.

14 Birth and death information for Albert Marro are not known.

15 "Calderonian" refers to Calderón de la Barca, the foremost Spanish dramatist of seventeenth-century Spanish Golden Age theater.

16 *Costumbrista* refers to a simplified or romanticized representation of local, everyday manners and customs.

17 There were several other avant-garde films in this period: Giménez Caballero's *Noticiero Cine Club* and *Esencia de la verbena* (1930); Ramón Gómez de la Serna's *El orador* (1929); Sabio Micón's *La historia de un duro* (1927); Nemesio M. Sobrevila's *Al Hollywood madrileño* (1927–8) and *El sexto sentido* (1929). For more information see Manuel Palacio's "Vanguardia." Palacio provides information about the avant-garde from its origins to contemporary films.

18 Regarding Buñuel's involvement and the ambiguity about the film and its screening, see Hammond's chapter "A Sixth Vesicular Joint, the Poison Sac" (pp. 52–68) in his *L'Âge d'or*. Also see Hammond, "Lost and Found: Buñuel, *L'Âge d'or* and Surrealism" (pp. 16, 17).

19 *L'Âge d'or* is "a sort of sound remake of *Un chien andalou*. There are even a few lines of dialogue 'left over' from *Un chien*." Furthermore, it is "a work of *bricolage* that grew from a twenty-minute short, a sort of remake of *Un chien andalou*, into a heterogeneous hour-long feature" (Hammond, "Lost and Found: Buñuel, *L'Âge d'or* and Surrealism," p. 15).

20 For more detailed discussion on the trauma of sound transition see Gubern's "El cine sonoro (1930–1939)."

21 See Gubern, "El cine sonoro (1930–1939)." Joinville was a powerful production facility owned by Paramount and geared toward mass-produced multilingual films. Eventually it became a dubbing studio for American-made films (Cook, *History of Narrative Film*, p. 374).

22   Six films were made in 1932; 17 in 1933; 21 in 1934; 37 in 1935; 28 in 1936. This data is taken from Gubern, "1930–1936 (II República)."

23   According to the Real Academia de la Lengua Española, an *españolada* is an "action, spectacle or literary work that exaggerates or falsifies the Spanish character." In film it refers to productions that represent Spanishness in a clichéd or stereotypical way, through the use of reified symbols like flamenco, bullfighting, gypsies, etc. It is usually associated with Spanish folkloric films from the 1930s and 1940s, but comedies from the 1950s, 1960s, and 1970s can also have *españolada* characteristics, sometimes with parodic overtones, as in Luis García Berlanga's 1952 masterpiece *¡Bienvenido Mister Marshall!*.

24   Luis Buñuel was Urgoiti's executive producer from 1935 to 1936.

25   For a detailed discussion of Rosario Pi see Susan Martin-Márquez's book *Feminist Discourse and Spanish Cinema: Sight Unseen*.

26   Buñuel's comment preceding the publication of the film's script in *La Révolution surréaliste* 12 (1929).

27   As we study two films by Buñuel here, the "Director (Life and Works)" section follows the discussion of the next film.

28   Remark on filming *Julio 1936*, cited in Gubern, "El cine sonoro (1930–1939)," p. 169. The original quotation comes from "La guerra civil a través de los objetivos cinematográficos," *Estampa*, February 20, 1937.

29   We have only translated the titles of certain films in the Spanish Civil War (1936–9) section, as they are illustrative of the ideological posture of the filmmakers.

30   See Ramón Sala and Rosa Alvarez Berciano, "1936–1939," and Gubern, "El cine sonoro (1930–1939)."

31   On the film's trajectory and its various versions after it left Spain see Ferrán Alberich, "*Sierra de Teruel*: una coproducción circunstancial."

32   See n. 23.

33   María A. Escudero writes that the concept of *hispanidad* incorporated conservative notions, "such as the defense of Catholicism, race, and the Spanish language, as well as the idea of the *Madre Patria*, and defended the need to develop closer ties with Latin American republics in order to create an ideal Hispanic Community. Franco's regime used the idea of *Hispanidad* during the Spanish Civil War, both as a way to give coherence and purpose to its own supporters and as a political-ideological weapon against the Republicans" ("Hispanist Democratic Thought versus Hispanist Thought of the Franco Era: A Comparative Analysis," p. 171).

34   Jo Labanyi argues that Martín Patino's use of "superimpositions and dissolves give[s] the human figure in the documentary footage a ghostly quality appropriate to this evocation of the 'disappeared'" (Labanyi, "History and Hauntology," p. 71).

35   *"Casticismo*: cultural nationalism. The adjective *castizo* means 'typically Spanish'; derived from *casta* ('caste'), the term has strong racial overtones, and was much abused in Francoist ideology. It first became widely used in the late-nineteenth century, at a time of growing nationalism, and was popularized by writers of the so-called 1898 Generation. Its association with the belief in the need for a strongly centralized nation-state has meant that, in practice, what is meant by the 'typically Spanish' is the Castilian" (Graham and Labanyi, *Glossary*, p. 420).

36   See n. 16.

37   The acronym NO-DO stands for Noticiarios y Documentales Cinematográficos (News and Documentary Films), which is also the name of the state film company that made the films. NO-DO had a monopoly on cinema news coverage and documentary making. Created in December of 1942, NO-DO was a compulsory official newsreel screened in all Spanish cinemas. It offered the regime's official interpretation of Spanish and world news and was an instrument of Francoist propaganda and disinformation. It remained compulsory until 1976, one year after General Franco's death.

38   A unit of Spanish volunteers that served in the German Army during World War II. Although Spain was officially neutral, Spaniards were allowed to volunteer for the German army on condition that they fought against Bolshevism on the Eastern Front. The Russians captured hundreds of Blue Division soldiers, who eventually returned to Spain on the *Semiramis*.

39   The "years of hunger" are those immediately following the end of the Civil War. This period was marked by a profound economic crisis in Spain due to the near-complete destruction of the country's industrial fabric and basic agricultural crops (wheat, potatoes, and corn). Furthermore, the majority of people were left homeless after bombs destroyed their houses during the war. International aid collapsed as most foreign countries were involved in World War II, also taking place during that time. As a result of these circumstances, hunger was endemic throughout the entire country. Epidemic illnesses multiplied and the state began to ration the few foods that were available. Food was dispersed to families that had a "ration card," which indicated the weekly amount of food each family could receive. For example, in Madrid in 1940, each family member was given no more than a quarter of a liter of oil, rice, and soap each week. The crisis and general hunger were lessening by the end of the 1940s. Ration cards were no longer used after 1952.

40   See n. 39.

41   The word *caudillo* translates literally as "chief" or "leader," but in Spain and Latin America often refers to a dictator; in other words, a self-proclaimed leader.

42   For a more detailed analysis see José Enrique Monterde, "El cine de la autarquía (1939–1950)."

43 "Cinematographic projection in any language other than Spanish is strictly prohibited, with the exception of that authorized by the National Syndicate of Spectacles, in agreement with the Ministry of Industry and Commerce, and given that the film in question has been previously dubbed. The dubbing should be completed in Spanish studios residing within the national territory by a Spanish national (April 23, 1941)" (Monterde, "El cine de la autarquía (1939–1950)," p. 192).

44 See nn. 33 and 35.

45 A reference to larger-than-life historical epics and superproductions.

46 José Antonio Primo de Rivera was shot in Alicante prison on November 20, 1936. After his death, Primo de Rivera became known as *el ausente* (the absent one).

47 *Raza* was scripted and released in the middle of World War II. It cost 1,600,000 pesetas (an extremely high amount for the period), and had 50 sets and 500 costumes.

48 Isabel the Catholic (1451–1504), ruler of all of the territories that comprised the Iberian peninsula, was considered Spain's first queen. She was born queen of Castile, and through her marriage to King Ferdinand was also the queen of Aragón. The different regions of the peninsula were unified under the power of the crown after the wars of the Reconquista (Reconquest), which ended in 1492 with the retaking of Granada. The Muslims and the Jews were either expelled or forced to convert to Christianity. Isabel created the Tribunal of the Inquisition in 1478 in order to expel reformist intentions from the Catholic church, whose power and influence grew under her reign. In 1492 she supported Christopher Columbus's expedition to the Indies, which resulted in the colonization of the "new" American continent for Spain. After her death in 1504, Isabel the Catholic's daughter Juana the Mad succeeded her.

49 See Inman Fox, "Spain as Castile: Nationalism and National Identity."

50 Teresa de Ávila (1515–82) was a mystic nun, founder of the religious order of the Discalced, or Barefoot, Carmelites, and a clerical reformer. The Catholic church sanctified her in 1622. She elaborated her theology in the books *Camino de perfección*, *Fundaciones*, *Las Moradas*, and *Castillo interior*, in which she explains the steps to reaching spiritual and mystical peace, and how to live a contemplative life based on poverty, meditation, and obedience. Santa Teresa and San Juan de la Cruz – a great Spanish mystic, poet and church reformer – represent the mystical current in peninsular literature.

51 La Sección Femenina was a social organ of the Falange founded in 1942 by José Antonio Primo de Rivera and presided over by his sister, Pilar Primo de Rivera. Its purpose was to organize the so-called Feminine Social Service, which required women to serve for a minimum of six months. The service consisted of taking care of the elderly and sick, and learning domestic chores.

52 However, the entry of López Rodó and the technocrats into the new cabinet was not altogether smooth and indeed was riddled with crisis. It was a period in which "public debt, inflation and balance of payments problems continued . . . being largely the legacy of autarky" (Preston, *Franco*, p. 670).

53 See J. L. García Delgado, "Estancamiento industrial e intervencionismo económico durante el primer franquismo."

54 The government assigned certain categories, similar to those of a rating system but tied to the amount of subsidy that a project received, to Spanish films.

55 See n. 23.

56 See Kathleen M. Vernon, "Culture and Cinema to 1975," and "Reading Hollywood in/and Spanish Cinema: From Trade Wars to Transculturation." Also see Marsha Kinder's chapter "The Ideological Reinscription of Neo-realist and Hollywood Conventions in Spanish Cinema of the 1950s" in her *Blood Cinema*.

57 For a detailed analysis of neorealism and its relation to Spanish cinema see Carlos F. Heredero's chapter "La larga sombra del neorrealismo" in his *Las huellas del tiempo: cine español 1951–61*.

58 The papers given at the Salamanca congress were published in the film magazine *Objetivo* 6 (June 1955).

59 Hollywood conventions were reinscribed in a similar hybrid manner. For detailed analysis see Marsha Kinder's chapter "The Ideological Reinscription of Neorealist and Hollywood Conventions in Spanish Cinema of the 1950s" in her *Blood Cinema*.

60 Some other examples of *cuplé* cinema include: *Aquellos tiempos de cuplé* (1958), *Miss Cuplé* (1959), *La violetera* (1958), *Mi último tango* (1960), *Pecado de amor* (1961), *La bella Lola* (1962), and *La reina del Chantecler* (1962).

61 See Jo Labanyi, "Race, Gender and Disavowal in Spanish Cinema of the Early Franco Period: The Missionary Film and the Folkloric Musical."

62 For more information on Opus Dei, see chapter 6.

63 The Ley de Prensa e Imprenta (Law of the Press and Print) was passed in 1966, while the Ley de Libertad Religiosa (Law of Religious Freedom) and the Ley Orgánica del Estado (Organic Law of the State) were passed in 1967.

64 The original quotation is from José María García Escudero's book *La primera apertura: diario de un director general*.

65 José María Nunes filmed *Noches de vino tinto* (1966) and Gonzalo Suárez made *Ditirambo* (1967). Jorge Grau worked in both Madrid and Barcelona.

66 Bronston Studios was linked to the Francoist establishment. Samuel Bronston was honored with the Cruz de Isabel la Católica and in return produced the propagandistic documentary *El valle de la paz* in 1961, a film that catered to a Francoist rewriting of Spain's past.

67 In August 1969 a great financial scandal hit Spain, which ultimately led to a Cabinet crisis in October of the same year. It concerned an important

industrial conglomerate: Maquinaria textil del norte (Matesa), which folded when it was alleged that some members of the conservative Catholic group Opus Dei were involved in the misappropriation of government funds.

68 Pedro Almodóvar takes up this same issue decades later in *¿Qué he hecho yo para merecer esto!*, which depicts how for many families that immigrated to the large cities, modernity failed to deliver on its promises.

69 In "Loss and Recuperation in the *Garden of Delights*" Katherine Kovacs analyzes these five narrative planes, which Saura himself outlined in his shooting-script. The complexity of the script was necessitated in part by the strict politics of censorship in the period during which the film was made. The staged past centers on significant early events from Antonio's life, re-enacted to trigger his memory. The present continuum is an attempt at reinsertion of the amnesiac Antonio into the family and work place. The evoked past consists of brief glimpses into what little Antonio does remember; the oneiric world is a series of Antonio's fantasies, mostly violent in nature; and the future plane is Antonio's attempt to assume agency over his own life and destiny.

70 See n. 8.

71 The Socialist Party established the Goya Awards in 1987 as part of their policy of supporting national film. Since then, the Goyas have grown in prestige and importance each year. In recent years the awards have been extended to Latin American film.

72 In Spain, the *maquis* were clandestine soldiers or guerrilla fighters who fought against the Franco regime, hiding in the mountainous zones of France (*maquis* is originally the French term for a scrubland vegetation on the lower slopes of mountains in the Mediterranean area).

73 Originally there were two independent projects, *No se os puede dejar solos* and *Atado y bien atado* (1979–81), which were later combined under the title *Después de. . . .*

74 See n. 3. Another important text is Kathleen M. Vernon's "Screening Room: Spanish Women Filmmakers View the Transition," which centers on Cecilia Bartolomé, Pilar Miró, and Josefina Molina.

75 See n. 71.

76 Riambau analyzes Imanol Uribe's *El rey pasmado* (1991) as a prototype of this cinematic trend.

77 Previously, in 1979, during the period of the transition, Aranda had adapted another Marsé novel, *La muchacha de las bragas de oro*.

78 Starting with the same historical figure, Lope de Aguirre, Werner Herzog filmed *Aguirre, the Wrath of God* in 1972.

79 Borau cleverly cast an icon of 1930s cinema, Imperio Argentina, as Elvira's nanny, and Alfredo Landa, an icon of 1970s cinema, as Elvira's childhood friend Teo, thus reinforcing Elvira's struggles with personal/collective history

and memory through another layer, that of Spain's cinematographic history. For a more detailed discussion see Marvin D'Lugo, "Heterogeneity and Spanish Cinema of the Eighties."

80   The Ministry of Culture subsidized Almodóvar's sixth film, *La ley del deseo* (1987), despite its controversial and explicit gay and transsexual themes, which were not the type of cinema the ministry generally supported. However, as Marvin D'Lugo emphasizes, official support for Almodóvar's projects "was itself part of an agenda to help undo the legacy of the Franco years by supporting those artistic efforts that might contribute both within Spain and abroad to the climate of greater toleration of cultural and social diversity" (*A Guide to the Cinema of Spain*, p. 26).

81   There is a great deal of critical disagreement around *la movida*. Vernon and Morris see 1982, the year in which the Socialists came to power, as marking *la movida*'s "new, more self-conscious phase" ("Introduction: Pedro Almodóvar, Postmodern Auteur," p. 8) and Bradley Epps reminds us that from the very beginning *la movida* and Almodóvar were tied to a "marvel of marketing" because "constraining as it is, capitalism is also the condition of possibility of the style-conscious, fashion-oriented, trend-setting vision of Almodóvar" ("Figuring Hysteria: Disorder and Desire in Three Films of Pedro Almodóvar," p. 102). Epps also emphasizes that this does not "deny the critical power of Almodóvar's work but acknowledge[s] the commercial power of cultural critique itself." Eduardo Subirats, a critic of *la movida*, claims that it is a "regressive social and cultural movement . . . a shameless display of intellectual incompetence and meaningless eloquence . . . an intellectual and aesthetic revolution that didn't change anything, and a big, self-gratifying, putrid, and empty party" ("De la transición al espectáculo," pp. 21, 22, 23).

82   For a detailed discussion of *¿Qué he hecho yo para merecer esto!* as Almodóvar's crossover film, see Paul Julian Smith's *Desire Unlimited* (p. 61).

83   *Ultras*, short for *ultraderecha* or "ultra-right," is the term used in Spain to describe individuals or groups that support at least one right-wing political position, expressed in an extreme manner through their political, religious, or social behavior. They are usually characterized by their extreme and at times violent defense of conservative or Nationalist ideologies.

84   It is important to note that Almodóvar returns to this theme in a less frivolous way in his films *¿Qué he hecho yo para merecer esto!* (1984) and *Volver* (2006).

85   It is interesting to note that the exteriors that introduce this scene are as claustrophobic as Gloria's cramped apartment. As she and Juani walk toward the shops, they are overwhelmed by the background: a depressing block of working-class housing that saturates the frame and the characters.

86   See Nuria Vidal, *El cine de Pedro Almodóvar*, p. 145.

87 Paul Julian Smith emphasizes that the "evidence of foreign popularity changed the perception of Almodóvar at home, lending credence to his claim to represent post-Franco Spain to the outside world" (*Desire Unlimited*, p. 102).

88 For a discussion on the blue period see Paul Julian Smith, *Contemporary Spanish Culture: TV, Fashion, Art and Film.*

89 Screen quotas protect Spanish/EU films against the domination of foreign films (mostly US) and as Peter Besas explains, the dubbing licenses "require any distributor releasing Spanish dubbed films to obtain a license. These licenses can only be obtained by releasing Spanish (and now EU) films" ("The Financial Structure of Spanish Cinema," p. 249). Besas adds, "for decades now these two measures have been a constant source of friction between local producers and the government on one side, and the American majors and local exhibitors on the other" (p. 248).

90 For a detailed discussion of this phenomena see Jaime Pena, "Cine español de los noventa: hoja de reclamaciones." Pena claims that members of this generation were seen as bastards of 1980s postmodernism because of their "de-ideologized and apolitical cinema" (p. 48).

91 Such as Spielberg's *Saving Private Ryan*, Michael Bay's *Armageddon*, or Roland Emmerich's *Godzilla*. It was the first time that Spanish film was able to compete on the market. *Torrente* was financed by a well-known producer, Andrés Vicente Gómez, and his production company Rocabruno (at a cost of 300 million pesetas).

92 See n. 23.

93 Sánchez-Biosca centers his analysis on two films, Manuel Gómez Pereira's *El amor perjudica seriamente la salud* (1997) and Alex de la Iglesia's *Muertos de risa* (1999).

94 While these films and their directors bring Spain's social problems to the forefront, they have nevertheless been attacked for simply creating a "reality in parentheses" (*la realidad entre paréntesis*). For a critical reading of the "social realism" phenomenon see Angel Quintana's "El cine como realidad y el mundo como representación: algunos síntomas de los noventa."

95 As Pedro Almodóvar has clearly stated: "If there is one thing that characterizes the end of the twentieth century it is precisely the rupture of the traditional family. Now you can form families with other members, other ties, other biological relations, and they should be respected just as they are. What's important is that the components love each other" (Strauss, *Conversaciones con Pedro Almodóvar*, p. 162).

96 Most of the critical work on immigrant cinema tends to center only on canonized films. For a more comprehensive and complex reading see Alberto Elena's "Representaciones de la inmigración en el cine español: la producción comercial y sus márgenes." Elena centers his discussion on various recent

documentaries as well as the emergence of films directed by immigrants themselves. Also see Isabel Santaolalla's and Isolina Ballesteros's work on the representation of immigration in contemporary Spanish cinema (Santaolalla, *Los "otros": etnicidad y "raza" en el cine español contemporáneo* and "Ethnic and Racial Configurations in Contemporary Spanish Culture;" Ballesteros, "Foreign and Racial Masculinities in Spanish Immigration Film," "Embracing the Other: The Feminization of Spanish 'Immigration Cinema'," and "Screening African Immigration to Spain: *Las cartas de Alou* and *Bwana*").

97   See Josep Lluís Fecé, "La excepción y la norma: reflexiones sobre la españolidad de nuestro cine reciente."

98   See n. 3.

99   Further detailed analysis can be found in María Camí Vela's *Mujeres detrás de la cámara: entrevistas con cineastas españolas de la década de los noventa*; Carlos Heredero's *La mitad del cielo: directoras españolas de los años 90*; and the already cited Susan Martin-Márquez, *Feminist Discourse and Spanish Cinema: Sight Unseen*.

100 For this humanist turn in Almódovar see Susan Martin-Márquez's "Pedro Almodóvar's Maternal Transplants: From *Matador* to *All About My Mother*" and Paul Julian Smith's *Desire Unlimited*, especially the chapter on *Todo sobre mi madre*.

101 For more details on the Escuela de Barcelona, see chapter 6.

102 As Paul Julian Smith points out "in Catalonia, a nation without a state . . . 'independence' necessarily goes beyond the aesthetic and economic to embrace the political dimension" (*Contemporary Spanish Culture*, p. 118).

103 The Carlist Wars were civil wars that took place in Spain during the nineteenth century, between 1833, when the first confrontation occurred, and 1876, when the Third Carlist War ended. The term "Carlism" arose because its adherents believed the successor to Fernando VII should be his brother, Carlos de Borbón, not his daughter, Isabel (the future Queen Isabel II). In addition to this dynastic conflict, the Carlists defended the role of the Catholic church in institutions and supported a protectionist, not liberal, economy. Later, given the Carlists' monarchic nature, they opposed the Second Republic, aligning themselves with Franco during the Civil War. The Carlist soldiers, called *requetes*, fought specifically in the rural areas and the mountains of the Basque Country and Navarra. In 1937 they were incorporated into the Falange, but after the monarchy was not incorporated into the government at the end of the Civil War, and the *fueros* or regional laws and rights, along with the federal system, were not respected, the Carlists ultimately opposed Franco.

104 For a detailed discussion of Medem's cinema and its relation to history and mythology see Isabel Santaolalla's "Julio Medem's *Vacas* (1991): Historicizing the Forest."

105   Alex Gorina, "Las Carícies de Ventura Pons." Ventura Pons. www.venturapons. com/filmografia/cariciasp.html, accessed September 9, 2007.

106   Nuria Bou and Xavier Perez, "Carícies." Ventura Pons. www.venturapons.com/ filmografia/cariciasp.html, accessed September 9, 2007.

107   Speaking about her film *My Life Without Me* in an interview with the Spanish website *terra*: www.terra.es/cine/actualidad/articulo.cfm?ID=4838, accessed October 29, 2007.

Bibliography

Alberich, Ferran. "*Raza*: cine y propaganda en la inmediata posguerra." *Archivos de la Filmoteca* 27 (1997): 50–61.

Alberich, Ferran. "*Sierra de Teruel*: una coproducción circunstancial." *Actas del VII Congreso de la A.E.H.C. Madrid, Academia de las Artes y Ciencias Cinematográficas de España* (1999): 43–57.

Almodóvar, Pedro. *Patty Diphusa y otros textos*. Barcelona: Editorial Anagrama, 1991.

Ballesteros, Isolina. "Embracing the Other: The Feminization of Spanish 'Immigration Cinema'." *Studies in Hispanic Cinemas* 2.1 (2005): 3–14.

Ballesteros, Isolina. "Foreign and Racial Masculinities in Spanish Immigration Film." *Studies in Hispanic Cinemas* 3.3 (2006): 169–85.

Ballesteros, Isolina. "Mujer y nación en el cine español de posguerra: los años 40." *Arizona Journal of Hispanic Cultural Studies* 3 (1999): 51–70.

Ballesteros, Isolina. "Screening African Immigration to Spain: *Las cartas de Alou* and *Bwana*." *Chasqui: revista de literatura latinoamericana* special issue 2: *Bridging Continents: Cinematic and Literary Representations of Spanish and Latin American Themes* (2005): 48–61. Eds. Nora Glickman and Alejandro Varderi.

Benet, Vicente José. "La nueva memoria: imágenes de la memoria en el cine español de la transición." www.hum.gu.se/ibero/publikationer/ anales3.4/pdf_artiklar/ benet.pdf, accessed September 10, 2005.

Besas, Peter. *Behind the Spanish Lens: Spanish Cinema Under Fascism and Democracy*. Denver, CO: Arden Press, 1985.

Besas, Peter. "The Financial Structure of Spanish Cinema." *Refiguring Spain: Cinema/Media/Representation*. Ed. Marsha Kinder. Durham, NC: Duke University Press, 1997, pp. 241–59.

Bou, Nuria and Xavier Perez. "Carícies." Ventura Pons. www.venturapons.com/ filmografia/cariciasp.html, accessed September 9, 2007.

Boyd, Carolyn. "History, Politics, and Culture 1936–1965." *The Cambridge Companion to Modern Spanish Culture*. Ed. David T. Gies. Cambridge: Cambridge University Press, 1999, pp. 86–103.

Buñuel, Luis. *Viridiana*. Mexico D.F.: Ediciones Era, 1971.

Camí Vela, María. *Mujeres detrás de la cámara: entrevistas con cineastas españolas de la década de los noventa*. Madrid: Ocho y Medio, 2001.

Cook, David. *A History of Narrative Film*. New York: Norton, 1981.

D'Lugo, Marvin. *The Films of Carlos Saura: The Practice of Seeing*. Princeton, NJ: Princeton University Press, 1991.

D'Lugo, Marvin. *A Guide to the Cinema of Spain*. Westport, CT: Greenwood Press, 1997.

D'Lugo, Marvin. "Heterogeneity and Spanish Cinema of the Eighties." *España contemporánea* 5.1 (1992): 55–66.

Drummond, Phillip. "Textual Space in *Un chien andalou*: Donkeys and Pianos." *Screen* 18.3 (1977): 55–119.

Elena, Alberto. "Representaciones de la inmigración en el cine español: la producción comercial y sus márgenes." *Archivos de la Filmoteca* 49 (2005): 55–65.

Epps, Bradley S. "Figuring Hysteria: Disorder and Desire in Three Films of Pedro Almodóvar." *Post-Franco, Postmodern: The Films of Pedro Almodóvar*. Eds. Kathleen Vernon and Barbara Morris. Westport, CT: Greenwood Press, 1995, pp. 99–124.

Escudero, María A. "Hispanist Democratic Thought versus Hispanist Thought of the Franco Era: A Comparative Analysis." *Bridging the Atlantic: Toward a Reassessment of Iberian and Latin American Cultural Ties*. Ed. Marina Perez de Mendiola. New York: SUNY Press, 1996, pp. 169–86.

Fernández Valentí, Tomás. "Julio Medem: el cine de azar." *Dirigido por . . .* 304 (2001): 48–57.

Fox, Inman. "Spain as Castile: Nationalism and National Identity." *The Cambridge Companion to Modern Spanish Culture*. Ed. David T. Gies. Cambridge: Cambridge University Press, 1999, pp. 21–36.

Fuentes, Victor. *Buñuel: cine y literatura*. Barcelona: Salvat Editores, 1989.

Gallero, José Luis, ed. *Sólo se vive una vez: esplendor y ruina de la movida madrileña*. Madrid: Ardora Ediciones, 1991.

García de Cortázar, Fernando and José Manuel González Vesga. *Breve historia de España*. Madrid: Alianza Editorial, 1994.

García Delgado, J. L. "Estancamiento industrial e intervencionismo económico durante el primer franquismo." *España bajo el franquismo*. Ed. Josep Fontana. Barcelona: Editorial Crítica, 1986, pp. 170–91.

García Escudero, José María. *La primera apertura: diario de un director general*. Barcelona: Planeta, 1978.

Gorina, Alex. "Las Carícies de Ventura Pons." Ventura Pons. www.venturapons.com/filmografia/cariciasp.html, accessed September 9, 2007.

Graham, Helen and Jo Labanyi. "Culture and Modernity: The Case of Spain." *Spanish Cultural Studies*. Eds. Helen Graham and Jo Labanyi. New York: Oxford University Press, 1995, pp. 1–23.

Graham, Helen and Jo Labanyi. "Glossary." *Spanish Cultural Studies*. Eds. Helen Graham and Jo Labanyi. New York: Oxford University Press, 1995, pp. 419–25.

Gubern, Román. "1930–1936 (II República)." *Cine español (1896–1988)*. Ed. Augusto M. Torres. Madrid: Ministerio de Cultura, 1989, pp. 87–103.

Gubern, Román. *1936–1939: la guerra de España en la pantalla: de la propaganda a la historia*. Madrid: Filmoteca Española, 1986.

Gubern, Román. *Benito Perojo: Pionerismo y supervivencia*. Madrid: Instituto de la Cinematografía y de las Artes Audiovisuales, 1994.

Gubern, Román. "El cine sonoro (1930–1939)." *Historia del cine español*. Eds. Román Gubern, José E. Monterde, Julio Pérez Perucha, Esteve Riambau, and Casimiro Torreiro. Madrid: Cátedra, 2000, pp. 123–79.

Gubern, Román. "Precariedad y originalidad del modelo cinematográfico español." *Historia del cine español*. Eds. Román Gubern, José E. Monterde, Julio Pérez Perucha, Esteve Riambau, and Casimiro Torreiro. Madrid: Cátedra, 2000, pp. 9–17.

Gubern, Román. "Teoría y práctica del star-system infantil." *Archivos de la Filmoteca* 38 (2001): 9–15.

Hammond, Paul. *L'Âge d'or*. London: BFI, 1997.

Hammond, Paul. "Lost and Found: Buñuel, *L'Âge d'or* and Surrealism." *Luis Buñuel: New Readings*. Eds. Peter Evans and Isabel Santaolalla. London: BFI, 2004, pp. 13–26.

Heredero, Carlos F. *Las huellas del tiempo: cine español 1951–61*. Madrid: Filmoteca, 1993.

Heredero, Carlos F. *La mitad del cielo: directoras españolas de los años 90*. Málaga: Ayuntamiento Málaga, 1998.

Hopewell, John. *Out of the Past: Spanish Cinema after Franco*. London: BFI, 1986.

Juliá, Santos. "History, Politics, and Culture, 1975–1996." *The Cambridge Companion to Modern Spanish Culture*. Ed. David T. Gies. Cambridge: Cambridge University Press, 1999, pp. 104–20.

Kinder, Marsha. *Blood Cinema: Reconstruction of National Identity in Spain*. Los Angeles: University of California Press, 1993.

Kinder, Marsha. "The Nomadic Discourse of Luis Buñuel: A Rambling Overview." *Luis Buñuel's The Discreet Charm of the Bourgeoisie*. Ed. Marsha Kinder. Cambridge: Cambridge University Press, 1999, pp. 1–27.

Kovacs, Katherine S. "Loss and Recuperation in the *Garden of Delights*." *Cine-Tracts* 4.2–3 (1981): 45–54.

Labanyi, Jo. "History and Hauntology; or, What Does One Do with the Ghosts of the Past? Reflections on Spanish Film and Fiction of the Post-Franco Period." *Disremembering the Dictatorship: The Politics of Memory in the Spanish Transition to Democracy*. Ed. Joan Ramon Resina. Amsterdam: Rodopi, 2000, pp. 65–82.

Labanyi, Jo. "Musical Battles: Populism and Hegemony in the Early Francoist Folkloric Film Musical." *Constructing Identity in Twentieth-Century Spain: Theoretical Debates and Cultural Practice.* Ed. Jo Labanyi. Oxford: Oxford University Press, 2002, pp. 206–21.

Labanyi, Jo. "Race, Gender and Disavowal in Spanish Cinema of the Early Franco Period: The Missionary Film and the Folkloric Musical." *Screen* 38.3 (1997): 215–31.

Llinás, Francisco. *Cuatro años de cine español (1983–1986).* Madrid: IMAGFIC, 1987.

Lluís Fecé, Josep. "La excepción y la norma: reflexiones sobre la españolidad de nuestro cine reciente." *Archivos de la Filmoteca* 49 (2005): 83–95.

Martín Gaite, Carmen. *Usos amorosos de la postguerra española.* Barcelona: Editorial Anagrama, 1987.

Martin-Márquez, Susan. *Feminist Discourse and Spanish Cinema: Sight Unseen.* Oxford: Oxford University Press, 1999.

Martin-Márquez, Susan. "Pedro Almodóvar's Maternal Transplants: From *Matador* to *All About My Mother.*" *Bulletin of Hispanic Studies* 81.4 (2004): 547–59.

Martin-Márquez, Susan. "A World of Difference in Home-Making: The Films of Icíar Bollaín." *Women's Narrative and Film in Twentieth-Century Spain: A World of Differences.* Eds. Kathleen Glenn and Ofelia Ferrán. New York: Routledge, 2002, pp. 256–72.

Moix, Terenci. *Suspiros de España: la copla y el cine de nuestro recuerdo.* Barcelona: Plaza y Janés, 1993.

Monterde, José Enrique. "El cine de la autarquía (1939–1950)." *Historia del cine español.* Eds. Román Gubern, José E. Monterde, Julio Pérez Perucha, Esteve Riambau, and Casimiro Torreiro. Madrid: Cátedra, 2000, pp. 181–238.

Monterde, José Enrique. "Continuismo y disidencia (1951–1962)." *Historia del cine español.* Eds. Román Gubern, José E. Monterde, Julio Pérez Perucha, Esteve Riambau, and Casimiro Torreiro. Madrid: Cátedra, 2000, pp. 239–93.

Palacio, Manuel. "Vanguardia." *Cine español (1896–1988).* Ed. Augusto M. Torres. Madrid: Ministerio de Cultura, 1989, pp. 309–25.

Pena, Jaime. "Cine español de los noventa: hoja de reclamaciones." *Secuencias* 16 (2002): 38–54.

Pérez Perucha, Julio. "Narración de un aciago destino (1896–1930)." *Historia del cine español.* Eds. Román Gubern, José E. Monterde, Julio Pérez Perucha, Esteve Riambau, and Casimiro Torreiro. Madrid: Cátedra, 2000, pp. 19–121.

Preston, Paul. *Franco: A Biography.* New York: Basic Books, 1994.

Quintana, Angel. "El cine como realidad y el mundo como representación: algunos síntomas de los noventa." *Archivos de la Filmoteca* 39 (2001): 9–25.

Riambau, Esteve. "El periodo 'socialista' (1982–1995)." *Historia del cine español.* Eds. Román Gubern, José E. Monterde, Julio Pérez Perucha, Esteve Riambau, and Casimiro Torreiro. Madrid: Cátedra, 2000, pp. 399–454.

Sala, Ramón and Rosa Alvarez Berciano. "1936–1939." *Cine español (1896–1988)*. Ed. Augusto M. Torres. Madrid: Ministerio de Cultura, 1989, pp. 129–61.

Sánchez-Biosca, Vicente. "Paisajes, pasajes y paisanajes de la memoria: la historia como simultaneidad en la comedia española de los noventa." *Archivos de la Filmoteca* 39 (2001): 55–67.

Santaolalla, Isabel. "Ethnic and Racial Configurations in Contemporary Spanish Culture." *Constructing Identity in Twentieth-Century Spain: Theoretical Debates and Cultural Practice*. Ed. Jo Labanyi. Oxford: Oxford University Press, 2002, pp. 55–71.

Santaolalla, Isabel. "Far from Home, Close to Desire: Julio Medem's Landscapes." *Bulletin of Hispanic Studies* 75.3 (1998): 331–7.

Santaolalla, Isabel. "Julio Medem's *Vacas* (1991): Historicizing the Forest." *Spanish Cinema: The Auteurist Tradition*. Ed. Peter William Evans. Oxford: Oxford University Press, 1999, pp. 310–24.

Santaolalla, Isabel. *"New" Exoticism: Changing Patterns in the Construction of Otherness*. Amsterdam: Rodopi, 2000.

Santaolalla, Isabel. *Los "otros": etnicidad y "raza" en el cine español contemporáneo*. Madrid: Ocho y Medio, Libros de Cine, 2005.

Santos Fontela, César. "1962–1967." *Cine español (1896–1988)*. Ed. Augusto M. Torres. Madrid: Ministerio de Cultura, 1989, pp. 235–67.

Smith, Paul Julian. *Contemporary Spanish Culture: TV, Fashion, Art and Film*. Cambridge: Polity, 2003.

Smith, Paul Julian. *Desire Unlimited: The Cinema of Pedro Almodóvar*. London: Verso, 1994.

Smith, Paul Julian. *Laws of Desire: Questions of Homosexuality in Spanish Writing and Film 1960–1990*. New York: Oxford University Press, 1992.

Strauss, Frédéric. *Conversaciones con Pedro Almodóvar*. Madrid: Ediciones Akal, 2001.

Subirats, Eduardo. "De la transición al espectáculo." *Quimera* February/March (2000): 21–6.

Talens, Jenaro. *The Branded Eye: Buñuel's Un chien andalou*. Minneapolis: University of Minnesota Press, 1993.

Torres, Augusto M. "1896–1929." *Spanish Cinema 1896–1983*. Ed. Augusto M. Torres. Madrid: Ministerio de Cultura, 1986, pp. 16–27.

Vázquez Montalbán, Manuel. *Crónica sentimental de España*. Madrid: Espasa-Calipe, 1986.

Vernon, Kathleen M. "Culture and Cinema to 1975." *The Cambridge Companion to Modern Spanish Culture*. Ed. David T. Gies. Cambridge: Cambridge University Press, 1999, pp. 248–66.

Vernon, Kathleen M. "Reading Hollywood in/and Spanish Cinema: From Trade Wars to Transculturation." *Refiguring Spain: Cinema, Media, Representation*. Ed. Marsha Kinder. Durham, NC: Duke University Press, 1997, pp. 35–64.

Vernon, Kathleen M. "Screening Room: Spanish Women Filmmakers View the Transition." *Women's Narrative and Film in Twentieth-Century Spain: A World of Differences*. Eds. Kathleen Glenn and Ofelia Ferrán. New York: Routledge, 2002, pp. 95–113.

Vernon, Kathleen and Barbara Morris. "Introduction: Pedro Almodóvar, Postmodern Auteur." *Post-Franco, Postmodern: The Films of Pedro Almodóvar*. Eds. Kathleen Vernon and Barbara Morris. Westport, CT: Greenwood Press, 1995, pp. 1–23.

Vidal, Nuria. *El cine de Pedro Almodóvar*. Barcelona: Ediciones Destino, 1988.

Index